The Abbeys & Priories of Medieval England

The Abbeys & Priories of Medieval England

COLIN PLATT

271
Platt

BARNES
&NOBLE
BOOKS
NEW YORK

1 - 230

This edition published by
Barnes & Noble, Inc.
by arrangement with
Reed International Books Limited

1996 Barnes & Noble Books

British Library Cataloguing in Publication Data

Platt, Colin
        The abbeys and priories of Medieval England
        1. Monasticism and religious orders - England
        - History
        I. Title
        271'.00942   BX2592

ISBN 0 76070 055 9

Printed in the United Kingdom by Bath Press, Avon

M 10 9 8 7 6 5 4 3 2 1

Contents

Reform in Normandy; the conquerors reward their home monasteries;
the alien priories; great houses of the Conquest period – Battle Abbey,
Lewes Priory and the Cluniac 'family'; the impact of the Conquest on
existing Anglo-Saxon houses – histories and a concern for the past;
buildings, relics and the cult of the saints.

The new asceticism; problems of choice among the reforming orders; the
Augustinian canons – their patrons and their endowment with parish
churches; Tironensians, Savigniacs and Cistercians – arrival and first
settlement; Cistercian expansion, Fountains Abbey (foundation
narrative, site, building process), lay brethren and the Cistercian plan.

Tarnishing of the Cistercian image, the merger with Savigny,
architectural elaboration, the admission of nuns to the order;
Augustinians and Gilbertines after 1150; the Premonstratensians as
successors to the Cistercians; problems of proximity; Carthusian
asceticism and its initially limited appeal in England.

The monasteries resume alienated lands, cultivate their own demesnes
and become prosperous; the land market favours the monks; forest
clearance and fenland reclamation; the importance of a famous relic –
Glastonbury and Canterbury; relic collections at Hailes, Vale Royal and
Reading; rebuilding programmes, frequently beginning with the saint's
resting-place in the presbytery; over-ambitious works, collapses and
other failures.

List of Illustrations

Preface and Acknowledgements

Monastic buildings, like parish churches or like castles, need to be seen in context. For most of us, our everyday built environment is of some importance to the way we conduct our lives. However, for none is this more true than it is for the monk, whose central beliefs are enshrined in his buildings and whose Rule would be meaningless without them. Monks, accordingly, are natural builders, and a monastic building, more than most, reflects changes in the climate of belief. Great churches, once up, are expensive to transform; tradition, too, may stand in the way of change. Yet it is probably true that there were more alterations of significance in the domestic arrangements of the English monasteries than in those of any other buildings of the period. It is the purpose of this book to chart these changes and to place them securely in the social context that brought them successively to pass. Of course, anybody acquainted with David Knowles's great works on English monasticism, published between 1940 and 1959, will not find here that splendidly broad canvas on which he painted so well. Nor is there likely to be a book about nuns that will compare, in its depth of understanding and genial insights, with Eileen Power's *Medieval English Nunneries*, now approaching its sixtieth birthday. Nevertheless, neither David Knowles nor Eileen Power found a place in their major works for the study and analysis of religious buildings. By deliberate choice – for they were both perfectly capable of such studies had they wished to incline that way – they stood on one side of a major divide; the architectural historians stood (and still stand) on the other. My book is directed at the middle.

Although I have not written at length about any one building, I have held it to be desirable, wherever possible, to illustrate the religious houses that I mention. In this, I have been assisted most capably once again by Alan Burn and his staff at the Southampton University Cartographic Unit, to whom I owe every line-drawing reproduced here. For permission to work from their originals for this purpose, I am grateful to John Allan and S. R. Blaylock for Fig. 59 (*Med. Arch.* 23 (1979), p. 251), to Elizabeth Eames and British Museum Publications for Fig. 63 (*Catalogue of Medieval Lead-Glazed Earthenware Tiles*, 1980), and to David A. Walsh and Philip Rahtz, the excavator, for Fig. 106 (*J.B.A.A.*, 122 (1979), pp. 44, 46–7). With the permission of the Inspectorate of Ancient Monuments and of the Director of Publishing at Her Majesty's Stationery Office, we have been able to base our plans of St Augustine's, Canterbury (Fig. 9), Roche (Fig. 29), Hailes (Fig. 48), Talley and Cymmer (Fig. 57), and Fountains (Fig. 123) on the official published guides to these houses, a series of high quality to which, in the course of writing this book, I have found myself returning many times.

I am deeply conscious too of my very great good fortune in obtaining plates – their copyright still – from three of the finest architectural photographers of this era. I am grateful to A. F. Kersting for Figs 6, 12, 17, 23, 24, 25, 30, 32, 34, 43, 45, 51, 52, 58, 62, 65, 68, 71, 72, 77, 89, 92, 97, 100, 101, 103, 104, 111, 114, 117, 122, 125, 127, 128, 131, 135, 136, 140, 141, 142, 143, 149, 151, 152, 159, 165, 167, 170, 173, 174, 175, 176, 181, 182, 183, 184 and 186; to Olive Smith, widow of the late Edwin Smith, for Figs 1, 2, 3, 4, 8, 10, 14, 16, 19, 22, 36, 39, 46, 53, 54, 55, 78, 84, 105, 119, 156, 157, 160, 161, 162, 172 and 179; and to Hallam Ashley for Figs 47, 50, 61, 66, 76, 80, 81, 82, 83, 108 and 144. David Wilson introduced me to the remarkable archive of the Committee for Aerial Photography (University of Cambridge), to which I owe Figs 20, 21, 26, 28, 44, 60, 67, 79, 98, 118, 124, 129, 137, 148, and 171 (*Cambridge University Collection: copyright reserved*); and Figs 27, 31, 38, 41, 42, 75, 99, 112, 115, 134, 138, 139, 154, 166, 177, 178, 180, 185 and 187 (British Crown copyright reserved). In addition, I am indebted to Patrick Greene and to the Norton Priory Museum Trust for Figs 40, 87 and 121; to David Baker for Fig. 13; to Evelyn Baker and to the Bedfordshire County Council Photographic Unit for Figs 15, 85 and 86(a–c); to Philip Rahtz for Fig, 56; to Aerofilms Ltd for Fig. 107; to the Bodleian Library, Oxford, for Figs 7, 11, 18, 37, 69, 70, 93, 94, 95, 96, 102, 109, 126 and 147; to the Property Services Agency (Photographic Library) (Crown copyright – reproduced with permission of the Controller of Her Majesty's Stationery Office) for Figs 33, 49, 64, 73, 90, 113, 116, 130, and 169 (also sanctioned by Mark Sorrell), 132, 153 and 164; to the Royal Commission on Historical Monuments (National Monuments Record) for Figs 74, 88, 110, 150 and 155; and to IPC Magazines Ltd for Figs 91, 120, 145, 146, 158 (also courtesy of Milton Abbey School); 163 and 168, published here by kind permission of *Country Life*.

Professor Giles Constable kindly gave me his permission to reproduce (below, pp. 32–3) Earl Robert's letter to Pope Alexander III, originally published in his own *Monastic Tithes* (Cambridge, 1964). Finally, it is a pleasure to acknowledge my constant dependence, in this as in other earlier books of mine, on Nikolaus Pevsner's great series *The Buildings of England*. Frankly, I do not know how I could have managed without it.

Glossary

The Orders

Arrouaisian   the contemplative branch (like the Victorines) of the Augustinian 'family'; canons

Augustinian   communities of clerics (also known as Austin or Regular Canons) who adopted the Rule of St Augustine; first officially recognized during the second half of the eleventh century

Austin Friars   originally congregations of hermits; brought together in 1256 under the Rule of St Augustine; also known as the Hermit Friars of St Augustine

Benedictine   the oldest of the orders, being monks (also known as 'black monks' from the colour of their habits) who observed the Rule of St Benedict; first brought under a collective discipline by St Benedict of Aniane in 817

Bridgettine   founded by Bridget of Sweden in the mid-fourteenth century; a double order of nuns with resident monks as spiritual advisers; introduced into England by Henry V

Carmelite   originally the mid-twelfth-century Order of Our Lady of Mount Carmel; reorganized as friars (the 'white friars') in the thirteenth century

Carthusian   a contemplative order of monks, bound to silence, founded by St Bruno in 1084 at La Grande Chartreuse, near Grenoble

Cistercian   reformed Benedictines, established at Cîteaux by Robert of Molesme in 1098 and later greatly expanded under the leadership of Bernard of Clairvaux (d. 1153); also known as the 'white monks'

Cluniac   reformed Benedictines of an earlier generation, taking their example from Cluny (Burgundy), founded in 909 and later organized into a great 'family' with the abbot of Cluny at its head

Dominican   founded by St Dominic (d. 1221) for the purposes of preaching and study; also known as the Friars Preachers or 'black friars'

Fontevraldine   founded by Robert d'Arbrissel at Fontevrault in 1100; a double order of monks and nuns, headed by the abbess of Fontevrault

Franciscan   founded by Francis of Assisi in 1209 and vowed, like the Dominicans, to corporate poverty; also known as the Friars Minor or 'grey friars'

Gilbertine   a community of nuns observing the Cistercian discipline, founded by St Gilbert at Sempringham, in Lincolnshire, in c. 1131; later reorganized as a double order of nuns and canons, of which many of the houses came to be for canons alone, living by the Rule of St Augustine

Grandmontine   founded at Grandmont by Stephen of Muret (d. 1124) and dedicated to extreme austerity, poverty and silence; distinguished initially by the power and responsibilities of the lay brethren

Hospitallers   a military order of knights dedicated, since the early twelfth century, to the provision of hospitality for pilgrims, to the care of the sick and to the protection of the Holy Land; also known as the Knights of the Order of the Hospital of St John of Jerusalem

Observants   friars of the Franciscan order advocating (from the later fourteenth century) a return to the primitive Rule of St Francis

Premonstratensian   founded at Prémontré by St Norbert in 1120 and observing the Rule of St Augustine, modified towards greater strictness; also known as the 'white canons'

Savigniac   founded at Savigny in 1105 by Vitalis of Mortain, originally as a colony of hermits; later developed as an order of monks which merged with the Cistercians in 1147

Templars   a military order, like the Hospitallers, founded by Hugh de Payens in 1118 for the protection of pilgrims in the Holy Land; also known as the Poor Knights of Christ and the Temple of Solomon; suppressed in 1312

Tironensian   founded by Bernard (d. 1117) at Tiron, and much influenced by the contemporary Cistercians although (unlike the Savigniacs) a merger never took place

Victorine   the Augustinian canons of St Victor (Paris), noted for the scholars and mystics among their number, especially in the twelfth century; influential in England in the founding of houses like Wigmore (Herefordshire)

*

Aisle   the part of a church on either side of the nave, usually separated from it by a row of columns

Alien priory   a religious establishment, sometimes fully conventual but very often not, owing obedience to a mother-house outside England

Ambulatory   the walking-place, or aisle, round the east end of a church, behind the high altar and usually giving access to additional chapels

Amice   a linen cloth worn round the neck by a priest when celebrating the Eucharist

Appropriation   the transfer to a monastic house of the full receipts of a parish church, usually accompanied by the undertaking to support a vicar

Apse (apsidal)   the semicircular termination of a chancel or chapel at its eastern end

Arcade   a series of columns supporting arches (as in 'nave arcade')

Bay   the division of a building, as marked by a unit of roof-vaulting etc.

Blind arcade   the decorative treatment of a wall by setting blank arches, carried on columns, against it

Canon (regular canon)   a priest living with others under a common Rule, usually that of St Augustine

Capacity   a sum of money allowed to a departing religious on the occasion of the suppression of his house

Capella ante portas   the chapel by the gate of a Cistercian house, for the use of travellers and other visitors

Cellarer   the official, or obedientiary, at a monastic house charged with supervision of its stores

Chancel   the east end of the church, by the high altar, usually reserved to the clergy

Chantry   a chapel, or just an altar, endowed by its founder with sufficient funds to maintain a priest to sing masses for his soul

Chapter-house   the chamber, usually centrally placed in the east claustral range, where the community met daily to transact business and to receive instruction, including the reading of a chapter of the Rule

Choir (quire)   the part of a church, equipped with choir-stalls, where services were sung

Cloister (claustral)   an open space, usually square and surrounded by an arcaded and roofed passage, for exercise and study

Conventual   of or belonging to a religious house (as in 'conventual life', 'conventual discipline' etc.)

Corona   the crown of radiating chapels sometimes found at the eastern ends of the greater monastic churches

Corrody (corrodian)   a pension or agreed maintenance in food, clothing and lodging, usually obtained by the individual corrodian in return for a gift of money or land

Crossing   the space in a church where nave, transepts and chancel intersect

Crypt   the chamber, usually below ground and under the east end of the church, where relics were commonly housed and displayed

Demesne   land kept in hand by its owner and not leased out to another

Denizen   native, not foreign (as in 'denizen status')

Dormitory (dorter)   the common sleeping-chamber of the monks

Farm out   to lease (as in 'the farming out of lands')

Feretory   a shrine specially constructed to house important relics

Friar   a member of one of the Mendicant orders (the chief of these being the Franciscans, the Dominicans, the Carmelites and the Austin Friars), vowed to corporate poverty

Garderobe   a privy or lavatory

Grant in fee   land given to another in return for services

Infirmary (infirmarer)   a building assigned to the sick

Lavatorium (laver)   the wash-place, usually a trough with running water, sited in the cloister for the use of the monks before meals

Lay brother   a man, of lower status than the monk, who had nevertheless taken the vows of the order and was employed in manual work

Misericord   the chamber in a monastery where meat, otherwise not permitted by the Rule, might be taken

Narthex   the vestibule, also known as a Galilee, at the west end of a church, sometimes taking the form of a porch

Nave   the western arm of a church, usually its main body west of the crossing

Obedientiary   an official in a monastic community, charged with a particular 'obedience' or duty

Peculium   the annual allowance of pocket money granted to a monk or nun in lieu of free distributions of clothing and other necessities

Possessioner   an endowed religious community (as in 'possessioner houses')

Presbytery   the eastern arm of a church, east of the choir and containing the high altar

Pulpitum   a partition or screen separating the monks' choir from the nave

Rebus   an arrangement of letters, in a badge or other device, signifying the name of an individual, sometimes displayed on a building or monument

Refectory (frater)   the common eating-chamber of the monks

Reliquary   a box or other container for relics

Rere-dorter   a building, at the far end of the dormitory from the church, housing the monks' latrines

Seyney   a recreational break, also called a *minutio*, during which the holidaying religious (*minuti*) might live away from the monastery and enjoy a more nourishing diet

Spiritualities   properties and revenues (e.g. a church and its tithes) obtained in return for spiritual services (e.g. the maintenance of a vicar to undertake the cure of souls)

Stalls   the monks' seats, often carved and canopied, in the choir

Temporalities   the material possessions and revenues (estates, receipts from sales of produce, and rents) of a religious community

Transept   the transverse arm, north or south, of a cross-shaped church, linking nave and chancel at the crossing

Triforium   the arcade, usually purely decorative, above the nave arcade and below the upper range of windows, or clerestory

Undercroft   a chamber, frequently vaulted, underlying an important apartment like a dormitory, refectory or chapel

Vault   an arched roof with variants as in 'tunnel vault' (a single vault of continuous semicircular section), 'groined vault' (formed by intersecting tunnel vaults) and 'ribbed vault' (made up of diagonal ribs supporting the vault spaces between them)

Warming-house   the common chamber, also known as the calefactory, where the monks might warm themselves at the fire

Chapter 1

An Alien Settlement

Monasticism was already old in Edward the Confessor's England, and it had come to bear the scars of its age. There were great monasteries and nunneries too, among them Glastonbury and Ramsey, Peterborough and Worcester, Shaftesbury, Romsey and Barking. But huge resources – an appreciable fraction of England's total wealth – had been allowed to accumulate in very few hands. Moreover, the communities they supported were aristocratic and conservative, backward-looking, traditionalist and out of date. Of course the Anglo-Saxon Church, like any other, had its saints. Wulfstan of Worcester, transcending the troubles of the post-Conquest decades, was one of them. Yet even a man like Wulfstan, the cream of the Anglo-Saxon system and its justification, would find himself having to learn new ways. 'Wretches that we are,' he said, 'we destroy the work of saints because we think in our pride that we can do better.'[1] In his own cathedral enclosure at Worcester, an old church, as venerable as it was ancient, would have to be demolished to make room for the saint's new cathedral. For Wulfstan, brought up in the Anglo-Saxon tradition of respect for the past, such a decision could be reached only with tears.

For the Normans, in contrast, every emphasis was on the virtues of the new. They belonged themselves to a new aristocracy. Their monastic reform, at home in Normandy, was of no great antiquity – a generation or two at most. Lanfranc, the Conqueror's choice in August 1070 for the crucial archbishopric of Canterbury, had little understanding of Anglo-Saxon spirituality and less sympathy still for its saints. Talking frankly one day to his friend and former pupil Anselm, he confessed, 'These Englishmen among whom we are living have set up for themselves certain saints whom they revere. But sometimes when I turn over in my mind their own accounts of who they were, I cannot help having doubts about the quality of their sanctity.'[2] Lanfranc learnt to moderate his opinions, but there were others more resolute than he. Abbot Scotland who, in the same year that Lanfranc took up his appointment, came himself to Canterbury to head the great Anglo-Saxon community at St Augustine's, made it among his first tasks on arrival to sweep the site clean of all the buildings it owed to his predecessors. Abbot Paul of St Albans (1077–93), Lanfranc's nephew and rebuilder of the church there, did not trouble to conceal his contempt for the former abbots, however 'venerable' and 'noble' his monks believed them, whose tombs he disturbed in the works. He was accustomed to describe them, so the chronicler reported, as *rudes et idiotas*.[3]

Within his own terms, of course, he was right. Paul of St Albans was the product of a monastic system radically different from the one that he had now entered. He had been a monk at Duke William's own foundation at St Stephen's, Caen, and had probably known the abbey of Bec as well, where he may have taken his vows. At these two centres of the newly vigorous Norman monasticism, enthusiastically sponsored by the duke and by his baronage, he would have come into daily contact with intellectuals of the stature of Lanfranc and Anselm; through their eyes, he would have looked south of the Alps into Italy. The insularity of England, unbroken even by its own native monastic revival under Edgar (959–75), was entirely foreign to Normandy. William of Dijon, the acknowledged founding father of Norman monasticism and abbot of Fécamp from 1001 to 1031, came originally from Volpiano, in Piedmont. John (d. 1079), his successor at Fécamp, was another North Italian, from Ravenna. Archbishop Lanfranc was a native of Pavia; Anselm had his roots in Aosta. The conversion of Normandy from the indifference to the Church of its Viking days, from which even William of Dijon had shrunk, to the pioneering zeal of native centres of excellence like Bec, had taken effect within less than two generations. Norman monasticism, internationally respected and a lure to the ambitious wherever they originated, had every advantage of youth.

The vigour of the Norman monastic reform might have been expected to have major consequences in England. And so, at the great centres of English monasticism – at Canterbury and Peterborough, Glastonbury and Bury St Edmunds – it not infrequently did, although not always with happy effects. In the localities, its results were more equivocal. In almost every case, the great Norman baronial families, only recently engaged in the monastic reform at home, had exhausted their zeal for the foundation of new religious houses well before they came to England at Duke William's side or in his footprints. Like the Conqueror himself, many of them had primary allegiances to Norman communities, as yet to be adequately endowed. While the invaders might have considered, with good reason, that the English monasteries were in need of reform, their first thoughts, inevitably, turned to their houses at home, some twenty-five of which had been either founded or refounded during the time of Duke William alone. These were the communities to which vows had been made. It had been as a consequence of these monks' prayers that the miracle of the Conquest had occurred. In 1070, after the first round of fighting was over, Bishop Ermenfrid of Sitten drew up a model tariff of penances which included the following clause:

> Anyone who does not know the number of those he wounded or killed [at Hastings] must, at the discretion of his bishop, do penance for one day in each week for the remainder of his life; or, if he can, let him redeem his sin by a perpetual alms, either by building or by endowing a church.[4]

To many of those who accepted the penance, it could have been interpreted only as an instruction to assist by their alms the struggling new communities at home. It was in no sense a requirement to engage in a further campaign of reform.

Duke William's vow that, if he won the battle, he would establish a monastery at Hastings, and his reward to the abbey of Saint-Valéry (where he awaited the crossing) for the fair wind that blew him to England, are well known. But such undertakings, clearly, were repeated during those tense days throughout the army, to bear fruit in the calmer times ahead. The manor of Takeley (Essex), given by the Conqueror to the monks of Saint-Valéry, was to become a diminutive priory in its own right, one of

1 The late-eleventh-century arcade, re-using Roman bricks, in the south transept at St Albans, attributable to Abbot Paul (1077–93), nephew of Archbishop Lanfranc and the first Norman abbot of this formerly great Anglo-Saxon community

those dependent 'alien' priories which would bring such confusion on their owners. Yet the gift initially had been little more than a straightforward financial transaction, the understood repayment of a debt contracted to the saint of Picardy who had sent the fleet a suitable wind for the passage.

In the first flush of his success, the duke made many such gifts, rewarding the great monasteries of his Norman homeland and in particular his own foundations (St Stephen's and La Trinité) at Caen. Jumièges and Fécamp, Grestain, Saint-Wandrille and Mont-St-Michel all got their reward, while each of these attracted other gifts also from the Conqueror's companions-at-arms.[5] Matching the fortunes of their donors, these gifts were widely scattered through the conquered territories, as well as being frequently on a very small scale. They met the requirements of Bishop Ermenfrid's penitentiary, for they increased the endowment of the Church. They fulfilled vows, exactly suiting the exultant mood of the invaders and costing them no more than a tolerable fraction of what the gamble as a whole had earned. But they were not conceived as a contribution to monastic reform in England, nor were they handled as such at the time. The Normans had not come, at least in the first instance, as monastic reformers, but they came from a land of reform. In this lies the key to the settlement.

What the Norman monasteries then made of this bounty was usually up to them, and certainly it brought them problems along with the rewards. Almost immediately, there were squabbles between them as competition developed for the richest pickings and as charters of gift, imperfectly drawn up, came under scrutiny and dispute. However, what is abundantly clear is that neither the home abbeys nor their patrons were primarily concerned with the life of religion in England. They would have viewed England still as a barbarous land, no place to send monks of their brotherhood. And if, in due course, they found themselves compelled to put together small 'priories', as Saint-Valéry would do on its estate at Takeley, as the best means to protect and administer their cross-Channel endowment, their entire purpose was financial not missionary, having nothing to do with some grand strategy of reform. Significantly enough, even the greatest and the most progressive of the Norman houses, among them that nursery of the pre-Conquest reform at Bec, showed little interest in the foundation of satellite communities. Indeed, it hardly paid them to do so, for they would have lost revenues in the support of such subordinate houses and have gained very little in return. When Bec found monks to colonize St Neot's, a decayed priory until then dependent on the ancient Anglo-Saxon monastery at Ely, it was undoubtedly the urging of Richard fitzGilbert, their patron, that brought them to do it, rather than any missionary impulse of their own. And St Neot's, conveyed to Bec no earlier than 1079, was yet among the first of the Norman monastic colonizations in England.[6]

A few years later, in 1093, Hugh d'Avranches, earl of Chester and one of the closest personal companions of the Conqueror, was to entice monks of Bec to Chester itself, where they made up the first community at St Werburgh's. Similarly, Gilbert de Clare, by giving Bec the collegiate church of St John Baptist of Clare, attempted to persuade the monks to establish the priory, within the bounds of his castle, which they later moved to Stoke by Clare, on a site more convenient for the purpose.[7] Nevertheless, each of these colonizations, as their terms make obvious, was carried out not on the initiative of the monks themselves but on the insistent importuning of their patrons. Bec had estates throughout south-east England and through much of East Anglia as well. But although many of these, at one time or another, might be called a 'priory', the great majority of the Bec manors had no conventual life of their own, nor were they ever intended to have one.

England was indeed a hostile land, and the first generation of Norman settlers, understandably enough, continued to look back with nostalgia at its home estates and at the monastic houses it had been instrumental in founding there. However, hostility and homesickness, combined together, had another effect as well. Most Normans, like their great Archbishop Lanfranc, would have found themselves out of sympathy with the Anglo-Saxon collegiate and parish clergy which they discovered already established on their lands. Clergy were not easy to displace. But there was no reason why a French-speaking lord should welcome, or need expect, his spiritual consolation from an Anglo-Saxon rural priest. Accordingly, the demand grew for Norman chaplains, and it would be a short step only to the further thought of attracting a more congenial community of French monks. This could not have been done in a rush. French monks themselves were reluctant to come. They feared the disorders of the times, disliked the sea crossing and believed with good reason that it would be difficult to pursue their monastic vocations in the new and small communities they were offered. Occasionally though – and increasingly as time went on – they allowed these objections to be overruled. Gilbert de Clare's lure to the monks of Bec, without which it is doubtful whether he could have got them to Suffolk at all, was an existing collegiate church, already established and endowed, being ripe for the smoothest of take-overs. And in exactly the same way, it was a college of canons that by degrees gave place to the monks of Séez at Roger de Montgomery's baronial headquarters at Arundel.[8]

The link between *caput baroniae* and monastery was obviously close from the beginning. With the associated town, these two other elements – castle and priory – comprised a unit of colonization already well tried in Normandy itself and thereafter one of the most important instruments in the conquest and settlement of England.[9] Earlier than most others, William fitzOsbern, the Conqueror's first earl of Hereford, brought the monks of Cormeilles (a Norman house of his own foundation) to his castle and borough at Chepstow, in Monmouthshire, before his death in battle in 1071 and burial at Cormeilles itself.[10] In the same Welsh Marcher lands, within the following generation, the abbeys of Saint-Florent (Saumur) and Saint-Vincent (Le Mans) were to be persuaded to find monk-colonists for new castle-associated priories at Monmouth and Abergavenny, while the use of monks to serve castle chapels was to result in the formal foundation of dependent priories at Carisbrooke and Folkestone, Tutbury and Eye, Blyth, Wareham and Castle Acre.[11]

Many of these priories were to serve another purpose as the parish churches of the boroughs with which, along with the castles, they were associated. And it was this need to exploit and to protect their spiritualities which became, over the course of the immediate post-Conquest decades, another powerful incentive for the importation of communities of monks. Such a need might arise in a new borough or at a manor carved out of the waste. But it was just as likely to occur where a Norman monastic house had been endowed with English churches, formerly the personal property of

Anglo-Saxon landowners and now transferred with their estates to the Normans. Groups of these churches, even more than collections of lands, must have suggested to their new Norman monastic owners the establishment of some form of headquarters, usually to be based at the collegiate or parish church already most important in the locality. In due course, the use of the same building for both parish and conventual purposes was to prove a nuisance, with the result that the monks might go to great lengths to rid themselves of their troublesome neighbours. In the twelfth century, too, inhibitions would grow about cloistered monks serving the churches that they owned. Yet in the aftermath of the Conquest, neither restraint yet applied, while still at their suppression in 1536 the naves of the priory churches at Monmouth, at Chepstow and at Abergavenny, as elsewhere, continued in the use of the parish.[12]

In practice, then, the foundation of diminutive priories dependent on the abbeys of Normandy and of other regions of western France, which was a characteristic of the post-Conquest years, could come about in a number of ways. It might follow from the desire of a great nobleman, with estates in both England and France, to bring French-speaking monks (very likely from a Norman foundation of his own or of his family) to serve his castle chapel. It might have occurred where a lesser man, a soldier of fortune at the Conquest, felt the need to establish, at relatively low cost to himself, a community of his own on freshly acquired estates: some sort of spiritual prop and guarantee of his new line. However, more pressing as a motive than either of these was the urgency experienced by every Norman monastic house with substantial holdings in England, particularly when times became harder in the following century, to find some method of protecting its endowment. Overseas estates were already vulnerable enough, but still more vulnerable were the gifts of churches and their associated tithes, which had come to the Norman abbeys in such great numbers and which they now discovered difficulties in retaining. If the experience of the abbey of Conches was typical – as indeed it probably was – the only effective recipe for securing the abbey's rights against the raids on its endowment conducted even by its original founder-patrons, was to set up its own agency in England. The priory of Wootton Wawen (Warwickshire) was the result, and the abbey's interest there lasted, much longer than at most alien priories, as late as the mid-fifteenth century. In contrast, an early casualty was Conches's parish church, with tithes, at Walthamstow (Essex), regranted within decades to the canons of Holy Trinity, Aldgate (London), by Alice de Tony, herself a member of the family, founders of Conches in about 1035, who had given the church to Conches in the first place. Not much more than a century later, Conches was to lose the tithes of Flamstead (Hertfordshire) and Kirtling (Cambridgeshire) as well.[13]

Whatever the motives, the organization of the dependent, or alien, priories could not be hurried, being certainly far from complete when, quite early in the twelfth century or even a few years before, new fashions in monasticism overtook them. Plainly, too, neither the purpose nor the location of these so-called priories ever had very much to do with the spiritual needs of the territories they controlled. What they served instead was the convenience of the baronage and the economic interests of the monasteries of Normandy. With their diminutive communities, usually no more than two or three strong, and with their chronically inadequate endowments, they did

2 The great dormitory undercroft (*c.* 1200) at Battle Abbey, illustrating the considerable scale of the buildings erected on this favoured royal site

little for the monastic vocation but weaken it. Yet they should be seen for what they were. They had never been intended as the spearheads of reform. Their purpose lay in the collection of revenues, not in the instruction and the cure of souls.

In just the same way, even the most important of the post-Conquest foundations – the Conqueror's Battle Abbey being prominent among them – have usually to be recognized less as instruments of reform than as the conscientious paying-off of debts. William, in dedicating the site of his major feat of arms to God, had marked as the position of the high altar of his new church the exact spot where Harold had been observed to fall. There were many objections to this ruling. Hastings had been fought on a dry sandy ridge, exposed and inhospitable, among scrublands of little use to man or beast. The first monk-colonizers, alarmed principally by the lack of water, established a base elsewhere. But William dismissed their complaints. His abbey, dedicated to the former soldier St Martin, was to be built on the battle-field and nowhere else. Once he had finished with it, William promised, wine would flow as freely at Battle as water at abbeys less fortunate.[14]

3 The fine twelfth-century door and decorative blind arcading on the west front of the church at Castle Acre (Norfolk), one of the earliest and the richest of the English Cluniac houses

The Conqueror's purpose was plain. The church of St Martin de Bello, otherwise known as Battle Abbey, was to be a war memorial first, a house of religion only second. William's endowment, whatever it cost him, would serve to keep a memory alive. His choice of a community from which to settle Battle Abbey was already of some considerable significance. Marmoutier, on the Loire in Touraine, was itself dedicated to St Martin. It had been suggested to the Conqueror by William 'the smith', one of his retinue and a monk professed at that house. But Marmoutier, although recently reorganized from Cluny, was not among the more important reforming houses of its day, nor was it even in Normandy.[15] In the event, Marmoutier was no bad choice, and Battle flourished under Abbot Gausbert and his successors. Nevertheless, it could never have been as if the Conqueror saw his expensive English foundation, isolated in the wastes of the inhospitable Sussex Weald, as a further stage in the development of that monastic reform of which, at home in Normandy, he had been one of the principal patrons. Like his baronage, he was rewarding God while reinforcing his self-esteem in the process.

In quieter times attitudes would change, and although the settlement of debts remained an important motive in the major new foundations of the period, founders themselves, before the end of the reign, had begun to discriminate more carefully in favour of houses of a purer observance. William de Warenne's choice in 1078–81 of Cluniac monks to settle his new foundation at Lewes (Sussex), although influenced, we are told, by his own reception at Cluny while travelling to Rome on a pilgrimage, was not arrived at entirely by accident. Under its great abbots Odilo (d. 1049) and

Hugh (d. 1109), Cluny had regained its tenth-century eminence. It had become deeply engaged in the contemporary reform of the papacy. It had itself spawned many new houses and had reformed others (Marmoutier among them), setting a new standard of excellence unmatched elsewhere in the West. Before he set out for Rome, William de Warenne was already resolved to establish French monks at the headquarters of his barony at Lewes. At Cluny, he found himself a model.

In some respects, clearly, the response of the Norman monasteries to the challenge of the Conquest had by this time disappointed their patrons. The Conqueror's search for clergy beyond the borders of Normandy, and his own first approaches to Cluny, are likely to date to the mid-seventies; at contemporary Canterbury, the influence of Cluny on the reforming legislation of Archbishop Lanfranc is plain.[16] But Abbot Hugh was not easily persuaded to lend a hand. Neither the Conqueror nor William de Warenne were at first successful in inducing him to part with monks who, as he told the king emphatically, were not for sale at any price. And it was only after prolonged negotiations and the meticulous exchange of guarantees that Cluny made its entrance to England. Abbot Hugh, who must have heard something of the hardships already experienced by monks of his acquaintance in England, was especially unwilling to risk the spiritual health of his brethren in the isolation of an unwelcoming English-speaking land. He had had his own difficulties in recruiting men he considered of adequate calibre, and it was natural for him to insist on the most exacting undertakings concerning the endowment and support of the new community. The surviving foundation charter of St Pancras, Lewes, with its unusual double guarantees by the founder and his king, is thus a document of considerable significance: a milestone in the post-Conquest settlement as it opened the way to a new wave of monastic migrations. It began with William and Gundrada, his wife, publishing to the faithful how they 'for the redemption of our souls, and with the

4 High-quality blind arcading on the north wall of the twelfth-century chapter-house at Wenlock Priory (Shropshire), another important Cluniac foundation, settled from La Charité-sur-Loire

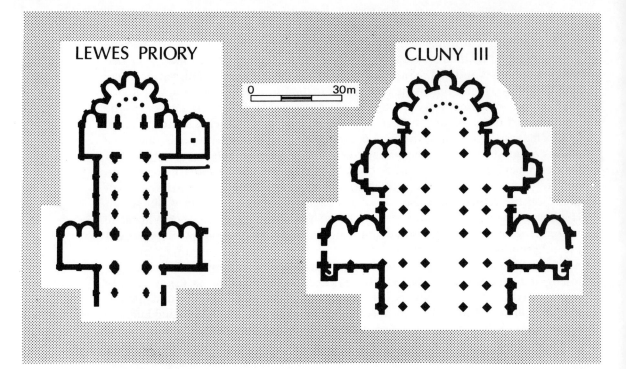

LEWES PRIORY

CLUNY III

0   30m

5 The east ends, each with its characteristic double transepts and *corona* of radiating chapels, of the great monastic churches at Lewes and Cluny, demonstrating the dependence of late-eleventh-century Lewes Priory on its Burgundian mother-house and model

advice and assent of our lord, William, king of the English, gave to God and to the holy apostles Peter and Paul at the place called Cluny where the lord abbot Hugh presides, the church of St Pancras in the same land of the English with all the things which pertain to it'. After other valuable gifts, the charter met Abbot Hugh's requirement for a copper-bottomed settlement by including the guarantee of the Conqueror himself. William declared himself moved 'by divine inspiration, and for the safety of my kingdom and the salvation of my soul, and at the fervent request and petition of William of Warenne and Gundrada, his wife', to confirm with his seal 'the gift here recorded which they make to the holy apostles of God at the place called Cluny'. He added, 'with my royal authority I ratify it in order that it may remain firm and unimpaired'.[17]

Cluny's role in England has been overshadowed by later developments, in particular the twelfth-century reform. Yet in the late eleventh century and still during the first decades of the twelfth, houses of Cluniac allegiance multiplied throughout the country, attracting a succession of rich patrons. Monastic orders, properly constituted with formal general chapters (meetings) and with a common observance published by statute, were as yet unknown in Europe. And what distinguished the Cluniacs, separating them most clearly from other more run-of-the-mill Benedictines, was that they saw themselves uniquely as a 'family' of priories to which the abbot of Cluny stood as father. Of course, the organization of the Cluniac family was still very rudimentary. Abbot Hugh's disciplinary powers were defective. Increasingly, the multiplication of Cluniac houses had led to the growth within the system of competing centres, including La Charité-sur-Loire, so-called 'eldest daughter' of Cluny and very influential, after Cluny itself, in the Cluniac colonization of England. Nevertheless, the family's cohesion, light though it was, proved sufficient to endow it with a colonizing potential quite unlike that of any individual abbey which, alone and unsupported, might soon exhaust its impulse to expand. Furthermore, Cluny had other advantages. Abbot Hugh was an aristocrat of the very noblest blood, and it was the barons who took Cluny to their hearts. Within a very few years, William de Warenne's foundation at Lewes, the first and always the richest Cluniac house in England, had become the father of a family of its own. Among the more successful of its daughter houses were Castle Acre (Norfolk), founded by the next William, the Warenne son and heir, and Thetford, in the same county, the major work of piety of Roger Bigod, a former boon companion of the Conqueror himself and father of a line of Norfolk earls. In Shropshire, it was Roger de Montgomery, first earl of Shrewsbury (1074–94), who imported Cluniac monks to Wenlock from La Charité-sur-Loire, while other foundations that recruited from La Charité included Pontefract (Yorkshire), adjoining Robert de Lacy's great castle, and Bermondsey (Surrey), endowed by a wealthy Londoner, Alwin Child, but supported additionally by William Rufus. Later, both Reading Abbey (Berkshire) and Faversham Abbey (Kent) were to start life under the auspices of Cluny, even if their rich endowments as the royal foundations of Henry I and Stephen respectively later enabled them to achieve independence.

Not all Cluniac houses were rich. Their siting had depended on the caprice of great patrons, and it was not uncommon for a small community to find itself stranded in the depths of the countryside, eventually to wither there and fail. Indeed the Cluniac family, a pioneer of centralized government but with no clear rules as yet to define and protect its new recruits, had more than its share of such catastrophes. However those that thrived – about a third of the houses of the initial Cluniac colonization – included such obviously successful communities as Bermondsey and Castle Acre, Thetford and Pontefract, with Daventry (Northamptonshire), Lenton (Nottinghamshire) and the especially prospering Montacute Priory, in Somerset. Lewes Priory, twice as rich as Montacute, never lost its position as the star in the Cluniac firmament. In obvious tribute to its founding house and to the original source of its inspiration, the church at Lewes, with its distinctive double transepts and its *corona* (crown) of radiating chapels, was laid out as a replica of Cluny. On a smaller scale it repeated the arrangements of Abbot Hugh's great church, the third rebuilding on the Cluny site, begun in 1088.[18]

With few exceptions, Wenlock being prominent among them, the Cluniacs built from nothing on vacant sites, without existing communities of Anglo-Saxon monks to discipline, reorganize or displace. Like Margaret, daughter of Edward the Etheling, whose marriage to Malcolm III in 1069/70 brought the new monasticism to Scotland for the first time, they had enjoyed the not inconsiderable advantage of starting with a *tabula rasa*.[19] The Conqueror and Archbishop Lanfranc, his lieutenant in the ecclesiastical settlement of England, were less fortunate.

Lanfranc was over fifty when he took up his appointment at Canterbury, and he came with many misgivings. Less than three years after his arrival in England, he addressed a *cri de coeur* to Pope Alexander II, pleading to be released from the responsibilities that both the pope and the Conqueror had urged upon him. He had yielded, he said, only to the command of the pope, 'the highest pastor of the holy Church', as transmitted to him in Normandy by Alexander's legates, Bishop Ermenfrid, author of the post-Conquest penitential (above, p. 2), and Cardinal Hubert.

I pleaded failing strength and personal unworthiness, but to no purpose; the excuse that the language was unknown and the native races barbarous weighed

6 The massive Norman arcade at Gloucester Abbey (now the cathedral), completed by *c*. 1120; the overlying rib-vault is of mid-thirteenth-century date

7 A self-portrait of the illuminator, Hugo *pictor*. Norman, late eleventh century

nothing with them either. In a word: I assented, I came, I took office. Now I endure daily so many troubles and vexations and such spiritual starvation of nearly anything that is good; I am continually hearing, seeing and experiencing so much unrest among different people, such distress and injuries, such hardness of heart, greed and dishonesty, such a decline in holy Church, that I am weary of my life and grieve exceedingly to have lived into times like these.[20]

Some of this passion no doubt was rhetorical, and Lanfranc certainly was never reluctant to lift a choice phrase from the scriptures. Yet this was no conventional expression of personal inadequacy before a task otherwise cheerfully assumed. At much the same date, Lanfranc snatched a moment to write to his friend, Archbishop John of Rouen, about the 'wretched' life he led: 'I am for ever enmeshed – by what hidden judgement of God I know not – in so many of the world's great snares: I have constantly to endure so many wrangles both on my own behalf and in other men's affairs; when I contemplate the disasters of this present time I foresee so many still to come.'[21]

It was Lanfranc's belief that things must grow worse before they could be expected to get better. 'While the king lives,' he wrote, 'we have peace of a kind, but after his death we expect to have neither peace nor any other benefit.'[22] And it is certainly true that at St Augustine's, Canterbury, the alienation of the Anglo-Saxon monks was never more complete than under Abbot Guy, appointed by Lanfranc in 1087 in succession to the already over-vigorous Abbot Scotland. Nevertheless, before the Conqueror's death in September that year, much had already been achieved. Neither William nor his archbishop believed in change for its own sake, and their religious settlement was to be conservative in many ways, even to the point of adopting and multiplying an institution like the cathedral priory which, although familiar in England since the reforming days of Edgar and Dunstan in the tenth century, had no precise equivalent in Normandy. Yet both recognized that their hold on the Church depended principally on good judgement in the filling of key posts. A recital of the 'acts' of Archbishop Lanfranc, written after his death and then inserted in the A version of the Anglo-Saxon Chronicle, is very largely a record of depositions and appointments which, at least to the native-born English reader, must have made it a dismal catalogue. At Winchester, Abbot Wulfric of the New Minster was deposed, and Rualo took his place; Thurstan (in the event not a good choice) replaced the deposed Aethelnoth of Glastonbury; Wulfketel of Crowland was removed from his

8 Bishop Herbert Losinga's early-twelfth-century nave arcade at Norwich Cathedral Priory, begun soon after the transfer of the see from Thetford to Norwich in 1094/5

abbacy in favour of Ingulf, formerly a monk professed at the Norman house of Saint-Wandrille.[23]

There were many more changes like these, especially obvious in the transformation of the episcopacy; so much so that, by the end of William's reign, an almost complete sweep had taken place. But at all times the calculated deposition of an abbot, or deprivation of a bishop, was less characteristic of the Conqueror's settlement than the filling of a voidance due to death. Heritability of lands presented few problems with the upper clergy. Furthermore, the Wessex kings' clear right to appoint to a vacant abbacy, acknowledged since the tenth-century reforms, gave William in his turn a control of the monasteries which he understood very well how to use. In practice, all he had to do was to wait.

The passage of time was one healing element; the quality of the Anglo-Norman clergy was another. Inevitably there were black sheep among them, perhaps none more unfortunate than Abbot Thurstan of Glastonbury whose heavy-handed insistence on liturgical reform ended in riot and bloodshed.[24] However, it says something for the firmness of purpose of the king that Thurstan was immediately despatched home to Normandy, while encomiums of good government and of improved observance at the religious houses were at least as common as stories of insensitivity and oppression. Thurstan had been a monk at Caen and it was to that abbey that he was later returned in disgrace. Another monk from the same community was Paul, abbot of St Albans (1077–93), more usually remembered with affection and gratitude although certainly no respecter of the past (above, p. 1). Similarly, Serlo of Gloucester (1072–1104), Crispin of Westminster (1085–1118) and Simeon of Ely (1082–93), among many others, each had his recordable successes.[25] From the list of his acts in the Anglo-Saxon Chronicle, Lanfranc of Canterbury emerges as a tough-minded administrator, brutal if called upon to be so. However, his good deeds also – 'his buildings, his alms and his labours' – were 'very many', and he was sorely missed. As for his successor, Anselm of Bec, archbishop from 1093: 'He was an upright man, being both good and full of learning. He was indeed the most notable man of his time.'[26]

Of course, Anglo-Saxon monks had no more reason to love their new masters than had their relatives and friends in the world beyond their walls. Grumbles and shuffling indifference were common enough, as they must surely be in any disaffected community. Yet there was to be at least one characteristic product of these difficult times which we can remember still with gratitude. The attacks on Anglo-Saxon institutions, on property and on the reputation of the saints, all of which characterized the immediate post-Conquest decades, stirred a concern for the past which found expression in numerous written histories.

In this work of remembrance, practical in purpose as well as merely nostalgic, the monks of the old houses were especially active. Some communities had been luckier than others. Under its French abbot Baldwin, formerly the physician of Edward the Confessor to whom he owed his preferment in 1065, Bury St Edmunds continued to grow and to prosper. At Canterbury, Lanfranc and Anselm similarly protected the endowment of their cathedral priory of Christ Church. But Peterborough's greatest days seemed already to be over by 1066, after which its first Norman abbot, Turold (1070–98), formerly a monk of Fécamp, brought disaster down upon his house. We

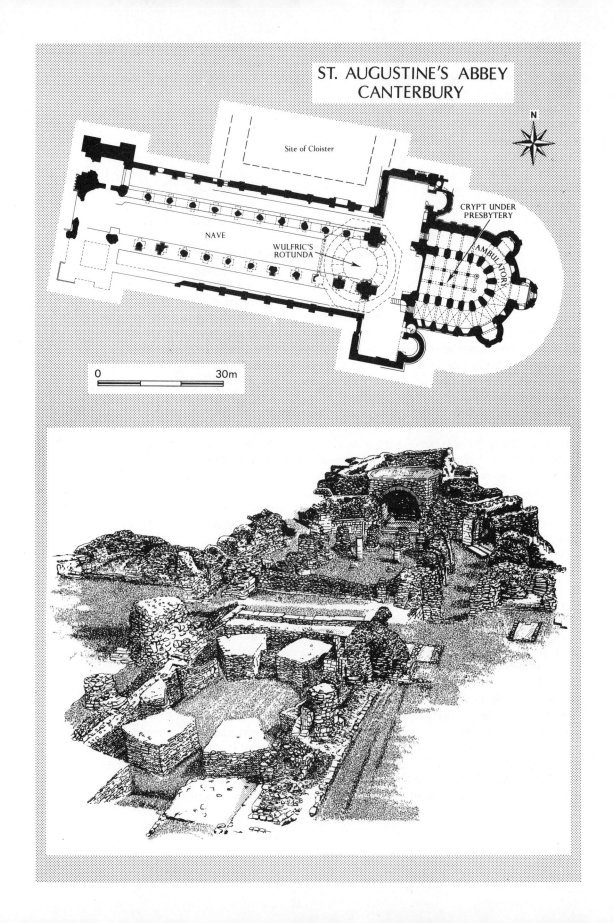

ST. AUGUSTINE'S ABBEY
CANTERBURY

N

Site of Cloister

CRYPT UNDER
PRESBYTERY

NAVE

WULFRIC'S
ROTUNDA

AMBULATORY

0   30m

9 *Opposite* Abbot Scotland's late-eleventh-century crypt at St Augustine's, Canterbury; in the foreground, the remains of Abbot Wulfric's remarkable rotunda, left unfinished on his death in 1059. Crypts of this kind, characteristic of the greater Anglo-Saxon churches, were used for the safe-keeping of relics; they are hard to parallel in contemporary Normandy

10 The crypt at Christ Church (Canterbury), built in *c.* 1100 to underlie a great new choir already replacing Archbishop Lanfranc's recent but much smaller work

know now that the damage at Peterborough was not permanent. Within a century of Abbot Turold's death, the losses had very largely been made up. Yet from the perspective still of the mid-twelfth century, the past looked black and the future scarcely less gloomy. In the words of Hugh Candidus, sub-prior of Peterborough and a resident there since his childhood:

> Then [in Turold's abbacy] a monastery that had once been very rich was reduced to penury. From that day up to the present time nothing has been added or restored, and many things have been taken away. For the same Abbot Turold not only added nothing, but he badly broke up his compact estate, and gave lands to his kinsfolk and the knights who came with him, so that scarcely one third of the abbey estate remained in demesne. When he came the abbey was valued at one thousand and fifty pounds, which he so squandered that it was scarcely worth five hundred pounds.[27]

At Ramsey and at Abingdon, as their chroniclers explained, lands leased out before the Conquest had failed to return to those abbeys after it. The Conquest had been a disaster, following which, as William of Malmesbury wrote, 'the newcomers devour the riches and entrails of England, and there is no hope of the misery coming to an end'.[28] But what brought the Ramsey chronicler to set down his thoughts was yet another round of catastrophes in the 'dark and gloomy days' of King Stephen. He explained:

At the end of these troubles, which had resulted in the loss of almost everything, we decided that somehow or other what remained should be preserved when, by the kindness of God, the darkness and gloom had been changed into tranquillity. So we collected together in one volume our cyrographs and the charters of our privileges (documents saved from the destruction of time . . .), as a warning for future ages and to instruct readers.[29]

Such growing awareness of the past can only be applauded: it has made the task of later historians of the Norman settlement of England very much easier. However, it had at the time its own serious purpose which Hemming, a monk of the cathedral priory at Worcester and the collector of its charters, was among the first of these writers to express. A very strong instinct in the Anglo-Saxon Church, continued after the Conquest, had been to hold onto the patrimony of the saints. It was to be recognizable again much later, for example, among the monks of Durham, seeing themselves as the 'mynistres of Saynt Cuthbert', fighting the saint's wars against the Scots who had appropriated his lands.[30] In the late eleventh century, the continuing losses of recent years had made these emotions especially sharp, nowhere more so than at a great house like Worcester which, under the protection of St Oswald (d. 992), had prospered during an earlier regime. As the monk Hemming recorded it:

Wulfstan, bishop of this see, caused this book to be written to teach his successors about the things which have been committed to their care, and to show them which lands justly belong (or ought to belong) to the church, and which have been unjustly seized by evil men – first, during the Danish invasions; later, by unjust royal officials and tax collectors; and most recently, by the violence of Normans in our own time, who by force, guile and rapine have unjustly deprived this holy

church of its lands, villages and possessions, until hardly anything is safe from their depredations.[31]

Hemming made his collection in 1095 or thereabouts, within months of the death of his patron. He very well knew what he wrote.

If times were hard at Worcester, under its saintly protector Bishop Wulfstan, they must have been very much worse elsewhere. The Normans, it has sometimes been argued, brought about a reconciliation with their Anglo-Saxon monks by setting them up in new buildings. Yet this activity can hardly have been easy to live with at the time, and it is difficult to see it making friends. One of the more active of the builders was Herbert Losinga, a Norman by birth, whose transfer of his see from Thetford to Norwich in 1094/5 became the occasion for a programme of works. The results were admirable and they have left us still a cathedral church of exceptional size and quality, substantially complete by Herbert Losinga's death in 1119, although the nave had yet to be finished on the plan originally laid out. Bishop Herbert had been a monk of Fécamp, in Normandy, and he understood the needs of the monks he installed at Norwich, for whom he added a fine set of buildings. But none of this could have been achieved without cost. The same chronicler who tells us about Bishop Herbert's 'most beautiful church' and about the 'spacious offices' of his monks, records the bishop's purchase of 'a large part of the town of Norwich', how he 'tore down houses and levelled the ground for a great space'.[32] While the work was in

11 *Opposite* Stephen (d. 1112), first abbot of St Mary's, York, seated with monks to his right and the abbey church to his left. English, thirteenth century

12 The nave arcade and contemporary vault at Durham, one of the outstandingly innovative building projects of its age, begun in 1093

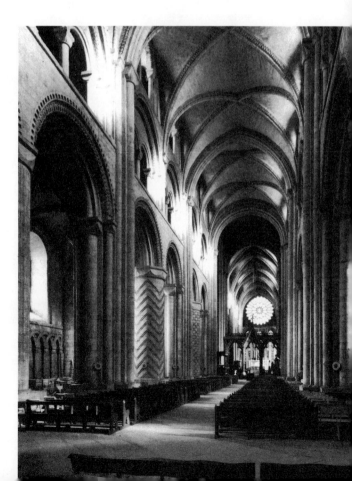

13 An Anglo-Saxon burial at Elstow (Bedfordshire), cut at the knees by the foundation trench of an early Norman building and at the head by the footings of the fourteenth-century cloister

progress, driven on by the bishop with the support of the king, the monks plainly failed to be infected by Herbert Losinga's urgency. As he told them with impatience:

> Behold the servants of the king and my own are really earnest in the works allotted to them, gather stones, carry them to the spot when gathered, and fill with them the fields and ways and houses and courts, and you meanwhile are asleep with folded hands, numbed as it were, and frostbitten by a winter of negligence, shuffling and failing in your duty through a paltry love of ease.[33]

Herbert's cathedral was conceived on the grandest scale; larger, in point of fact, than his means. And it was this quality of size that came to distinguish the greater

Anglo-Norman churches not merely from their predecessors in pre-Conquest England but from those of Normandy itself. When Lanfranc rebuilt Canterbury after the fire there shortly before he took office, he replaced the ruined buildings he found on the site with others 'which greatly excelled them both in beauty and size'. Maurice, bishop of London (1086–1107), 'a man of vast ambition', began the new St Paul's on such a scale that it became a burden to his successors, yet 'it is of such magnificent beauty that it is worthily numbered amongst famous buildings. Such is the breadth of the crypt, such is the spaciousness of the upper building, that it would seem to be large enough for any crowd that could be brought together.' At Bury St Edmunds, the memorialist recorded how Abbot Baldwin (1065–97/8) 'by the order of the elder King William . . . laid the foundations and began a more artistic and more beautiful church, wrought with work of columns, vault and marble, than which many who have seen it declare that they have never seen one more handsome and delightful'.[34] Just as Baldwin, Edward the Confessor's man, felt moved to take the same initiatives as his colleagues who had come over with the Conqueror, so Bishop Wulfstan of Worcester, for all his attachment to the things of the past, was driven to new building in his turn. Characteristically, he placed special importance on the crypts which 'I myself built from their foundations, and which later by the mercy of God I dedicated.'[35] It was there that he set the shrine of 'the pious father Oswald', with the relics of those other native saints and martyrs he revered.

Anglo-Saxon relic cults may indeed explain the relatively high incidence of elaborate crypts in the greater churches of the post-Conquest decades, for which there is no real parallel in Normandy. Wulfstan's crypt at Worcester has itself survived, and there are other important examples remaining at Abbot Serlo's Gloucester and at St Augustine's, Canterbury, where its builder, Abbot Scotland, was to be buried among the tombs and relics of many of his predecessors in office.[36] However, another difference from Normandy which can only be explained in the context of the settlement, owing nothing to native survivals, was the very common stretching of the ground plans of churches, to make them much longer, although rarely any broader, than their models in western France. The first churches at Battle Abbey and at Old Sarum, laid out in the 1070s within a few years of the landing, were still comparatively modest buildings, directly matching their equivalents in the Norman homeland. But Abbot Paul's St Albans, Herbert Losinga's Norwich and William of St Calais' Durham were conceived in more secure times, and they display this security in their scale. Except at Durham, the vaulting of which was technically very advanced, the Anglo-Norman builders did not show themselves to be innovative by nature. They took over something from the Anglo-Saxons in the widespread, if short-lived, emphasis on the crypt, out of fashion again by the mid-twelfth century. Quite commonly, too, they employed Anglo-Saxon ornament in their buildings. But they entered the main stream of European architectural innovation only once, at Durham. And the greater churches of the Norman settlement of England are conspicuous chiefly for their extraordinary size, a proof of ambition more certainly than of good taste.

This ambition, in Durham's case, was given special meaning by a revival of monasticism in the North which owed everything to the cult of St Cuthbert. It was the Cuthbert legend, as preserved most particularly in the writings of Bede, which drew three monks of Evesham northwards in the mid-1070s, to be welcomed there by Bishop Walcher of Durham (1071–80), another student of Bede, and to result in the resettlement of the Cuthbert holy places at the ancient monasteries of Wearmouth and Jarrow. Other great northern houses that owed their origins to this initiative were Whitby, already in existence by 1077, and St Mary's, York, established there by 1088. However, it was the cathedral priory at Durham itself that was to be the most important product of the migration from Evesham, for it was to Durham that William of St Calais, Bishop Walcher's successor, brought the communities already settled at Wearmouth and Jarrow, and it was at Durham that the incorrupt body of St Cuthbert, the perpetual inspiration of his legend, was re-housed. Like Bishop Walcher, William of St Calais had studied the Cuthbert legend. He must have recognized the value of the Cuthbert association to his own Christian ministry in the North, nor would he have had any objection, as a former abbot of Saint-Vincent-du-Mans, to having monks as custodians of the saint. Bishop William died in 1096, to be succeeded after a three-year interval by Ranulf Flambard. But though his cathedral was not consecrated for another generation, its plan and very likely its innovatory vaulting system were established before his death. The simple tunnel vault had been used before, with the groined vault developing by the early 1060s as identical tunnel vaults were made to meet at right angles. However, at Durham for the first time diagonal arches spanned the bays, and the ribbed vault, with all its potential for future sophistications of roofing, had been born.

Ranulf Flambard (1099–1128), as one of the monks of his community at Durham remarked, 'concerned himself with the work of the church with greater or less energy according as money from the offerings to the altar and burial fees flowed in or was lacking'.[37] Nevertheless, so much had been achieved by his predecessor, and even by the monks themselves during the vacancy, that the translation of St Cuthbert's body to its new resting-place behind the high altar could already take place as early as 1104, with the entire east end of the cathedral by then complete. From that time on, St Cuthbert's miracles multiplied, while the money of his devotees poured in. Both the saint and his tomb-church were secure.

The energy of the monks of Durham in promoting their saint paid off very handsomely and very soon. It enabled them to complete what was to remain one of the greatest churches in Europe within a comparatively short space of time. And of course it inspired many imitators. Among the first of these were the Cluniac monks brought by Roger de Montgomery to Wenlock (Shropshire) in 1080/81, where they were to re-settle the site of an existing minster and former house of nuns dedicated to its first abbess, St Milburge (d. 722). Finding the shrine of the saint empty, so the story goes, the monks pursued their researches into the whereabouts of the body until, one day, they found a document telling them where to dig for it. As is so often the case even in modern archaeology, the wish became father to the deed. St Milburge's bones were found, greeted with joy by their discoverers, washed, and laid with reverence in a new shrine upon the altar. Miracles at once began.[38]

It is, of course, in stories like these that some of the contradictions of the Norman settlement become most obvious. Anglo-Saxon myths, we know, were not always revered. At Elstow, for example, being one of the very few nunneries founded in these decades, the new abbey church was cut roughly through a pre-existing Anglo-

Saxon graveyard on this Bedfordshire site, and although some of the skeletons found in the work were re-buried with reasonable care in charnel pits, others were merely truncated by the foundations and left in place.[39] Lanfranc, too, had deliberately failed to find space for the Anglo-Saxon relics he mistrusted, even in the great cathedral he reconstructed at Canterbury. Yet at Wenlock the legend of St Milburge retained its importance through all the traumas of the Conquest, while at Durham the Anglo-Saxon element, far from weakening over the years, seems on the contrary to have become stronger. Certainly, Durham was among those buildings of the late eleventh century where Anglo-Saxon ornament, after the lapse of some decades, was coming back once again into fashion. At Durham, the pre-Conquest tradition of manuscript illumination, distinguished by its outline drawing in the lively English manner, found talented continuators throughout the twelfth century. Durham's saint, St Cuthbert, was as English as the monks by whom he came to be surrounded, with a prestige in the region which not even the Conqueror could bring himself ever to disavow. In practice, then, the Norman settlement brought discomfort and unease to many in the existing English monastic community, but permanent dislocation to very few. The real revolution in Western monasticism – Europe-wide, in any event, rather than English – was yet to come.

Chapter 2

The Reforming Summer

When William de Warenne brought Cluniacs to Lewes and when Roger de Montgomery chose monks of the same 'family' to colonize the former nunnery at Wenlock, they were backing the best cause that they knew. But Cluny, despite its re-invigoration under its great abbots Odilo and Hugh, was beginning to experience problems of its own. Sixty years in office, Abbot Hugh (d. 1109) had ruled Cluny for too long. In his middle years, as the trusted associate of the papacy and the adviser of princes, he had presided over a community at its peak; in his old age, he would witness a decline. Too rapidly and with too few organizational safeguards, Cluny's recent expansion had taken it into such alien lands as England and, pre-eminently, Spain. It had undertaken commitments, not least of these to Abbot Hugh's great church, which it found difficult to continue. Under the good management of Peter the Venerable (1122–57), many of these problems could still be resolved. And certainly Cluny's special relationship with the papacy, inherited from Abbot Hugh, continued to stand it in good stead. The Cluniac economy survived in reasonable health for many centuries. More serious by far in its long-term consequences was Cluny's failure to retain its leadership in the faith.[1]

Already in the eleventh century, a new asceticism was finding favour. Against Cluny's magnificence and its near-complete identification with the upper ranks of contemporary feudal society, could be set the primitive austerities of the apostolic life as it was thought to have been practised in the earliest – and by implication the purest – years of Holy Church. Until this time, most monastic houses (Cluniac included) had clustered in centres of population. They had conceived their purpose to be the glorification of God, and had spent lavishly on buildings to achieve it. Now the emphasis was to be radically different. Stephen of Muret's Order of Grandmont, founded in the later 1070s, was one of the pioneers of a return to eremitical monasticism in which the primitive teachings of the early Fathers of the Desert figured prominently. The so-called *Rule of St Stephen* was a posthumous compilation, but its main precepts were those of the founder himself and it well caught the mood of his period. 'My brethren,' Stephen is reported to have said, 'you will go to some poor place where there are neither buildings nor books, and you will not shrink from poverty. A wood is a suitable spot in which to build a cell and live by toil. . . . Wherever you build, see that you harm no one; those who hated you when you first began to build in solitary places will love you afterwards and confer many benefits on you. . . . If you are reduced to such straits of poverty that you have no food left you must send two of your brethren to the bishop to ask him for help, and if he will not hear you, and you have eaten nothing for two days, send two of the brethren to ask alms at mills and houses, as other poor folk must, but do not go to beg from your

14 'A religious site truly suited to the monastic life . . . in a wilderness far removed from the bustle of mankind': Llanthony Priory, in Monmouthshire

friends. I have remained in my hermitage for nearly fifty years, some of them years of plenty, others of scarcity, but I have always had enough. So will it be with you if you keep my commandments.'[2] True to St Stephen's teaching, the English Grandmontine houses, although founded much later and never more than three in number, were established in remote places – Grosmont in the forest of Egton in North Yorkshire, Alberbury and Craswall in the Welsh Marches. All remained poor throughout their history, and only Grosmont survived until 1536 and to the general dissolution of the lesser houses.

The original desert fathers, St Antony (d. 356) and St Pachomius (d. 346), both of Upper Egypt, had sought solitude in the wilderness as the best aid they knew to contemplation. In Western Europe, in the late eleventh century, these beliefs were dusted off, to take their place among the principal axioms of the new monasticism. Gerald of Wales, himself no friend of monks or canons, contemplating Llanthony Priory (Monmouthshire) towards the end of the next century, nevertheless recognized there 'a religious site truly suited to the monastic life and more adapted to canonical discipline than all the convents of the British isle . . . in a wilderness far removed from the bustle of mankind . . . a place truly suited to contemplation, a happy and pleasant spot'.[3] Nothing could point the contrast with the perennial activity of Cluny more clearly. It was just these distractions – the comings and goings of important people, the large and noisy congregations, the everlasting tumult of the building site – that the reformers most wanted to avoid.

Of course, it is easier now to see some pattern in such twelfth-century developments than it was for those who lived amongst them. The new orders of monks (Tironensians and Grandmontines, Cistercians, Savigniacs and Carthusians) and of regular canons (Augustinians, Premonstratensians and Gilbertines) were not sprung upon the world fully formed. Originating in an ideal of isolation and of a return to the letter of the Rule, they were rarely well adjusted to expansion. Their founders – Stephen of Grandmont, Robert of Molesme, Bruno of La Grande Chartreuse, Norbert of Prémontré, Gilbert of Sempringham – were inspirational dreamers rather than organizers. They borrowed precepts from each other, and not infrequently changed their minds. St Gilbert, founder of the only English order to survive these years intact, was one of the heaviest borrowers of them all. He was legislating for a mixed order of regular canons (priests living the 'regular' or monastic life) and nuns, with the additional complication that the manual work and most of the day-by-day business of his communities were handled by specially recruited and similarly celibate lay brethren. For these last, he took the existing Cistercian *Use* as his model; his nuns were to live according to the Cistercian interpretation of the Rule of St Benedict, his canons by the Rule of St Augustine. Gilbert knew the Cluniac-influenced nunnery at Fontevrault, of which Amesbury (Wiltshire), re-founded in this allegiance in 1177, became the most successful English daughter-house. He drew upon its customs for the care and custody of his own nuns, and looked similarly for inspiration to St Stephen's Grandmont.[4] That 'clearly extraordinary man', Gilbert of Sempringham, was to be judged soon after his death as 'of singular grace in the care of women'.[5] Yet it had been he who, at an advanced age and 'most unsuited for the purposes of lust', had chosen to make a point about chastity among his nuns by parading naked in front of the community, 'hairy, emaciated, scabrous and wild'.[6] It is of such that saints, more than organizers, are made.

Usually, indeed, it was in the second generation that the success of the new orders was established. And the greatest of these – the Cistercian, or 'white' monks – owed more without question to Bernard of Clairvaux (1090–1153) than to Robert of Molesme, their founding father, or even to Stephen Harding, their original legislator. In the meantime, and frequently for years afterwards as well, confusion between the emergent orders was extreme. Few perhaps were to match the bemusement of Margaret de Lacy who, 'in her simplicity' and a full century after most had begun to come to grips with the problem, made over her new nunnery at Aconbury (Herefordshire) to the Knights Hospitaller, while fully intending to subject her community to the more congenial Rule of St Augustine.[7] But many were uncertain to which group of religious they should direct their benevolence, or how consistent they really ought to be. Walter Espec, founder in the early 1120s of a community of Augustinian canons at Kirkham, in East Yorkshire, was to become in the next decade one of the most generous of the supporters of the Cistercians, taking a prominent part in the endowment of Rievaulx (1132), in the same county, and then of Warden (1136), its Bedfordshire daughter-house. For a time it seemed as if Kirkham itself might be directed, under Walter's influence, towards the rival Cistercians.[8] In the event, Kirkham survived in its original allegiance, yet its canons could scarcely have welcomed the changing emphasis of their founder's affections, nor were they alone in the experience. The Tony family, founder-patrons of Conches, in Normandy, swung inconstantly first to the Austin canons of Holy Trinity, Aldgate, then to the endowment of a small nunnery at St Giles in the Wood, Flamstead (Hertfordshire), finally turning in another direction altogether with a project, ultimately unsuccessful because insufficiently endowed, to support the Cistercians of Cwnhir (Radnor) in the foundation of a daughter community.[9]

What sent Ralph de Tony to the assistance of the Cistercians was his view of them still, in the early thirteenth century, as an ascetic order, better able to look after his soul than monks of a slighter observance. And while opinions would differ, at this as at any time, about the respective merits of the orders, what remained important to founders of every rank was the degree of sincerity they thought they perceived among the communities to which they directed their investment. Wulfric, a West Country recluse of some local fame in the mid-twelfth century, preferred the Cistercians, tolerated the Cluniacs and actively disliked the Augustinians. When asked to advise on a proposal to establish an Augustinian priory at Haselbury Plucknett (Somerset), his own village, he was able to deflect the generosity of the founder, William fitzWalter, into what he considered better paths.[10] William of Malmesbury, Wulfric's contemporary, would probably have concurred in this action. He had himself witnessed the birth of the Cistercian colonization of England, and was especially proud of the role of the Englishman, Stephen Harding, in the early promotion of the order, for 'it redounds to the glory of England to have produced the distinguished man who was the author and promoter of that rule'. Like others of his day, what he admired about the Cistercians was their austerity and the discipline with which they maintained it. 'So intent are they on their Rule,' he reported, 'that they think no jot nor tittle of it should be disregarded.' Indeed, 'to sum up all the things which are or can be said of them, the Cistercians at the present day are a model for all monks, a mirror for the diligent, a spur to the indolent'.[11]

It would have been surprising if the Cistercians had held this eminence for long, and of course their claim to it was very quickly challenged. Ranulf de Glanville's choice of Augustinian (black) canons and Premonstratensian (white) canons for his two Suffolk foundations at Butley (1171) and Leiston (1183) respectively, may not have occurred exactly as Gerald of Wales tells the story. Gerald himself had a grudge against the Cistercians, whom he held to be avaricious in the accumulation of lands, and thought as little of the Cluniac monks, whom he judged slothful and too fond of their food. And these were the opinions he would attribute in his turn to the justiciar.[12] Yet it is plain that Ranulf de Glanville did indeed think hard about the orders he supported, and other patrons, unless restricted in their choices by some necessary precondition, are likely to have done the same. When Bishop Alexander of Lincoln (1123–48) believed it tactically desirable to turn his energies to the foundation of monastic houses, his selection of good causes was significant. It was Arrouaisians, the contemplative branch of the Augustinian family, that he installed at Dorchester (Oxfordshire) in about 1140 and that he supported in preference to the more pastoral canons of the order throughout his large Lincoln diocese. Furthermore, this enclosed and ascetic flavour in the Arrouaisians was still more apparent in Bishop Alexander's other works. Within a very few years, he had founded two Cistercian houses at Louth Park (Lincolnshire) and Thame (Oxfordshire), had been prominent in the early support of the double priory at Sempringham, St Gilbert's home base, and had himself been instrumental in setting up another Lincolnshire Gilbertine house at Haverholme, near Sleaford, on a site originally intended for Cistercians. Of these, it is probable that support of the native Gilbertine order was the cause dearest to Alexander's heart, for Gilbert of Sempringham, besides being a Lincolnshire man, had also been a member of the bishop's household for some years. Nevertheless, a conscious decision in favour of the new asceticism is apparent in all three choices, being obviously what links them most firmly. And Alexander's neglect of the old black monk communities – the Benedictines and Cluniacs of the Anglo-Norman settlement – is as apparent as his favour for houses of the new wave.[13]

Among Bishop Alexander's associates, at least one of whom helped actively in the foundation and endowment of Louth Park, were Ranulf, earl of Chester (d. 1153), William, earl of Lincoln and Cambridge (d. about 1161), and Robert, earl of Leicester (d. 1168), with his twin brother Waleran, count of Meulan. All of these were energetic patrons of the Cistercians, promoting between them a proliferation of ascetic communities which would have been impracticable in the absence of such leadership. When their work was complete, the main period of Cistercian expansion was already over. But this is not to say that founders of the next generation looked any less carefully for proof of devotion amongst those they assisted with their gifts. The canons of Wigmore (Herefordshire) went through many vicissitudes before settling on their final location in the 1170s. However, what recommended them still to their helpers at that time was the sincerity they preserved from their Victorine origins and which had brought them to England in the first place. Back in the 1140s, their founder, Oliver de Merlemond, had stayed at the abbey of St Victor, just outside Paris, where he had been 'most handsomely and courteously received with great honour [a graunt honour]'. While there, having clearly a foundation of his own in mind at the church he had newly built at Shobdon on his Hertfordshire estates, he 'examined and carefully considered all things which he saw in the guesthouse, the cloister and the choir, and particularly [nomement] the service which was performed around the altar, and his heart was moved by the orderliness which he saw in all places'. St Victor just then, as the home of the great Victorine theologians Hugh and Richard of St Victor, was at the peak of its intellectual eminence. Its prestige, through the troubled early years of its English daughter-house, characterized by repeated changes of site, kept the infant community from foundering.[14]

The canons' final move had been away from their village site in Wigmore itself, where they had found the speech of their neighbours 'very vulgar and coarse' and where solitude and contemplation were impossible. It was an attitude that found favour with patrons unable to maintain such discipline themselves. As William of Malmesbury had said of the Cistercian Stephen Harding – 'I am anxious to extol his praise, because it is a mark of an ingenuous mind to approve that virtue in others, the absence of which you regret in yourself.'[15] Similarly, the great men of the time, among them the king, looked to the monks for a standard of excellence that their own lives of action denied them. Henry II was no clean-mouthed ascetic, and his language

15 The foundations of the domestic range at Grove Priory (Bedfordshire). Grove's excavators are stand-
    ing at the four corners of the chapel (top), of the porch (top right), and of the hall (centre). Grove
    was a non-conventual priory, and was more secular than monastic in its plan

no doubt was only a degree or so less vulgar than that of the villagers of Wigmore.
Nevertheless, he appreciated a sincere man of religion when he saw one, and his
support of religious of the stricter observance undoubtedly goes back earlier than
that penance, following Thomas Becket's murder, which is so often advanced to
explain it. The archbishop died on 29 December 1170, and many of Henry II's more
expensive works of piety do indeed fall within the following two decades. But his
interest in the Cistercians, which he shared with his mother Matilda, dated back to
his youth, while it was at that time also that his benefactions in Normandy included
support for the more dedicated and austere of the canons, among them the Victorines
of Notre-Dame-du-Voeu, near Cherbourg.[16] Later he was to give exceptionally
generous aid to the Augustinian canons of Waltham, in Essex, whose house, after its
refoundation in 1177, became one of the wealthiest of that order; he was a supporter
of the Carthusians, being the founder of their first house in England, at Witham
(Somerset); and gave help also to Gilbert of Sempringham as founder of Newstead
(Lincolnshire) and as patron of Bishop Alexander's double priory at Haverholme.
More significant though than any of these, and the cause of some perplexity among
his contemporaries, was Henry's particular favour for the hermit-monks of

Grandmont, among whom, before the squabbles within the order that characterized the 1180s, he had intended to enjoy his last rest. Henry did not himself bring the Grandmontines to England, for they came there only in the first decades of the next century. However, he spent heavily on the rebuilding of the church at Grandmont itself, as much before as after Becket's murder. It was at Grandmont, following the grisly fashion of the day, that the entrails of Henry the younger, Henry II's eldest son, were buried in 1183. Richard the Lion Heart, his second son, would be generous to Grandmont in his turn.[17]

In the event, neither Henry II nor Richard I were buried at Grandmont. The divisions within the order, as lay brethren and choir monks fought for its control, came out into the open in the 1180s. But even without this, Grandmont would hardly have seemed, to most contemporaries, a resting-place fit for a king. Henry's next choice, Robert of Arbrissel's mixed community at Fontevrault which became one of the wealthiest nunneries in France, was very much more appropriate. It was there that he was buried, to be joined by Richard (d. 1199), and by Eleanor of Aquitaine (d. 1204), his widow. The choice, once again, was significant. Fontevrault was no ordinary Benedictine nunnery. Its founder, Robert, had been one of those originators of the reform – the contemporary of Stephen Harding (of the Cistercians), Bernard (of the Tironensians), and Vitalis of Mortain (of the Savigniacs) – whose dissatisfaction with the complex rituals, elaborate buildings and financial preoccupations of the monasteries of their day, had led them into a life of fresh asceticism. Furthermore, Robert's original community at Fontevrault had included a number of high-born ladies who not only brought their individual wealth to the support of the house but established its social superiority. Both ascetic and noble, Fontevrault had just those qualities that would appeal to a king of Henry's predilections, as they had done already to the counts of Anjou and to the dukes of Aquitaine before his time. In

England, Henry had shown his interest in Fontevrault, and his belief in the continuing validity of its ideals, by re-founding the corrupt community at Amesbury (Wiltshire) as a house of Fontevraldine nuns, colonized by nuns from Fontevrault itself and very largely rebuilt at the king's expense in the late 1170s and early 1180s. Earlier still, in 1164, he had given the valuable manor of Leighton (Bedfordshire) to Fontevrault, perhaps intending it as the site for another Fontevraldine community, although it never grew in practice beyond the status of an alien priory.[18]

Leighton, subsequently known as Grovebury or (briefly) Grove Priory, was back in the king's hands in the fourteenth century, as were many alien priories of its kind. And the continuing interest of the Plantagenet kings in Amesbury, as a nunnery fit for their daughters, and in manors like Leighton, formerly their own, is a useful reminder both of the immediate purpose of such twelfth-century founders and of the nature of their preoccupations in the longer term, as later developed by their heirs. The foundation story of St Botolph's, Colchester, an early swallow of the reforming summer, is unusual in that it seems to have been the priests themselves of this former Anglo-Saxon minster community who took the initiative in adopting the Rule of St Augustine. They sought advice from one of their number who had studied at Bec under Anselm, to be told by him – 'If you propose to assume the religious life, there is in foreign parts a certain way of life wise and fine enough, but entirely unknown in these parts – the life and rule, that is to say, confirmed by the authority of the most holy Augustine, the glorious doctor, which furthermore is termed by Catholics the canonical rule.'[19] And this, after further research at Beauvais and at Chartres, was what they brought back to England in the very last years of the eleventh century, or conceivably early in the twelfth. More commonly, though, it was laymen's initiatives that provided the necessary spur. Two other communities of regular canons, obscure in origin but each likely to be earlier than St Botolph's, were St Mary's, Huntingdon, and St Giles', Cambridge (later re-established at Barnwell). They were the foundations of Eustace the Sheriff and Picot the Sheriff respectively, and they foreshadow an association between the regular canons and the administrative or curial classes, which became one of the more outstanding characteristics of the first phase of the Augustinian settlement.

In an association of this kind, as was only to be expected, there was advantage to be gained by both sides. The king's administrators were hard-bitten and practical men. They identified easily with the regular canons who, playing Martha to the Benedictines' Mary, were quickly becoming the maids-of-all-work in the Church. St Augustine, bishop of Hippo (392–430), had never drawn up a monastic rule as St Benedict, founder of Monte Cassino in 529, would have understood it. Very much later, Augustine's 'Rule' was to be pieced together from advice he had once given to some religious ladies on the maintenance of a life in common. It was not systematic, making only simple points about obedience, about property-holding and about the designation of fixed hours of prayer. However, it possessed the advantage, especially valuable at such a time of flux as the Church was experiencing in the late eleventh century, of being interpretable in many different ways. Within the Augustinian movement, as it began to shape itself for the first time in these years, there was as much room for the 'broad' as for the 'severe' schools of thought. Existing communities of priests, like those of St Botolph's and St Giles, adrift in a sea of change, found themselves a safe resting-place in the bosom of St Augustine. As one of the Cambridge canons was later to explain it – 'The rule of the canons regular is the Rule of St Augustine, who drew his brethren to live together and tempered the rigour of his rule to their infirmity. Like a kind master, he did not drive his disciples with a rod of iron, but invited those who love the beauty of holiness to the door of salvation under a moderate rule.'[20]

In effect, St Augustine's Rule was better than none. It knit together communities with no other allegiance, and took its place in the contemporary monastic reform. But except in their more severe manifestations, prominent among these being the 'white' canons or Premonstratensians, the regular canons who followed St Augustine never made comfortable bed-fellows with the ascetics. They ran hospitals and retreats for the aged and for lepers; they were school-teachers, chaplains and confessors; they commemorated and buried the dead. Above all, they assumed the responsibility for the parish churches which, in the prevailing reforming climate, lay owners everywhere were shedding.[21] Lay proprietary rights in churches and their tithes, acceptable enough in the tenth and early eleventh centuries, had come increasingly to be denounced by the reformers. Additionally, the lord's entitlement in certain circumstances to give away the tithes of the lands he cultivated (his demesne) to whom he wished, was similarly under attack. Not all men of religion were prepared, and still fewer truly equipped, to take on responsibilities of this kind. There was strong opposition, certainly among the ascetics, to monastic ownership of tithes, the Cistercians rejecting them, along with much else, in a self-denying prohibition of 'churches, altar-dues, burial rights, the tithes from the work or nourishment of other men, manors, dependent labourers, land rents, revenues from ovens and mills and similar [property] which is not in accord with monastic purity'.[22] However, the Benedictines had rarely been bothered by inhibitions of this kind, while one of the chief purposes of the Augustinians from the start was to care for churches hitherto neglected by their lay owners and to recover misappropriated tithes. Under pressures like these, the attitudes of laymen swiftly changed. Before the mid-century, during Stephen's reign, the Benedictines of Winchcombe (Gloucestershire) had laid their hands permanently on the tithes of William de Solers' demesne at Postlip, in their own county, 'which I and my ancestors have been accustomed to give at will to men of religion, priests and poor clerks, now to some, now to others'.[23] Not much later, Roger de Flamville was giving the parish church of Norton to the Gilbertine canons of Malton (Yorkshire) only 'in as much as it is right for a lay person' to do so.[24] But the most complete statement of this kind is surely that of Robert, earl of Leicester (d. 1190), the third of his line, explaining his father's gift of English tithes to the Norman Benedictines of Lire. As he told the pope:

Ever since the Normans subjugated England, my ancestors were always accustomed to give these tithes [of Sopwich and Ringston] to whomever they wished. My grandfather R[obert de Beaumont], count of Meulan, gave them to the monks of Préaux, who after some time were seriously oppressed by the managers of these estates and complained to my grandfather that the violence of his officials made it so difficult to collect the tithes that they derived small benefit from them;

and the monks thus complained frequently until my grandfather took the tithes back into his own domain and in their place gave the monks an estate called Expectesberi. For some time my father the late Earl Rob[ert of Leicester, 1119–68] gave these tithes to his managers with his other farms. At last, being a just and devout man, he followed wiser counsel and was unwilling to use them for himself any longer, since he realized that they had once been tithes, although they had become part of his domain by the subsequent exchange for the estate mentioned above, and he gave them to his clerics, first to his doctor, Peter, and then to Adam of Ely. Since he was concerned over recent events, however, and wanted to grant them definitely, he gave the said tithes permanently to the monastery of Lire and to the monks serving God there, in the presence of myself and many others and at my request, and he confirmed [this grant] in writing and by his seal.[25]

Earl Robert's growing awareness of the special quality of these revenues was to be shared by many of his contemporaries. No longer morally able to hold onto the possessions of Holy Church, they looked about them for some more suitable custodian. Communities of regular canons, not infrequently brought together for this very purpose, were especially appropriate beneficiaries. It was not that the canons necessarily served the parish churches they acquired at this time, although as priests they were perfectly able to do so, and sometimes did.[26] However, they were willing to shoulder the general responsibility for the cure of souls in the parishes, while being able – and this, perhaps, was more important to the average patron of the period – to offer appreciable benefits in return. Patrons might take their duties seriously enough; as Picot the Sheriff's successor put it, re-establishing the failing community at St Giles (Cambridge) on its new and permanent site: 'As I have succeeded Picot in place of his heir in possessing his heritage, so I will succeed him in endowing and cherishing this house.'[27] Nevertheless, what they more usually gave up was an asset by that time recognizably of declining value to themselves, in favour of many long-term advantages. Chief among these always was the prominence given to the founder, as well as to every substantial benefactor after his day, in the prayers of the grateful community. Such permanent commemoration had its own value, not readily obtainable elsewhere. But it had another purpose too in reminding the community of persisting obligations to the founder's kin, his successors and assigns. Founders and their heirs, right through until the final suppression of the religious houses, continued to lay claim to hospitality in the communities with which they remained associated. Very often they enjoyed the privilege of nomination to a vacancy, whether one that had occurred at an appropriated church or one arising in the community itself. They might keep their horses and hounds in the priory stables, or lodge an elderly relative in its guest-house. Religious houses were convenient repositories for plate and other treasures; they might be touched for a loan, or their services enlisted in the business transactions of their patrons.[28]

The relationship was less unequal than it might seem. Whereas it is true that founders had comparatively little to lose by transferring their churches to the canons, these in their turn had very much more to gain. The profit, of course, was not always immediate, but one of the qualities of a perpetual corporation was that it could usually afford to wait. In later years, for which the figures for the first time become available, it is often apparent that the spiritualities (receipts from churches and their tithes) of an Augustinian house had come to equal, or even exceed, its temporalities (receipts from cultivated lands and rents). Moreover, this was at least as true of the larger houses as it was of the medium-sized and small. Notley Abbey, in Buckinghamshire, was one of the greater Augustinian houses, founded by Walter Giffard (d. 1164), earl of Buckingham, and originally (like Bishop Alexander's near-by Dorchester foundation) of the contemplative Arrouaisian persuasion. Earl Walter gave the canons his park at Long Crendon, as Bishop Alexander had set up the Cistercians in his park at Louth, to remove them from the society of laymen. But he endowed them too with all the parish churches on his demesne lands, several of them grouped tightly around Notley itself, and these were to become, with the other spiritualities subsequently acquired by the canons, twice as valuable as the abbey's temporalities.[29] In much the same way, when Ranulf de Glanville chose Augustinian canons for his new foundation at Butley (Suffolk) in 1171, he endowed them immediately with six or more churches in the vicinity, a total which they continued to augment. By the late thirteenth century if not before, spiritualities had become much the most important element in Butley's annual revenues. They were not to remain so throughout the Middle Ages. Nevertheless, before the Dissolution, Butley had established a claim to as many as twenty-nine churches in total, most in East Anglia but one of them as distant as London, and the canons may have had interests, although perhaps only temporary, in another five churches as well.[30] For smaller houses like Owston (Leicestershire) and Burscough (Lancashire), the accumulation of churches might very well have been the single most important element in their success. It was the glebe lands of Owston's parish churches that became the nucleus of the abbey's subsequent estates as they were to develop, for example, in the canons' demesnes at King's Norton and Stretton Parva.[31] At Burscough, a house of little wealth with a leper hospital to maintain from its revenues, the three parish churches of the founder's gift, although none of them valuable, brought in almost the entire income of the canons. A major coup of the priory's later history was the appropriation in 1381 of a fourth church at Ratcliffe on Soar, in Nottinghamshire, without which the community might easily have foundered.[32]

Robert, son of Henry, who had brought the Augustinian canons to Burscough late in the twelfth century, would have had a mixture of motives in doing so, one of them the enclosure and development of his own lands. Such, certainly, was a well-documented purpose of many contemporary Lincolnshire foundations where the monks played their part in the drainage of fenland, in the provision of ferries and in the maintenance of bridges and causeways.[33] Nor was it less essential in the remote and ill-developed North-West, where the close partnership of lay landowner and man of religion brought prosperity, if only patchily, to the region. Characteristically, it was only in the second phase of Augustinian expansion that the canons penetrated the area. However, the services they brought to Lancashire and Cumberland in the late twelfth century, recommending them to such leading county families as the Lathom founders of Burscough, were precisely those that had given the first wave of foundations its impetus in the more favoured and prosperous South. One of the most influential, and always among the wealthiest, of the new foundations was Merton Priory, in Surrey. On the initiative of Gilbert the Sheriff, a trusted royal servant who

17 A general view from the south-west of the remains of Furness (Lancashire), originally a Savigniac
community settled on an estate belonging to Stephen of Blois. After he became king in 1135, Stephen
richly endowed Furness and resisted its merger with the Cistercian order in 1147

owed his fortune to Henry I, it was colonized in 1114 by a small group of canons from
St Mary's, Huntingdon, itself established before the end of the previous century by
another official, Eustace the Sheriff, although on a very much smaller scale. Gilbert
used his connections at court and in the government service to build the fortunes of
the priory by which he expected to be remembered, and within a very few years
others of his kind were active in following his example. Prominent royal officials,
before the end of Henry I's reign, had brought the Augustinians to Leicestershire at
Richard Bassett's Launde, to Warwickshire at Geoffrey de Clinton's Kenilworth, to
Hampshire at William Pont de l'Arche's Southwick (originally at Portchester), and to
many other regions of the country.[34] Furthermore, the interest of leading churchmen
was engaged. When William Giffard, bishop of Winchester (1107–29), turned an
existing collegiate foundation at Taunton (Somerset) over to the regular canons, he
acknowledged the inspiration he had experienced himself from Gilbert the Sheriff's
Augustinians at Merton – 'Seeing therefore this congregation sublimely aspiring to
perfection, William, bishop of the church of Winchester, began thenceforth to
beseech the brethren [of Merton] with vows and prayers, desiring to introduce into
his church of Taunton those same observances which they themselves employed.
Which indeed came to pass.'[35]

   Taunton's colonization by the Augustinians can be dated to approximately 1120,
and it was in the latter part of Henry I's reign especially, between 1120 and the last

18 St Bernard writing, inspired by God (the hand from the cloud), with two pupils seated at his feet. English, mid-thirteenth century

months of 1135, that the annual totals of Augustinian foundations peaked most strikingly.[36] It was at this time too that the wealthiest communities of black canons were established, and they owed their support in very large measure to the friends and associates of the king. Some forty-three Augustinian houses had been founded in England and in Norman-held Wales before the end of Henry's reign, and of these, it has been calculated, three-quarters or more were connected in one way or another with the king's circle.[37] It was not, of course, that the king or his officials were alone in endowing these houses. They did not need to be so, for their initiatives could be relied upon, in almost every case, to attract substantial support in the locality. The

19 Rievaulx Abbey (North Yorkshire) in its remote valley-bottom situation on the banks of the Rye: the first of Bernard's 'fortifications' in the north of England where the Cistercians would soon become so numerous

Augustinians of Nostell, a rich West Yorkshire house, counted Hugh de Laval, lord of Pontefract, as their founder. But it was Henry I himself who could claim the credit for the collection, from 1122, of Nostell's substantial endowment. He gave it the church at Bamborough and a rent at his exchequer at York; furthermore, he moved his friends to do likewise. Archbishop Thurstan of York gave the canons a church at Tickhill; William de Warenne, earl of Surrey, contributed his part of the parish church at Woodkirk; Hugh de Laval assisted them with churches in his Pontefract honour and put pressure on his tenants to support the new foundation in whatever way they could.[38] On a much smaller scale, the canons of St Denys, near Southampton, established there by Henry I in 1127 or just before, experienced both the advantages and some of the snags of royal interest. They were to find, just as the monks of the king's abbey at Westminster had already begun to do, that 'nothing grows under a big tree', and neither community was especially lucky in attracting the support of its immediate neighbours.[39] But if the burgesses of Southampton were cool initially, the landowners in the region were more generous. Many of these, it is known, had connections at court, and it was royal curialists and administrators again who, for the rest of the century, were the chief prop of this diminutive community.[40]

Much depended at all times on the preferences of founders, and in the 1130s, just a few years after the Augustinian settlement at St Denys, these were already beginning to shift. The regular canons had answered a very real need. Accordingly, they had appealed to the men whose job it was to see that society ran smoothly. But they were not, before the arrival of the white canons (the Premonstratensians) later in the

20 Rievaulx from the air; it was here that recruits to the order, in Abbot Ailred's time (1147–67), swarmed 'like a hive of bees'

21 Fountains Abbey (West Yorkshire), first established in this 'place of horror and vast solitude' during the winter of 1132–3

century, well equipped to respond to the demand, increasing in urgency at just this time, for the promotion of a life of asceticism. To those among the higher aristocracy who sought the very best from their religious, the 'moderate' Rule of the Austin canons, tempered to the infirmity of the brethren, was clearly not adequate for their purpose. Moreover, there was no difficulty in finding an alternative.

In this new monastic invasion of Britain, the outriders were St Dogmael's, a Tironensian house in remote Pembrokeshire, founded in c. 1115 by Robert fitzMartin, the first Norman lord of Cemais, and Furness in Lancashire, a Savigniac community, settled on its second and final site in 1127 on lands of Stephen of Blois.[41] Neither the Tironensians nor the Savigniacs were to make much impact on England, the former being the initiators of the merest handful of communities, while the latter became the subject of a merger with the Cistercians which occurred only twenty years after the gift of the site at Furness. Nevertheless, both foundations, at St Dogmael's and Furness, held the seed already of much that was yet to come. They were sited remotely – St Dogmael's on the Pembrokeshire coast, under permanent threat from the Welsh, and Furness likewise in a coastal and forest location, desolate as yet and uncleared. That first condition (isolation) of the ascetic life had thus been met. A second, being the disinterested support of a magnate patron, was present at both houses as well.

Especially important in the promotion of the ascetic orders was the concern of the king himself. Stephen's reign (1135–54) began, as was only to be expected, with a substantial reaction against the policies of his predecessor. Already, in such foundations as Stephen's own Furness, past materialism was implicitly condemned. As king, Stephen continued to see himself as the lay patron of Savigny, having further Savigniac foundations at Buckfast (Devonshire) and Coggeshall (Essex) to his

22 The remains of the west porch (narthex or Galilee) at Fountains, such porches being a characteristic Burgundian import from the Cistercians' original homeland

23 *Opposite* Unadorned severity in the mid-twelfth-century nave at Fountains, following St Bernard's prescription

credit. Stephen's magnates, whatever side they favoured in the civil wars of his reign, followed the king's preferences in the support of the reforming orders – the Savigniacs, the Gilbertines and the Cistercians. It was not a political decision, yet politics sometimes gave it a special twist. The most influential figure in the contemporary Church was Bernard, abbot of Clairvaux (1115–53). He was never an easy man, and he thrived, like many great leaders, on controversy. One of these battles was with Stephen himself over the election to the archbishopric of York. It was Bernard ultimately who triumphed, although only at the cost of Stephen's continuing opposition to the merger of Cîteaux and Savigny.

Appropriately enough, a later chronicler of the successful Cistercian settlement of the North of England used military metaphors to describe it. The settlement had been anticipated at Waverley (Surrey) in 1128, one of the progeny, with Tintern (Monmouthshire) in 1131, of the Cistercian community at L'Aumône. However, it was Bernard's leadership, during the last years of Henry I, that drove forward the major colonization. From Clairvaux, we are told, this 'man of splendour, a strenuous worker at the business of God' sent 'the soldiers of his army to conquer distant lands', among them the promising territory of England. There,

his men were received with honour by the king and the kingdom, and they established new fortifications in the province of York. They constructed the abbey which is called Rievaulx [1131–2], which was the first plantation of the Cistercian

Order in the province of Yorkshire. Those who were sent were holy men, being monks who glorified God in the practice of poverty. They dwelt in peace with all men, although they warred with their own bodies and with the old enemy. They showed forth the discipline of Clairvaux whence they came, and by works of piety they spread the sweet savour of their mother-abbey, as it were, a strong perfume from their own house. The story spread everywhere that men of outstanding holiness and perfect religion had come from a far land; that they had converse with angels in their dwelling; and that by their virtues they had glorified the monastic name. Many therefore were moved to emulate them by joining this company whose hearts had been touched by God. Thus very soon they grew into a great company . . .[42]

That great company at Rievaulx, under the saintly Abbot Ailred (1147–67), would grow so large 'that the church swarmed with them like a hive of bees'. But in the meantime Rievaulx itself had been sending out colonizers to Melrose (Roxburghshire) and Warden (Bedfordshire), among others, and the influence of Clairvaux, whether through Rievaulx or through its many sister Cistercian foundations, was being felt throughout the land. Significantly, it was not the administrators and curialists – such strong supporters of the regular canons in Henry's reign – who were the most prominent patrons of the Cistercians. Rather, the friends of St Bernard's monks were men of Stephen's class, many of them numbered among his tenants-in-chief and most his associates from youth. Stephen himself was the patron of Red Moor (Staffordshire), later re-founded at Stoneleigh, south of Coventry; to his relative Robert of Gloucester, Henry I's natural son, went the credit of Margam (Glamorgan), one of the largest Cistercian communities in Wales. Revesby (Lincolnshire), founded in 1142 and a daughter of Rievaulx, was the work of William de Roumare, earl of Lincoln and Cambridge; Pipewell (Northamptonshire), in 1143, of Ranulph, earl of Chester; Forde (Dorset), in 1136, of Baldwin de Brionne; Bordesley (Worcestershire), in 1138, of Waleran, earl of Worcester and count of Meulan.[43]

Rievaulx's founder, Walter Espec, was himself one of this group. A man of great height and of 'trumpet voice', he was active as a law-keeper in the northern counties and in the defence of the region against the Scots. Like many of his class, and perhaps

24 The surviving undercroft of the lay brothers' range at Fountains, extended to meet the needs of this large community in the late twelfth century

25 The west front at Fountains, including the undercroft (right) of the lay brothers' range at its northern, and earlier, end

more than most, he had devotional interests as well. Kirkham, his Augustinian foundation north-east of York, was established in the 1120s following the death of the young Walter, his son and heir. It was to Kirkham that the old baron is said to have retired in 1152, to spend the last months of a long and active life in contemplation. In the meantime, though, his support had been engaged for the Cistercians. Not having heirs to consider, both Rievaulx and Warden, on Walter's Bedfordshire estates, could be comfortably endowed from the start. They were to remain among the wealthier of the Cistercian houses, sharing this quality with other major baronial foundations of the time, including the family-linked Revesby and Pipewell.

William de Roumare, earl of Lincoln, and Ranulf de Gernon, earl of Chester, were half-brothers. Founders of Revesby and Pipewell respectively, they were each as active in the support of the Cistercians as they were vigorous in the civil war against Stephen. It is hard to believe that the two activities were wholly unrelated. Both earls had much on their conscience; they had usurped lands and had violated oaths; Ranulf, indeed, is thought to have been poisoned by one of the many he had wronged. With little inclination or opportunity themselves for a life of religion, they were nevertheless aware of what was best in their time and were fully able to back up their preferences with gifts. Ranulf of Chester was a generous supporter of the Savigniacs even before the civil wars began. Before his death in 1153, he could count five Savigniac and Cistercian houses as his own foundations, while featuring also as a substantial patron of another six Cistercian communities. In addition to Revesby,

26 Strata Florida from the air, showing the boxing-in of the lay brothers' choir
by the low screen walls which carried the piers of the nave arcade

William de Roumare brought monks from Rievaulx in 1146 to colonize Rufford, in
Nottinghamshire. He was a benefactor of Garendon (Leicestershire), colonized from
Waverley, and of two Fountains daughter-houses at Vaudey and Kirkstall, in
Lincolnshire and West Yorkshire respectively. At Swineshead, again in his own
home county, the earl of Lincoln was a patron of the Savigniacs.[44]

Ranulf of Chester and William de Roumare had reasons of their own for welcoming St
Bernard's 'soldiers' to their estates. But they were not moved exclusively by self-
interest. Bernard of Clairvaux, at the height of his influence in the 1130s and 1140s,
was not a force easily resisted. From Clairvaux, Cistercian colonizers were to travel
westwards as far as Ireland and Portugal, north into Scotland and Scandinavia, and
south into Italy and the Balkans; from Morimond, before the saint's death, they
would begin the penetration of the central Slav lands and of the territories of the
Orthodox Church. Accordingly, it would be quite wrong to view the Cistercian
settlement of England in terms merely of family alliances, important though these
were, or even as a reaction, understandable enough, against the violence of the
Matildine wars. It was as unstoppable as the rising of the tide.

What gave Cistercian expansionism its special quality was in part the personal
drive of St Bernard himself. Yet it owed much also to the self-evident merits of the
message he so energetically preached. Both elements came together at Fountains
(West Yorkshire), the greatest English community of the order. Fountains was settled
by a splinter group from the Benedictine abbey of St Mary's, York, itself one of the
more important houses of the earlier northern reform and a community clearly able to

27 Neath (Glamorgan): in the church (left), a dividing wall separates the monks' choir at the east end and crossing from the lay brothers' choir in the nave; between the two, also, there was an intervening retro-choir, or pulpitum (*British Crown copyright reserved*)

attract recruits, before the arrival of the Cistercians, from among the noblest spirits of the time. St Bernard's monks, on their way to settle Rievaulx in March 1132, had passed through York. The spell of their example was irresistible. Within the year, and with the support of Archbishop Thurstan, the more intellectual element of St Mary's had split off from the remainder. Failing to reform the existing community, Prior Richard and his companions had sought refuge with the archbishop, to be found a site of their own on an estate of their patron, in the wastes south-west of Ripon. St Mary's itself had been established in this way, nor were the seceders at first concerned to break free from their Benedictine allegiance. However, what they were trying to achieve was clearly in tune with what was happening contemporaneously at Rievaulx. It seems likely that it was in the late summer of 1133 that the first approaches to Clairvaux were made, to be welcomed by St Bernard and to bring the community before 1135 into the growing family of the Cistercians.[45] Recruits flowed in, among them the wealthy Dean Hugh of York, and the future of the settlement was secure.

The quality of the first settlers at Fountains was already very high; four of them were to build reputations as men of letters, and nine were to win promotion as abbots. Nevertheless, the early days on the site were to prove very difficult, mirroring the experience of many similar communities thrust out into the waste by the reformers. For all its present beauty, the site at Fountains when its first settlers looked upon it was 'a place of horror and vast solitude'; it had been 'uninhabited for all the centuries back, thick set with thorns, and fit rather to be the lair of wild beasts than the home of human beings'.[46] While the monks cleared the ground, preparing it for cultivation and for building, they sheltered first under a rock overhang and then

28 Roche (West Yorkshire) from the air, showing clearly the divisions within the abbey church (left) and the line of the stream (right) which the Cistercians diverted and canalized to drain their site

beneath the branches of a great elm. Yet from 1135, under the benevolent eye of St Bernard and with the support of prominent local families, progress was astonishingly rapid. Before Abbot Richard's death in 1139, Fountains had sent out colonies to Newminster, in Northumberland, and to Kirkstead and Louth Park, in Lincolnshire; in the next decade, the communities of Woburn (Bedfordshire), Kirkstall (Yorkshire) and Vaudey (Lincolnshire) were to be recruited from the same rich source.[47] Although savagely interrupted in 1147 when disgruntled supporters of William fitzHerbert, Stephen's ill-starred choice for the archbishopric of York, sacked and burnt the house, building advanced very quickly.

In this first programme of works on the abbey site at Fountains, two characteristics especially stand out. One is the strong Burgundian influence, imported direct from the Cistercian homeland, apparent both in the initial layout and in details of finish and design; the other is generosity of scale. The Cistercians were not great architectural innovators. Almost everything they did had precedents outside the order. Nevertheless, St Bernard himself had very clear views on the architectural environment of his monks. To Fountains, the saint sent Geoffrey of Ainai, one of the two principal monk-architects of Clairvaux; his own choice of third abbot, the abrasive Henry Murdac (d. 1153), had been a monk of Clairvaux and abbot of Vauclair, with views identical to those of his patron. A guiding principle of the Cistercians was austerity. St Bernard was to carry these beliefs even further than his

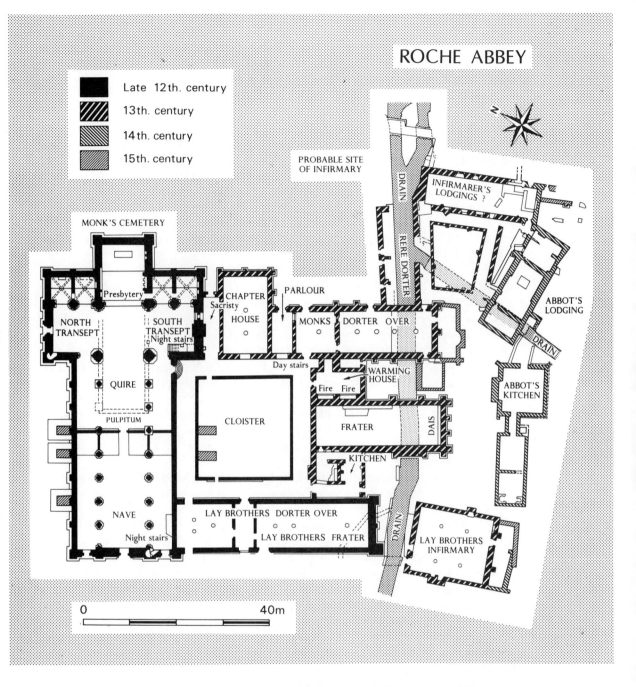

ROCHE ABBEY

Legend:
- Late 12th. century
- 13th. century
- 14th. century
- 15th. century

PROBABLE SITE OF INFIRMARY

INFIRMARER'S LODGINGS ?

ABBOT'S LODGING

MONK'S CEMETERY

DRAIN

RERE DORTER

Presbytery

CHAPTER HOUSE

PARLOUR

Sacristy

NORTH TRANSEPT

SOUTH TRANSEPT

Night stairs

MONKS DORTER OVER

Day stairs

ABBOT'S KITCHEN

DRAIN

WARMING HOUSE

QUIRE

Fire   Fire

DAIS

PULPITUM

CLOISTER

FRATER

KITCHEN

NAVE

LAY BROTHERS DORTER OVER

Night stairs

LAY BROTHERS FRATER

DRAIN

LAY BROTHERS INFIRMARY

0   40m

29 Roche Abbey in plan, showing the characteristic Cistercian layout of its claustral buildings; notice particularly the provision for lay brothers in the church west of the pulpitum, with their separate sleeping and eating quarters in the west claustral range, as well as an infirmary of their own

predecessors, but they were there already in the days of Stephen Harding and had become, by the time that William of Malmesbury wrote his eulogy of the order, an important element in an apparently inviolable code. 'A proof of his abstinence,' in William of Malmesbury's estimation of Stephen and Cîteaux, 'is that you see nothing there, as in other monasteries, gleaming with gold, blazing with jewels or glittering with silver. For as a Gentile says, "Of what use is gold to a saint?" We think our holy vessels to be lacking in something, unless the ponderous metal be eclipsed by precious stones; by the flame of the topaz, the violet of the amethyst or the green shade of the emerald; unless the vestments of the priests sparkle with gold; and unless the walls glisten with multi-coloured paintings and throw the reflection of the sun's rays upon the ceiling. These men, however, placing those things second which mortals foolishly esteem first, give all their diligence to improve their morals, and love pure minds more than glittering vestments.'[48] Fountains, after St Bernard's death, would be rebuilt in the 'far more festive' manner celebrated by its chronicler and still obvious to the visitor today. In the mid-twelfth century, it was fashioned with deliberate austerity.

For all its great scale, that is, the church plan of Fountains repeats the plain cross, obscured in the next century by the rebuilding of the east end, of the order's earliest houses. The cross is to be found again, for example, at the first church of Rievaulx, and was repeated contemporaneously at Tintern and Waverley in the initially modest plans of these abbeys. Another Burgundian characteristic, shared with Rievaulx, was the porch (also known as a narthex or Galilee) sheltering the main door at the west end, while the pointed barrel vaults of the aisles in each building are again purely Burgundian in inspiration. An un-English austerity was introduced at both buildings by the abolition of the run of decorative arcading (the *triforium*) commonly used in major Anglo-Norman churches to separate the nave arcade from the clerestory under the roof. At Rievaulx especially, the square piers of the nave – cylindrical at Fountains – were quite obviously the product of a self-conscious pursuit of Bernardine architectural severity.[49]

There were other important differences between these houses and the conventual buildings of contemporary religious communities. At both Fountains and Rievaulx the communities had grown very fast, and while work was in progress in the mid-twelfth century, the pace of recruitment had as yet shown no sign of slackening. Ailred of Rievaulx died in 1167, but as long as he lived, so his biographer reported, there came to his abbey 'from foreign nations and distant lands a stream of monks who needed brotherly mercy and true compassion, and there they found the peace and sanctity without which no man can see God. Yea, those who were restless in the world and to whom no religious house gave entry, coming to Rievaulx the mother of mercy and finding the gates wide open, freely entered therein.'[50]

An open-door policy on quite this scale was certainly not usual among Cistercians, nor would many abbots have exerted the draw claimed for Ailred of Rievaulx by his biographer. Yet there was one thing especially about the order that gave it a peculiar distinction. Ailred's welcome was not limited to men of the same class or inclinations as himself. Some two-thirds or more of the community at Rievaulx were recruited from amongst unlettered men whose contribution to religion was their labour. Of course, the Cistercians were not the first to use lay brethren in this way; a labouring element had always been necessary to support the life of prayer of the contemplatives.[51] Nevertheless, what Ailred and his contemporaries were among the earliest to emphasize was the spiritual advantage of hard manual work, giving both dignity and holy profit to labour.[52] In Cistercian houses to which the normal sources of monastic revenue – churches and their tithes, manors, mills and rents – were denied as 'not in accord with monastic purity', the only path open to economic survival was the intensive cultivation of their lands. At Fountains, back in its earliest months, the first actions of the monks had included the clearing of land for a garden. Before long, the abbey would become the hub of a complex network of estates, the most important of which were organized as home-farms or 'granges' at which the role of the lay brethren was crucial.[53]

Many lay brethren spent their lives on the granges, returning regularly but only for brief periods to the home monastery. Others, however, were found permanent employment at, or in the immediate vicinity of, the monastic establishment which had become, with the same sense of commitment the monks themselves felt, the only home they knew. Such a novel solution to the problems of labour, embraced with characteristic enthusiasm by the Cistercians, required heroic innovations in architecture. Inevitably there was some preliminary fumbling. At Fountains, the first plan, traditionally Benedictine, was for a relatively modest west claustral range and for a refectory parallel to the cloister on the south. Within just a few decades the west range, given over for the most part to the lay brethren of the community, had proved too small, needing to be extended to its later great length, with the lay brothers' refectory at ground-floor level at the southern end and with their dormitory across the top. To the south range also these alterations brought important changes, for it now became necessary to re-site the monks' refectory in a north-south position, giving space for a warming-house to the east of the new hall and for a great kitchen, common to both, between the hall and the lay brothers' refectory to the west.[54]

In effect, pressure of numbers had forced upon Fountains what was already becoming the standard Cistercian plan. At Rievaulx, strangely, the lay brothers' west range, although rebuilt at this time, remained comparatively modest, while at smaller and later houses like Cymmer (Merioneth), founded in 1198–9, the west range, coming last in the sequence of essential conventual buildings, might never have been built at all.[55] However, Cymmer was a poor house even by the already depressed standards of Wales, and the usual emphasis at Cistercian communities, in the thirteenth century as much as in the twelfth, was on a very different scale of accommodation. Melrose, in Roxburghshire, was one of the first houses to be colonized from Rievaulx, and there, in contrast to the provision at the mother community, the lay brothers' range at this Scottish abbey was already considerable before a further massive thirteenth-century extension.[56] When Devorguilla built Sweetheart Abbey (Kirkcudbrightshire) in the late thirteenth century, she similarly supplied it with lay brothers' quarters of such generous proportions as to exceed in scale those of the monks.[57] In the next generation, as work began on a new abbey at Whalley (Lancashire) for the monks of Stanlaw (Cheshire), driven from their previous site by floods, the by then traditional layout was maintained. The west range at Whalley, although of fourteenth-century build and consequently post-dating the decline in the Cistercian recruitment of lay brethren, was as large as its equivalents in the generations before; in the church, there was as much space in the nave for the lay brothers' choir as there had been originally at Stanlaw.[58]

Duplication of buildings at a Cistercian house was inevitably the consequence of division within the community. Even the church, although shared, was divided by screens, so that the monks might preserve the east end (presbytery) and crossing, while to the lay brethren was given over the nave. One of the clearest survivals of this arrangement is at Strata Florida (Cardigan), where the piers of the nave arcade were themselves set on the screen walls that boxed in the choir of the lay brethren.[59] But such separations were contrived, if less solidly, in all houses of the order, the lay brethren of Roche (West Yorkshire) getting four bays of the nave, while those of Fountains got six and of Rievaulx as many as seven. Beyond the church, the lay brothers' dormitory (dorter) and refectory (frater) at a house like Roche, closely modelled on Fountains to which it was related by way of its own mother-house at Newminster, balanced the similar but more lavish provision for the choir monks of the community, to the east and the south of the cloister. In the south-west angle of the site, the lay brethren were equipped with an infirmary of their own, paralleling the monks' grander infirmary to the south-east. The great kitchen, as at Fountains, was placed between the two refectories, and the main drain, still a very prominent and remarkable feature of the remains at Roche, carried away the waste of both groups together. Otherwise everything was separate.[60]

In due course, the separation of the communities would be the cause of major difficulties. Even while Roche was being built, in the last decades of the twelfth century, jealousies had troubled the Grandmontines and the Gilbertines, and both had experienced riots among their lay brethren which they had not found it easy to suppress.[61] However, the Cistercians had been more careful from the start in their definition of responsibilities, and although they too would know disturbances before the end of the century, especially among the more remote limbs of their order,[62] their experience of lay brethren over the first generations was more usually rewarding to both parties.

Indeed the lay brethren, made welcome by Ailred of Rievaulx and his contemporaries, were a manifestation themselves of that devotional movement which had brought the reform into being in the first place. They gave their labour to the service of God just as the knights, coming together in such orders as the Templars and Hospitallers, commended their swords to the battles of Christ. Stephen of Muret, founder of Grandmont, saw his ideal knight as a 'monk who wears a shield upon his neck'.[63] St Bernard, the most powerful advocate of them all, recruited successfully for the Templars. 'Every order,' wrote Gerhoh of Reichersberg, 'and absolutely every profession in the catholic faith and apostolic doctrine has a rule suited to its quality, and by fighting lawfully under this it will be able to attain to the crown.'[64] He was not talking of monks alone, nor even of those and their associated knights; what he meant was the entire community of the baptized.

Chapter 3

A Spirit of Compromise

In Cistercian history of the mid-twelfth century, three events especially stand out. Together, they marked the end of an era. First of these was the union with Savigny, agreed at the order's general chapter in 1147 and recognized immediately by Pope Eugenius III, himself once one of their number. Coincidentally, it was in that year that there were more Cistercian foundations in England than ever before, or than there ever would be again.[1] Second was a formal acknowledgement of over-rapid expansion, resulting in the prohibition from 1152 of further growth, whether by the foundation of new houses of the Cistercian allegiance or by the reception within the order of other monks. Third was the death of St Bernard.

Changes, even after 1153 and the removal of the strong hand of the saint, were not immediate; yet over the next generation they were significant. In the two decades of Stephen's reign, there had been no fewer than thirty-six Cistercian foundations, seven of those in 1147 alone. Over the following two decades, under Henry II, there were only five.[2] Furthermore, the quality of Cistercian patronage was changing. Of the houses of the order founded while Henry II was king, only two – Stanlaw (Cheshire) and Robertsbridge (Sussex) – were of any real substance. Such contemporary men of means as the justiciar Ranulf de Glanville (above, p. 27) clearly preferred in their own generation to place their investment with the regular canons. And while it is true that the Cistercians continued everywhere to accumulate lands through these years, they did so usually in much smaller parcels, often by purchase or exchange. With patrons no longer among the higher feudality, they found their friends more readily among the lesser gentry and swapped lands with the wealthier peasants.[3]

Some of these trends were to prove of less permanent consequence than others. In the next century, there were to be the great royal foundations at Beaulieu (Hampshire) in 1203/4, at Hailes (Gloucestershire) in 1246, and at Vale Royal (Cheshire) in 1274. For a prominent churchman and administrator like Peter des Roches, bishop of Winchester (1205–38), the foundation of Cistercian houses at Netley (Hampshire) and La Clarté Dieu (Touraine) could still be an important preoccupation of the patron's final years.[4] And it was in the thirteenth century also that the Cistercians greatly enlarged their numbers – and their problems – by the formal recognition for the first time of their responsibility for communities of nuns.[5] Nevertheless, the continuing prosperity of the Cistercian order was not without its less fortunate implications. The very success of the Cistercians as farmers brought upon them the hostility of their neighbours. In court circles in the late twelfth century, whereas the regular canons might be regarded with some favour, the Cistercians were chastized for their avarice, to be depicted in the writings of Gerald of

30 The ornate chapter-house and adjoining entrances at Furness, in Lancashire, illustrating the Savigniac taste for fine decoration which would later infect the Cistercians

Wales and Walter Map as heartless dispossessors of the poor.[6] Neither writer is wholly to be trusted, for both had grievances against the order to pay back. However, their closeness to the king made them, so long as this lasted, a force to be reckoned with in the wealthiest circles where the best patrons were to be found; nor were their criticisms, as contemporaries would have recognized, entirely baseless. The union with Savigny, where discipline was concerned, had not done the Cistercians much good. It had begun a process, hastened in 1153 by St Bernard's death, of compromise in the order's strictest observances. There was less to distinguish a Cistercian from a Benedictine – a white monk from a black – than there had been in the days in the wilderness.

Savigny, indeed, in its early years had been closer to Cluny than to Cîteaux, particularly in its constitutional framework.[7] And when the Savigniacs merged with the Cistercians in 1147, they brought with them what Cistercians of the purer observance clearly saw as a corruption of uses. In England, with Stephen's support, the Savigniac communities – prominent among them being the king's own foundation at Furness (Lancashire) – at first resisted the merger. They lost that battle soon enough, but continued nevertheless to hold onto properties and to practise an architecture of which the Cistercians, until then, would have disapproved. Certainly, whether for this or another reason, the Cistercians had begun to collect spiritualities, or the receipts from parish churches, some decades before the end of the twelfth century.[8] They were not to become regular appropriators of parish churches until the later fourteenth century, and the ownership of tithes, so frequently condemned in the early statutes of the order, was rarely to constitute the most important part of a Cistercian community's net worth. Yet a major element in the re-endowment of Dieulacres (north Staffordshire) in 1214, moved to its new site from Pulton, in Cheshire, originally a Savigniac foundation, was the gift of a church and its associated chapels, and this was a long time after the merger of the two orders should have made such donations unacceptable.[9] Before the Dissolution, the Cistercians of Dieulacres had come to depend on spiritualities, chiefly tithes, for as much as thirty per cent of their income.[10] It was a proportion not uncommon among the Welsh Cistercians by this later period, although certainly more exceptional in England.[11]

In architecture, the corruption of standards was more insidious. The generosity of founders was difficult to turn aside, for the early severity of Clairvaux and its affiliates, standing out like a rock against the currents of the day, had seemed to many at the time to do honour neither to God nor Man. Again former Savigniac houses led the way. The great church built at Byland (North Yorkshire) in the late twelfth century and laid out already in the 1170s, was to be highly influential in Cistercian building in the North, especially important in the introduction of early Gothic. What happened at Byland was imitated at Jervaulx, its daughter-house in the same county, with obvious effects also on contemporary building programmes at Roche and Newminster, Vaudey, Revesby and Abbey Dore. But Byland had begun life in the family of Savigny, colonized from King Stephen's Furness, and the persisting influence of its Savigniac origins continued to be visible in the character of its buildings, long after the merger with Cîteaux. Byland, at last settled on its final site after years of disruptive wanderings, was to be equipped with a church of exceptional grandeur. In direct contrast to Rievaulx, its nearest Cistercian neighbour, where the first church of St Bernard's original 'fortification' in the North had been finished with conspicuous severity, the architecture of Byland was sophisticated, expensive and ornate. With its richly decorated triforium, its fine mouldings and ornamental arcades, it owed more to new developments in cathedral-building in north-east France than to the traditions of Cîteaux's Burgundian homeland.[12] Furthermore, it was far from exceptional in this emphasis. The *corona* of radiating chapels at the east end of the church at Croxden (Staffordshire), founded in 1176, repeated the plan of its Norman mother-house, the former Savigniac community at Aunay-sur-Odon, being very much more Cluniac than Cistercian in its inspiration.[13] At Rievaulx itself, not very much later, the rebuilding of the choir and presbytery in the early thirteenth century provided new opportunities for display. Whereas the first church at Rievaulx, in accord with Cistercian practice at the time of

St Bernard, had extended only two bays east of the crossing, the choir and presbytery of the thirteenth-century rebuilding were seven bays long in total. The three-tiered arcading and fine decorative detail of the new work at Rievaulx, surviving largely intact to this day, were in absolute contradiction of all that St Bernard and 'the soldiers of his army' had maintained.[14]

The early Cistercians had upheld other standards as well, which were now similarly under attack by their patrons. On the Savigniac merger in 1147, the Cistercian community had had to accept three nunneries with the twenty-eight monasteries it absorbed. Yet in that same year, the Cistercian general chapter, under Bernard's guidance, had remained firm enough in its rejection of unwelcome extra responsibilities to deflect the request of Gilbert of Sempringham for affiliation to the order of the canons and nuns of his allegiance.[15] Nor was the Cistercian leadership yet in any way committed to the reception of nuns – even those who had explicitly adopted its life-style and its Rule – within the organization it controlled. Bishop Alexander of Lincoln (1123–48), although himself a very good friend of the Cistercians, was unable to persuade them to adopt the nuns he had established in 1139 at Haverholme, in his diocese, where they followed 'the life of the monks of Cîteaux as far as the strength of their sex allowed'. Instead, he gave them to St Gilbert.[16] Very commonly at this period, exceptionally prolific in the foundation of

31 Byland (North Yorkshire) from the air: a former Savigniac community which, after the merger of the orders in 1147, moved to its final site in the late 1170s, there to be built with exceptional richness (*British Crown copyright reserved*)

32 The west front at Byland, dating to the early thirteenth century and showing clearly the influence of the new Gothic style currently in vogue in France

new nunneries, the nuns wore the white habit of the Cistercians and followed their practices, even to heavy labour in the fields. But they had done so, it is clear, of their own free will, or at best under the guidance of a patron like Bishop Alexander who had no power to welcome them as new members of the order. The encouragement they received from the Cistercians themselves was still, at this time, insignificant.

Such resistance, however, could not continue. Partly because of the competing attractions of the native Gilbertine order, the Cistercian nunneries were never as thick on the ground in England as they would be in Flanders or northern France.

33 Foundations of the *corona* of radiating chapels at the east end of the church at Croxden, a Cistercian house where the earlier austerities of St Bernard and his followers had come to be forgotten or ignored by the late twelfth century

34 The extended choir and presbytery at Rievaulx, rebuilt in the early thirteenth century in a style more lavish than before

However, some thirty English houses of nuns were to enter the Cistercian allegiance at one time or another before the Dissolution, and many of these had first come into existence during precisely that surge in popular devotion that had assisted the expansion of the monks. Over half a century later, in 1213, the Cistercians bowed to the inevitable. For the first time, under pressure from prominent lay patrons like Alfonso of Castille, founder of the wealthy and aristocratic community at Las Huelgas, the Cistercian general chapter accepted the formal incorporation of nuns within the order. With the Premonstratensians at just that time contracting out of the care of further nunneries, swamped by the recruits they had accepted in large numbers since the days of St Norbert their founder, the Cistercians shouldered a burden of responsibility which, in better years, they had always been careful to avoid.[17] The decision, grudgingly made, was quickly regretted. The wealth of the nuns never caught up with their numbers, and to the problems of discipline and surveillance which the Cistercian fathers had anticipated from the first, were added those of inadequate endowments. The poverty and the purely local interests of the majority of the post-Conquest nunneries, very unlike the situation of the great Anglo-Saxon communities of nuns, left them exposed in an unusual degree to the disruptive interference of their patrons. Few nunneries could stand aside, as the monks of the reformed orders had been accustomed to do, from the many obligations of the feudal economy or from the insensitive demands of the rich. In undertaking the care of their weaker sisters, the Cistercians would find, as in the appropriation of parish churches, that they had jeopardized yet another of the main principles of their founding fathers, to the ultimate decline of their calling.

In some degree, the loss of the Cistercians was the gain of their rivals for lay patronage. Yet each order had its own characteristics, appealing to potential founders for different reasons, and it is clear, for example, that the limitation on Cistercian growth in 1152 was not to be reflected in any consequential upsurge among the Augustinians. These, since their great days in the early 1130s, had settled down to a long period of sustained but unspectacular growth lasting, at the rate of between ten and fifteen houses every decade, for the rest of the twelfth century and tailing off dramatically only in the middle years of the thirteenth.[18] What the Augustinians continued to offer was a useful service for their patrons, and communities of Austin canons grew easily from the seed of an isolated hermitage or were the natural successors to the secular priests who had earlier run colleges and hospitals.[19] But what recommended them especially to the less wealthy founder was the relative economy they offered him. New Augustinian houses were no less numerous in the second half of the twelfth century than they had been overall in the first, but they were significantly smaller and less wealthy. Thus Royston (Hertfordshire), raised from a chapel to a priory in the 1160s, was endowed initially for a community of only seven canons; Wymondley, in the same county, started life with five canons only; Latton, in Essex, with just three.[20] Modest endowments promised ill for the future, and the Augustinian communities, like the alien priories of the Norman Benedictines, had more than their share of later failures. But in the first instance the setting up of a regular community at minimum cost was obviously very attractive to founders and their heirs, while many of the smallest Augustinian establishments met genuine and immediate needs. Tandridge, in Surrey, grew from a hospital attended at first by three priests observing the Augustinian Rule; it never expanded to any great size and had only one canon in residence at the last, when dissolved in 1538. The three canons of Pynham (Sussex) looked after a hospital, or rest-home, for travellers, maintained a bridge and served the chapel annexed to it. Those of Maiden Bradley (Wiltshire), although richer than most, took charge from 1190 of a hospital for leprous women which they continued to maintain for the poor and infirm even when leprosy was no longer a problem.[21]

The practical qualities of the Augustinian canons were surfacing also among the Gilbertines. These too had begun to play their part in the care of parish churches, still largely spurned by their Cistercian contemporaries, while appealing once again to a class of founders unable to rise to something better. St Gilbert's great days, like those of the Cistercians, were already over before 1150. Only one double house, for both nuns and canons, was established successfully after King Stephen's death in 1154, and even this – at Shouldham, in Norfolk – was only moderately wealthy. However, the majority of Gilbertine communities for canons alone belong to the later period, many of them after 1200, and a good proportion of these priories had additional purposes, whether in the supervision of a hospital or in the care of some such other public utility as a bridge. Like the Augustinian houses of a similar date, the Gilbertine single-sex priories were small; with only two exceptions, at Malton and at Lincoln (both founded before 1154), they were very poor as well.[22] This had

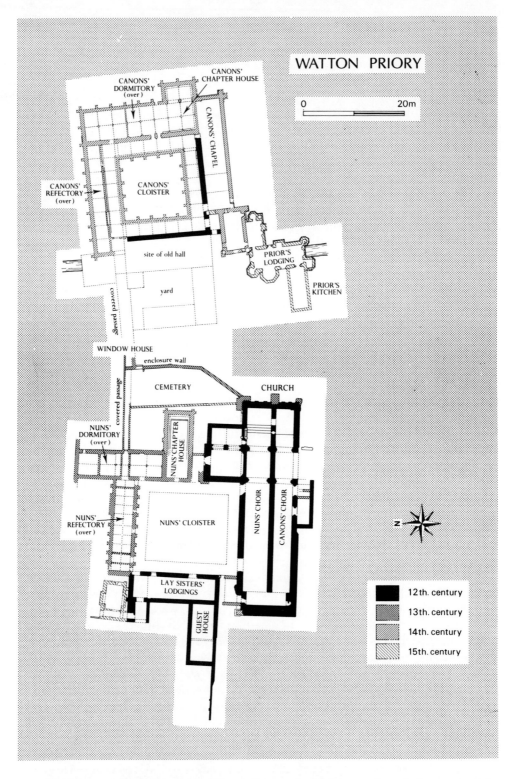

WATTON PRIORY

CANONS' DORMITORY (over)

CANONS' CHAPTER HOUSE

CANONS' CHAPEL

CANONS' REFECTORY (over)

CANONS' CLOISTER

site of old hall

covered passage

yard

PRIOR'S LODGING

PRIOR'S KITCHEN

WINDOW HOUSE

enclosure wall

covered passage

CEMETERY

CHURCH

NUNS' CHAPTER HOUSE

NUNS' DORMITORY (over)

NUNS' REFECTORY (over)

NUNS' CLOISTER

NUNS' CHOIR

CANONS' CHOIR

LAY SISTERS' LODGINGS

GUEST HOUSE

0   20m

12th. century
13th. century
14th. century
15th. century

35 The Gilbertine double priory at Watton (Yorkshire), founded in c. 1150 and always one of the richer of the Gilbertine communities. The two elements of the house, separated by a high enclosure wall, met at the window house (centre) and at the shared church (bottom right), the larger part of which was assigned to the nuns (after W. H. St John Hope, *Arch. J.*, 58(1901))

36 Shap Abbey: a Premonstratensian house in the isolated Westmorland setting to which the community moved in *c.* 1200, some ten years after the first foundation at Preston Patrick, in the same county

not always been the case, and St Gilbert at first had had little difficulty in attracting the minimum 'full convent' of thirteen inmates without which the Cistercians, from whom he took so much, had always refused to sanction a new foundation. Indeed, the Gilbertine double houses of the order's earlier years had usually been very much larger. However, patrons prepared to support St Gilbert's work on this scale were increasingly hard to find. Those lesser gentry and wealthy burgesses who had come to replace the higher feudality as the principal support of the order were less concerned with the pursuit of an ideal, and could not have afforded it anyway. From the Gilbertines, as from the Augustinians, they both expected and obtained a range of services otherwise denied to them by the monks.

In point of fact, the true successors to the Cistercians after 1152 were not the black canons but the white. Norbert's Premonstratensians had first come to England some ten years earlier with the foundation of Newhouse, in Lincolnshire. However, the expansion of the order in its English province occurred almost exclusively during the second half of the century, to constitute the final phase of the reform. As relatively recent arrivals, the white canons had not attracted the hostility already earned by the more pushing and aggressive Cistercians and long associated with the notoriously self-indulgent Benedictines. They were known to be followers of an ascetic Rule, and had friends in high places at court. When Ranulf de Glanville was a younger man and still fairly low in the royal service, his choice had fallen on the Augustinian canons whom he established at Butley, in his home county of Suffolk. By the time he founded Leiston in 1183–5, he had become chief justiciar of England. It was then that he could afford, like his predecessors in high office, to buy the best protection for his soul then available. Predictably, he selected the Premonstratensians.[23]

The white canons, although not as determinedly withdrawn from the world as the Cistercians, never matched the Augustinians in their engagement with it either. Their houses, like Shap (Westmorland) and like Leiston itself, were frequently established in isolated locations. They accepted churches but rarely served them, nor were they commonly in the business of caring for the sick or of undertaking responsibility for public works. This freedom from the world's cares was, of course, one of the chief attractions of the order to its benefactors. Ranulf de Glanville no doubt paid regard to what he knew of the reputation of the white canons. He would have heard of their frugal vegetarian diet, of their heavy labour in the garden and the choir, their verminous clothing (a deliberate penance), their 'pitiable poverty' and 'abundant want'.[24] Nevertheless, his piety was engaged by self-interest. The canons' prayers were of especial value in view of their extreme dedication. If he were successful in making Leiston the greatest English house of its order, the justiciar would enjoy an advocacy in the after-life undoubtedly second to none.

Leiston, in the event, was not the luckiest of houses. Ranulf de Glanville's dismissal from office in 1189 came too early in its history, and it was never, whatever may have been the original intentions of its patron, as richly endowed as his earlier foundation at Butley. Later, its exposed coastal site was to bring hardship to the canons and to force them to make an expensive move inland. Yet Leiston itself was only one of a distinct 'family' of Premonstratensian houses brought into being by the justiciar's relatives and closest associates. Coverham, in North Yorkshire, was one of these, founded by Helewise, Ranulf's daughter. Another daughter, Matilda, no doubt assisted her husband, William de Auberville, in selecting the white canons to colonize Langdon, in Kent, while two further Premonstratensian communities – Cockersand, in Lancashire, and West Dereham, in Norfolk – had links once again with the clan.[25] Premonstratensian houses were not always rich. Matilda's community at Langdon, founded from her father's Leiston Abbey, remained one of the smallest in the English province of the order. And there were instances among the Premonstratensians, just as there continued to be with the Augustinians, where the survival of a community, as at Bayham (Sussex), could be secured only by the merger of two houses each on the edge of bankruptcy.[26] However, of the thirty or so Premonstratensian abbeys that came into being at this period, the great majority were soundly based. The white canons were not, in general, as poor as the black. Even in their richest houses, they never approached the wealth of the Benedictines, nor were they usually as well off as the Cistercians. Theirs was the median role.

Indeed, the moderate cost of a Premonstratensian foundation was second only in appeal to the reputation of the order as an encouragement to those whose intention it became to establish a religious community on their estates. Broadly speaking, the higher feudality – the tenants-in-chief – who had been the patrons of the Norman abbeys and of the Cluniacs in the early years, and who had later switched their allegiance to the Cistercians, were no longer in need of such services. Each major family had a religious house of its own, to which it stood in a permanent relationship as founder and principal patron. As families inter-married, both the benefits and the responsibilities of these relationships multiplied, with the obvious result that the first claim on a patron's generosity would be the survival of the community he knew. Accordingly, late arrivals like the Premonstratensians had to find their support neither among the magnates, already obliged to other religious, nor among those who, in the same generation, were to befriend the Augustinians but who had not the resources to establish a community with no other role but prayer. Just as the Austin canons had done when first they came to England, the white canons appealed to the administrative classes, the new men who had risen to high office in the service of Henry II or who would do so under his sons. It was these who would constitute what has rightly been described as 'the last generation which took it for granted that the foundation of religious houses was among its spiritual obligations'.[27]

In essence, then, the Premonstratensians, for all their initial austerity and their high place in the story of the twelfth-century monastic reform, were themselves a compromise by the time they settled in England. They met a need, deeply felt but nevertheless essentially personal, among a class of newly prospering curialists. And they plugged a gap – for just as long as that deficiency continued to be recognized – that nobody else could fill. In the next century, the friars arrived with a different message and found another audience in the towns. Otherwise the map of monastic Britain, with very few exceptions, was complete.

Of course, coverage was far from equal throughout the country. In Lincolnshire, a particularly thickly settled county, Barlings and Tupholme, two prospering sister-houses of the first-generation Premonstratensian colonization, lay no more than five miles from each other in a direct line, with the wealthy Benedictines of Bardney in between. Bardney, certainly, was within easy hearing of both its neighbours' bells.[28] In Yorkshire, Byland and Rievaulx, troubled by a similar proximity, agreed to a separation when the sound of bells, disturbing their peace, 'could by no means be endured'.[29] In Glamorgan, when the rivalry between the Cistercians of Margam and of Neath became especially oppressive, the latter seriously contemplated moving their entire community to their estates in Somerset, having found their original site, only eight miles from Margam, very much too close for comfort.[30]

Such awkward sitings as these, quite as much as the greater areas bare of any monastic settlement at all, illustrate the dependence of the monks, at all times in their history, essentially on the convenience of their patrons. It was Ranulf de Glanville's family connections, not the interests of the order he supported, that scattered Premonstratensian communities through the land, from Lancashire and Yorkshire in the North to Kent in the South, with another concentration in East Anglia (above, p. 60). Yet there is some evidence, for all that, of a degree of forethought in the twelfth-century settlement, or at least of a sensitivity to over-crowding. Before they came to England, the Premonstratensians had already agreed with the Cistercians, whom they resembled in so many ways, that neither order would establish an abbey within two leagues of an existing community of the other.[31] And it is certain that one of the reasons why Wulfric laboured to prevent the establishment of Augustinians in his village of Haselbury, quite apart from his dislike of the order (above, p. 27), was that he considered the region too crowded as it was, with a consequential deterioration in local patronage.[32]

Over the country as a whole, the private interests of patrons are not the only explanation for an observable tendency among the new orders to concentrate in some areas or, more obviously, to avoid the spheres of influence of the black monks. The late arrival of the Premonstratensians, for example, undoubtedly determined their disproportionate representation in counties like Sussex, Derbyshire and Suffolk, where the new monasticism had remained, until that date, comparatively thinly spread.[33] Similarly the Augustinians, once their first most favoured days were over and the all-powerful patronage of Henry I and his administrators had been removed, showed themselves sensitive to Benedictine earlier interests in those classic areas of black monk settlement – Kent and Dorset, Gloucestershire and the Cambridgeshire fens.[34] When three important houses, as was to be the case in north-east Yorkshire, came to dominate a region between them, their careful delineation of individual spheres of interest is obvious in the distribution of their estates. Of these, Whitby, a Benedictine community re-founded in the post-Conquest northern reform, was the first to be established. It assembled a few interests in what was later to become the territory of the Augustinians of Guisborough (founded in 1119), but held most of its estates along the east coast, southwards in the direction of Scarborough. At Guisborough, the next to be settled, the lands and churches of the Austin canons clustered in the vicinity of the priory itself, with no more than a handful of outlying estates and no interests at all on the coastal strip that Whitby had made peculiarly its own. Rievaulx, founded in 1131/2, was the third to arrive in the region. The Cistercians were not as reluctant as the black monks and the canons had been to settle the North York moors, and some of their more important pastoral investment was concentrated on the granges of Bilsdale. But again they avoided completely the Whitby coastal settlement and were only sparsely represented near Guisborough. Like their brethren in religion, they would have preferred, obviously, to assemble their major interests within the immediate neighbourhood of their house. However, their late arrival was to result in a scatter of lands much wider than that of the religious communities which had initially opened up the region. Where they were least successful was precisely in those areas already dominated by Whitby and Guisborough.[35]

The dominance of established religious houses could become apparent in many ways, and it might well have seemed, towards the end of the twelfth century, that there was little room for any further development. At the Conquest, there had been some sixty houses of monks and nuns, with a total community of little more than a thousand; by the end of John's reign in 1216, the figures were nearer seven hundred for the first and an impressive thirteen thousand (out of a population somewhere in the region of three million) for the second.[36] Yet there were still areas in which the reform in England had lagged behind that on the Continent, in particular on the more extreme margins of asceticism. The interest that Henry II had shown, for example, in the Grandmontines, although strong in their Limoges homeland, never resulted in an English foundation, whether in his reign or in the next. When, under John, Grosmont in North Yorkshire was established, it was the first of only three Grandmontine foundations, none of them of any significance. Similarly the Carthusians, although much more successful in the later Middle Ages, attracted little support in twelfth-century England. What they had, they derived from the king.

It is probable that Witham (Somerset), founded in 1178/9, owed its modest beginnings to Henry II's penance after the murder of Thomas Becket (1170), which took the form of the foundation of monasteries. At Waltham (Essex) and Amesbury (Wiltshire), Henry spent lavishly on new buildings for the Austin canons and Fontevraldine nuns respectively, and both of them ended up as rich houses.[37] To the

Carthusians of Witham, his attitude was certainly more equivocal. Hugh of Avalon, the first effective prior of Witham, was Henry's man, coming to stand high in the affections of the king. Yet in the early years, progress was exceptionally slow. As Adam of Eynsham began the sad story:

> When the more important buildings had been erected, the king, absorbed in political matters, took little interest in the completion of the remainder. The masons became indignant when there was no money to pay them and abused the prior and brethren. The prior sent some of the monks to the king to tell him of the arrears and of what more was required. He promised that he would soon give the matter his attention and send what was needed. So the envoys returned merely with empty promises, and as the king did not fulfil his undertakings the building operations stopped altogether.[38]

At length, on another mission to the king led by the prior himself, Gerard ('a monk of rather harsh temperament') spoke his mind to Henry, rebuking him fiercely 'with the assurance of a good conscience, old age, and noble birth'. And although the issue was at first in doubt, Prior Hugh himself never being able to recall the incident in later years without embarrassment, Henry reacted favourably; the money was forthcoming, and the building work was brought to completion.[39]

Prior Hugh was too useful to the king to be left at Witham. In 1186, he was raised to the wealthy bishopric of Lincoln, which he held until his death in 1200. However, Hugh's departure from Witham was not the end of his connection with the community, which he visited regularly, nor did it diminish the appeal of the Carthusian life of silence to the more austere spirits of the time. Among those who found rest there were the Benedictine Robert fitzHenry, former prior of St Swithun's (Winchester), and the Premonstratensian Adam of Dryburgh, once abbot of the Scottish house of that name.[40] What they appreciated at Witham was the characteristic retreat of the individual Carthusian not just from the world outside his house but even from other members of the community. Yet it was exactly this Carthusian rejection of their fellow men, manifested in a life of individual devotions in the cell, that very quickly brought criticism upon them. The Carthusian, who seldom left his cell, shared very few beliefs with the Benedictine, who never entered it. A monk brought up in one form of discipline usually found it difficult – sometimes impossible – to adapt himself successfully to the other. Alexander of Lewes was one of those who, while Hugh of Avalon was still bishop of Lincoln, attempted unsuccessfully to return to Witham, having earlier left it in favour of the busy Cluniac community at Reading.[41] Much later, a monk of Rochester, an old and wealthy cathedral priory, tried the Carthusian way of life for just one month before returning to the routines that he knew. In the 1390s, which was when this happened, the choices open to the discontented were bewildering. Having failed as a Carthusian, the same monk of Rochester sampled the Cluniacs and then sought admission to each of the orders of friars in its turn. He ended his wanderings where he had begun them, back among his brethren at Rochester.[42]

Alexander of Lewes had not found within him the resources to endure a life of eremitical isolation. His private tragedy was that the unremitting liturgical routine of a Cluniac community suited him no better. Yet the latter, for all its by now old-fashioned look, remained undoubtedly better fitted to the religious climate of the times than the anti-communal individualism of the Carthusians. Before the end of the Middle Ages, devotional fashions would change. Two centuries after the foundation of Witham, the Carthusians were riding the crest of the wave, in the full flood of their belated expansion. In the meantime, progress was very slow. The next Carthusian settlement, at Hinton (Somerset), not many miles from Witham, again had connections with the crown, being established on the initiative of William Longespée (d. 1226), Henry II's natural son, subsequently confirmed and re-endowed by his wealthy widow Ela, countess of Salisbury in her own right. When, over a century later in 1343, Sir Nicholas de Cantilupe founded the third community at Beauvale (Nottinghamshire) in the appropriate isolation of his park, it belonged rather to the next phase of colonization among the English Carthusians, being remote both in time and place from their first settlements.[43]

Clearly, extreme asceticism was not for everybody. As the Benedictines were to tell Wolsey in the early 1520s, few in their day sought austerity,[44] nor were the majority of religious, even three centuries earlier, equipped for this harshest of roads. The competition between the orders was already divisive enough. Against the dull melancholy of which Alexander of Lewes accused the Carthusians could be set the busy greed of the Cistercians, the gluttony and torpor of the Benedictines, the imperfect discipline of the lesser Augustinian houses, and the moral laxity that many affected to see in the double communities of the Gilbertines. Criticism between the orders was at least as fierce as anything they could expect from outside. Samson of Tottington, abbot of Bury St Edmunds (1182–1211), was no admirer of the Carthusians to whom, in his own life and works, he offered the most extreme contrast. It was not that Samson was without ascetic impulses of his own. 'When he heard of the capture of the Cross and the fall of Jerusalem [1187],' his biographer tells us, 'he began to wear drawers of haircloth, and a shirt of hair instead of wool, and to abstain from flesh and meat.' But he was a man of action, well known in his day as a builder, a businessman, and a disciplinarian. He seemed, again in Jocelin of Brakelond's words, 'to love the active life better than the contemplative; he had more praise for good obedientiaries than for good cloister monks; and rarely did he approve of any man solely for his knowledge of literature, unless he were also wise in worldly affairs'. Such men as Abbot Samson were as necessary to the Church as those who, like Robert, prior of Winchester, and his sacrist Ralph, threw up their responsibilities at a rich cathedral priory to withdraw to the silence of Witham. However, there was not likely to have been – nor was there in practice – any great love lost between them. 'When he [Abbot Samson] heard of any prelate that he grew faint beneath the burden of his pastoral cares and turned anchorite, he did not praise him for so doing.'[45] In a similar spirit, the abbot of Prémontré, asked to pardon one of his English canons from Egglestone accused of forging a letter in his name, offered him a choice of punishments. For seven years, the guilty canon was to fast on bread and water every sixth day; he was to receive a correction and to repeat a psalter weekly during that period. Alternatively, he might join the Cistercians, which 'penance will suffice instead of all those abovementioned'.[46]

Chapter 4

Affluence, Investment and Growth

Abbot Samson's contempt for the instinct to retreat was informed by a very clear understanding of the dangers that threatened the Church and of the need to protect its endowment. He himself was the successor to Abbot Hugh (1157–80), formerly prior of Westminster, and he had watched the abbot in his later years bring Bury almost to ruin. 'At that time,' wrote Jocelin of Brakelond, 'Abbot Hugh was grown old and his eyes waxed somewhat dim. Pious he was and kindly, a strict monk and good, but in the business of this world neither good nor wise. For he trusted those about him overmuch and gave them too ready credence, relying always on the wisdom of others rather than his own. Discipline and religion and all things pertaining to the Rule were zealously observed within the cloister; but outside all things were badly handled, and every man did, not what he ought, but what he would, since his lord was simple and growing old. The townships of the Abbot and all the hundreds were given out to farm; the woods were destroyed, and the houses of the manors threatened to fall in ruin, and day by day all things went from bad to worse.'[1]

Abbot Hugh's age and infirmity were indeed responsible for many of the troubles of contemporary Bury, but they were not the cause of them all. It may be that the economic contrast between the twelfth and the thirteenth centuries has been exaggerated, and that the farming out (leasing) of manors, characteristic of the earlier period, did not imperil monastic finances to the degree that some historians have since argued.[2] Direct management of estates, widely practised in the thirteenth century, had its disadvantages also, not least to the life of the spirit. Nevertheless, Abbot Samson was not alone in recognizing the dangers of a leasing policy where there was no guarantee that the land so alienated might not become the subject of hereditary rights and thus difficult – perhaps impossible – to recover. At Westminster Abbey, his predecessor's house of origin, the services of patrons had been consistently rewarded with grants of land in fee which, before the end of the twelfth century, had placed between a quarter and a third of the monks' annual revenues under some threat of hereditary right.[3] When great men, among them the earl of Norfolk, came to Abbot Samson to solicit the re-grant at a fixed annual rent to Adam de Cockfield of the half-hundred of Cosford, arguing that both Adam's father and his grandfather had held it before him, the abbot refused them with vehemence and some drama: 'When he got a chance to speak, [Samson] put two fingers against his two eyes and said, "May I lose these eyes on that day and in that hour when I grant any hundred to be held by hereditary right, unless the King, who has power to take away my Abbey and my life, should force me to do so."' Adam's father, Robert, had earlier acknowledged to Abbot Samson that he claimed no hereditary right to the

Denuf pallefcic. qnden fedcra nefcie
lumuf equatof celo uide ire laconas
lumuf habec diefxtti Luna xti tr
                    Iuhil.
xix f iiii ko Sctium Marcellum J Petri ok.
iiii G iii ko
xti A ii ko
       B

37 A monk shearing a sheep. Illuminated initial from an English calendar from St Albans of *c.* 1140–58

hundred. As the price of a settlement, the son and heir found himself having to do the same, 'but no mention was made of our township of Cockfield, nor is it thought that he has any charter for it'.[4]

The argument at the time against hereditary leasing was framed principally, by Abbot Samson among others, in terms of a possible further alienation to the crown on the death or disinheritance of a tenant. But Samson's abbacy of Bury St Edmunds, lasting from 1182 to 1211 and even longer than that of his predecessor, coincided precisely with a period of inflation, one consequence of which was to increase the pressure on every landowner to resume control of alienated lands.[5] Long-term leases and fixed rents were especially disadvantageous at such a period, for the tenant's profit from rising prices was not reflected in the landowner's receipts, while inflated costs were everywhere causing the monasteries to re-calculate their revenues. Among those worst affected through the course of the twelfth century by the pressure to lease out their lands on favourable terms to the more prominent of their patrons and lay officials had been the Benedictines of William the Conqueror's great foundation at Battle. Already unusually subject to their de Lucy patrons even to the extent of finding one of the more prominent of their abbots, Walter de Lucy (1139–71), in the family, the monks of Battle had further allowed themselves to become dependent on lay servants who, as tenants also, came to hold former abbey lands on especially generous leases. As grants of this kind turned imperceptibly into freeholds, the threat to Battle's revenues became clear. Early in the thirteenth century, a campaign to resume the alienated lands was launched, using every weapon available to the community. A forged charter, dating to this time, puts the problems of its own period as if they had come to be recognized much earlier. In it, William the Conqueror is made to instruct Abbot Gausbert (1076–95) to keep the Battle *banlieu*, or *leuga* (the circular estate, three miles in diameter, which was the monks' initial most important endowment), free of hereditary leases of any kind. The abbot is to avoid at all costs the 'domination of servants', giving over to them only the land within the *leuga* which he could not himself farm directly: 'For I have been informed that you have given in fee the great part of that *leuga* to your servants whom you brought with you. This I completely forbid, and so that it [your grants] may be of no effect, I command it upon pain of forfeiture, lest the liberty I gave that church [Battle] be destroyed by others.'[6]

We cannot know how much use was ever made of this forgery. Nevertheless, it voices with peculiar clarity the fears of the monks and their new determination to take a tighter grip on their estates. Throughout the thirteenth century, the community at Battle, not content merely with recovering its lands, was actively engaged in enlarging them. Lands adjoining the abbey's demesnes were purchased as they became vacant; programmes of clearance, enclosure and drainage, begun in the previous century, were continued; the monks increasingly tightened their hold on the lay community which had grown up at their gates. In the town of Battle alone, the abbey's rent-roll was to swell before 1305 between four and five times above the receipts recorded in 1240. It was part only of a general pattern, throughout the estates, of increasingly successful exploitation.[7]

Other monastic communities, similarly placed, were likewise raising the receipts on their lands. The monks of Westminster, already impoverished before 1200 by their wholesale alienations of estates, had multiplied their difficulties in 1225 by a division of assets between abbot and convent which, in the setting up of the two separate households, was both expensive to negotiate and to continue. Nevertheless, before the end of the century they had improved their position to such an extent that their revenues had risen to more than twice the sum they had collected a hundred years before.[8] They had done this in part by the purchase of new lands. But more important than this had been the recovery of estates previously let out to farm, and the implementation of a policy of direct management. By this time, of course, they had many models to guide them, some of the more inspirational of which could be found among communities of black monks like themselves. Within a generation at Peterborough, for example, the economy of this ancient pre-Conquest community was to be transformed by the systematic resumption of estates. In the 1170s, all the manors of Peterborough had been let out to farm on the old pattern, yielding a respectable but in no ways exceptional income; thirty years later they were all in hand, the income of the abbey had more than doubled, and the monks, who were to double their revenues again before the Dissolution and who had probably been much wealthier in between, could consider themselves to be rich.[9]

The new affluence of the monks undoubtedly explains the impressive building campaigns, by this time largely self-financed, that came to characterize the period. Usefully, too, this fresh inflow of funds had been derived from more than one source. Thus whereas the produce of their home farms was certainly to result in increasing profits for the Westminster monks, it is probably the case that they benefited still more from the manorial rents now under their control, from the perquisites of their courts, and from such other incidental dues as the receipts to be expected at their mills.[10] Strong lordship, at all times in the Middle Ages, was quite as likely to be the source of profit on the estates as any improvements in agricultural techniques. For the first time, many monastic houses were to find themselves at this period in full charge of their principal assets. They became especially alert about their rights. It was early in the thirteenth century that the monks of Lewes, feeling themselves threatened by their own parish clergy and likely to lose pensions and tithes, resorted to forgery in self-defence. Like the contemporary Battle forgeries, the Lewes charters could be seen quite reasonably as a means of establishing, before a court of law and beyond all doubt, rights that the monks already knew in their hearts that they possessed.[11]

The times, in any event, were exceptionally favourable for those equipped to take a long view of their situation. A perpetual corporation like a monastic house had many advantages over its neighbours. It could suffer, of course, from the incompetence of individual administrators, and failures among these were undoubtedly the principal cause of the financial difficulties experienced by many communities even in a period of manifest economic growth. But it was spared the worst caprices of the laws of inheritance. While others might find it difficult to plan for the future, or to see any justification for so doing, such concerns were second nature to the monks. They had no fear for the continued life of their communities. An

38 Peterborough's already fine twelfth-century church acquired its remarkable west front in the early thirteenth century as the abbey recovered its prosperity (*British Crown copyright reserved*)

39 Late-twelfth-century work of characteristic elaboration and cost on the west tower and transept at Ely; the stone octagon at the top of the tower is a fourteenth-century replacement of the earlier spire

investment could be planned in the best possible way, not for an easy and immediate return but for what it might bring in due course.

We need postulate no crisis in the contemporary knightly class to recognize how the contemporary land market, throughout the thirteenth century and into the next, continued to favour the monks. Small lay estates could certainly survive and even prosper securely in these conditions.[12] However, it is obvious that the religious houses at this time were better placed than most to go on the economic offensive. Richard de Berking, whose election to the abbacy of Westminster in 1222, shortly followed by the separation of the abbot's and monks' portions at that house, was to precipitate such a crisis in the community, was also the originator of a policy of deliberate land acquisition, subsequently extended by his successors through the rest of the century and not confined to minor properties or to the rounding-off of

40 A decorative blind arcade in the recently uncovered west passage at Norton (Cheshire); the expansion of the community in *c*. 1200 was accompanied by the rebuilding on a more considerable scale of both the church and the claustral buildings at Norton, the west range being among the new works

41 Haughmond Abbey (Shropshire) was one of the greater Augustinian houses. It was extensively rebuilt in the thirteenth century as the fortunes of the canons improved, acquiring at that time a second cloister to the south of the refectory, the buildings of which included a generous infirmary hall (top right) (*British Crown copyright reserved*)

existing estates.[13] Similarly, there is good evidence of other great houses – Battle and Peterborough among them – buying out the holdings of lesser landowners in their areas as they enlarged and consolidated their demesnes; in effect, reversing the experience of the previous century when the monks themselves had lost land continually to their neighbours.[14] When the Augustinian canons of Oseney (Oxfordshire) entered the local land market shortly after 1200, they did so on such a scale that their purchasing activities can hardly have left the social structure of the region unaffected.[15] Like the monks of Battle whose still larger investment in East Sussex lands, alongside that of other great property-owners, may have caused an entire class to disappear, the canons of Oseney could only have acquired their new lands from those no longer in a position to compete with them. With land values rising as demand increased, the 'embarrassed English knights' who sold out to Peter

42 Netley Abbey (Hampshire), a Cistercian community founded in 1239, by which time its endowment could be put together from the estates of impoverished local gentry. The sixteenth-century rebuilding for William Paulet, first owner of Netley after the Dissolution, explains the unusual plan of the south claustral range (centre) where the former refectory, formerly at right-angles to the cloister, was demolished to make room for a gatehouse (*British Crown copyright reserved*)

43 The great west front at Peterborough, built in the early thirteenth century out of the profits of an expanding agricultural economy; the central porch, added in the fifteenth century, is a sad interruption of an otherwise perfect and very individual façade

des Roches and his executors in Hampshire, making possible the foundation in 1239 of the Cistercian community at Netley, had their equivalents all over the country, often with a purchasing abbey close at hand.[16] Of course, the monks' success need not have been won at the cost of ruin to the lesser gentry in their immediate vicinity. Nor need we suppose that it had this effect in any but a handful of cases. However, what is certain is that it was the monks who gained most by these transactions. Only the unlucky or the exceptionally ill-governed failed to boost their revenues at such a time.

Among the monasteries, the greatest purchasers of land at this period were also, not uncommonly, the most energetic clearers, enclosers and reclaimers. Ramsey, in Huntingdonshire, had great fenland holdings on which it spent lavishly through the years, at no time more so than in the thirteenth century. Yet it was at just this time too that abbots like Hugh of Sulgrave and William of Godmanchester were committing their house to extensive land purchases on which they laid out considerable sums.[17] A few miles to the north, in the Lincolnshire fens, other rich Benedictine communities like Spalding and Crowland were establishing in this century the great arable granges from which, on the model of the Cistercians before them, they tamed and then exploited the waste.[18] 'Concerning this marsh,' wrote Matthew Paris as a monk of the same order and a contemporary witness of their activity, 'a wonder has happened in our time; for in the years past, beyond living memory, these places were accessible neither for man nor for beast, affording only deep mud with sedge and reeds, and inhabited by birds, indeed more likely by devils as appears from the life of St Guthlac who began to live there and found it a place of horror and solitude. This is now changed into delightful meadows and also arable ground. What therefore does not produce corn or hay brings forth abundant sedge, turf and other fuel, very useful to the inhabitants of the region.'[19]

At opposite ends of the country, the monks of Glastonbury were reclaiming the Somerset Levels, those of Christ Church (Canterbury) were improving their lands on the north coast of Kent, the new sea defences of Pevensey were owed to the Benedictines of Battle, while the ambitious drainage schemes in the flat country east of Beverley were in large part master-minded by the Cistercian abbots of Meaux. A great house like Peterborough (Northamptonshire), midway between Ramsey and Crowland, might have interests as important in forest clearance as in the reclamation of the fens it adjoined. Before this work, as Robert of Swaffham described it, 'the foresters and the beasts of the forests in those days lorded it over men, and there was nobody living within the forest bounds – be he rich or poor, or even religious – who was not wronged by them'.[20] Yet the Peterborough granges, in both forest and fen, were to help bring these areas under control. In the Soke of Peterborough itself, the main thrust of the work of woodland clearance was to take place during the years 1175 to 1225, to continue actively for another quarter century but to fall off noticeably in the 1250s. And just as the monks of Battle were doing contemporaneously in their Sussex *banlieu*, so Peterborough in its soke enlisted the help of its own knights and freeholders in a campaign of clearance ultimately of more profit to the abbey than to its men. It was these separate holdings which, in the course of time, were most readily engrossed by the Peterborough abbots as the debts of their less lucky neighbours fell due.[21]

Peterborough's fine buildings, including the great west front which is a work of the early thirteenth century, have a lot to do with the wealth of the abbey at this period. However, they need to be seen in the larger perspective of a redistribution of wealth in England that was everywhere associated with the economic initiatives of the monks. The silt fens of Lincolnshire, especially favourable for agricultural development, were one area in particular which had advanced in wealth from the time of the Domesday Inquest of 1086 to the compilation of the lay subsidy accounts of 1334, our next useful point of comparison. Whereas in 1086 the uplands of Lincolnshire had been many times more prosperous than the fens, subsequent reclamations of waterlogged land had reversed the position by 1334, being very largely the work of the monks. Similarly, the yields on the Somerset Levels had been much improved, while among other regions significantly wealthier in 1334 were previously forested areas like north-east Northamptonshire, where Peterborough

Abbey had been active, or uplands like the Chilterns, exploited by the Augustinians of Missenden among others. Indeed, each of the three principal regions of growth during the period coincided strikingly with areas of known monastic investment. The first of these, a scatter of former marshlands and forest all over the country, recalls a work of reclamation and enclosure in which laymen had been at least as active as the monks. But of the other two regions, one was the Lincolnshire silt fens, dominated by the Benedictines, and the other was the North, where much of the work of post-Conquest restoration may be attributed to the Cistercians and their imitators.[22] Nothing establishes with greater clarity how the fortunes of the monks had advanced.

In a predominantly agricultural economy, the prosperity of the religious houses ultimately depended on the success of their exploitation of the land. For most communities, outright gifts of land had largely ceased by the mid-thirteenth century. If further growth were needed, it would have to come by purchase, by the

44 Glastonbury Abbey from the air: the grand scale of the church (left) is still obvious, although very little either of it or of the accompanying conventual buildings – except the abbot's kitchen (bottom right) – escaped demolition at the suppression in 1539

45 Glastonbury Abbey church from the east end, looking west through the choir and crossing

improvement of fields and buildings already held, or by the sort of agreement we know to have been reached between the nuns of Lacock and their local parson, one of their more cooperative neighbours. It was in 1308 that Robert of Durrington, parson of Lacock and the likely beneficiary of any improvement of tithable lands, 'granted to the religious ladies that they may inclose a certain furlong of their land called la Hele in the field of Lacock with certain land of theirs lying together unseparated beside it' for the very good reason that 'it is clear to him and may be well known enough that all improvement of agriculture and profit of land made in his parish would be not only useful to him and his church but also to those who will succeed him in it'.[23] However, such agreements as these might be hard to come by and were usually slow of issue. An ambitious abbot with a heavy building programme to complete would do better to look for his resources elsewhere.

One obvious source of funds, likely to appeal to men of religion as being so clearly within their control, was the exploitation of the saints and their relics. Glastonbury was already an unusually wealthy house at the Conquest. Yet it grew much wealthier in later years not merely by making good use of the estates it possessed, including reclaimed lands on the Somerset Levels, but by developing the abbey's role as a cult centre. The story of Glastonbury's rediscovery of the bodies of King Arthur and of Guinevere, his queen, artfully identified by a lead cross in the grave which was found to be inscribed 'Here lies buried the renowned king Arthur on the Isle of Avalon', is one of the least edifying of the Middle Ages. The excavations of 1191 were certainly a fraud, and the resurrection of the Arthurian myth at just this time,

46 The east end and choir of Canterbury Cathedral, as rebuilt by William of Sens after the fire of 1174; it was the successful cult of Thomas Becket, drawing pilgrims to Canterbury from all over England, that materially assisted this rebuilding

conceivably for political as well as religious purposes, was a cruel and cynical deception. Nevertheless, it is easy to see why, in general, the monks of Glastonbury felt the need for such a patron of indisputable prestige, as well as how, in particular, it suited them to find him so soon after the great fire of 1184 had reduced their church 'to a pile of ashes, its relics to confusion'.[24]

Before they agreed to put their money on King Arthur in the late twelfth century, the antiquaries of Glastonbury had already fumbled several times in the luckless promotion of other saints who, for one reason or another, had failed to catch on with the general public. Neither St Patrick nor St Dunstan had developed cults at Glastonbury, and it was probably, in the circumstances, at least as much the comparative success of their competitors elsewhere as the financial pressures of their rebuilding programme that drove the monks of Glastonbury to perpetrate their supreme deception in 1191, in which they knew they might remain unchallenged. Others certainly, among them most gallingly the monks of Canterbury, rivals for the patronage of St Dunstan, had been managing provokingly well. Thus Canterbury's own great fire in 1174, when Prior Conrad's 'glorious choir . . . by the just but occult judgement of God . . . was made a heap of ashes', had followed the martyrdom there of Thomas Becket, only four years before the catastrophe.[25] If Becket's cult had not so quickly developed, it seems highly unlikely that the rebuilding of the ruined east end of the cathedral could have been begun so soon, or that it could have been conceived on such an expensive and sophisticated scale.

For many years afterwards, the offerings at the martyr's shrine were to remain of importance to the monks of Christ Church, fully justifying the initial great cost of housing and promoting Becket's relics. It was, for example, the return of the pilgrims in 1318–19 that helped materially the recovery of the cathedral priory's finances after a period of severe famine and dearth.[26] But if Becket were still the principal draw at the cathedral, there was much else to be seen there as well. In 1315/16, during the first year of the great famine, a list of the Canterbury relics was drawn up which, although full, nevertheless omitted at least two of the most important. What was not featured was the so-called 'Crown' of St Thomas, being the crown of his head, severed by one of the knight's swords at the martyrdom. Nor was there listed the equally famous Sword Point with which, as Erasmus much later described it, 'the head of the most excellent prelate was cleft and his brain mixed together in order that his death might be more speedy'. But among the great multitude of miscellaneous 'skulls, jaw-bones, teeth, hands, fingers, and whole arms' which Erasmus also saw on his visit, were the entire bodies (all present in 1315) of St Dunstan and St Odo, St Wilfrid, St Anselm and St Aelphege, each counting, along with the splendidly enshrined body of St Thomas, as one of the greater relics of the cathedral, with other bone boxes (the 'lesser' relics) of St Aelfric and St Blase, St Audoen, St Salvius, St Wulgan and St Swithun. In an ivory coffer, under lock and key, were many personal memorabilia of Archbishop Becket: his hairshirt, the white mitre in which he had been buried, his gloves, his sandals, his buskins (half-boots) and part of his bed and girdle.[27] As for Becket's shrine, it was the verdict of a well-travelled Venetian who came to Canterbury in 1496/7 that:

The magnificence of the tomb of St Thomas the Martyr, Archbishop of Canterbury, is that which surpasses all belief. This, notwithstanding its great size, is entirely covered with plates of pure gold; but the gold is scarcely visible from the variety of precious stones with which it is studded, such as sapphires, diamonds, rubies, balas-rubies, and emeralds; and on every side that the eye turns, something more beautiful than the other appears. And these beauties of nature are enhanced by human skill, for the gold is carved and engraved in beautiful designs, both large and small, and agates, jaspers and cornelians set in relievo, some of the cameos being of such a size, that I do not dare to mention it: but every thing is left far behind by a ruby, not larger than a man's thumbnail, which is set to the right of the altar. The church is rather dark, and particularly so where the shrine is placed, and when we went to see it the sun was nearly gone down, and the weather was cloudy; yet I saw that ruby as well as if I had it in my hand.[28]

If the feretory of St Thomas surpassed them all, it was nevertheless the case that many religious houses had similar treasures of their own, some of which were of crowd-pulling appeal. Thus the great wealth of the nuns of Shaftesbury, which enabled them to remain from pre-Conquest days the largest such community in England, was closely related to the prestige they continued to earn as custodians of the body of Edward the Martyr, murdered in 978. Edward had been done to death at Corfe, not far from Shaftesbury, and the same successful exploitation of a local saint had already made Bury, the final resting-place of Edmund, king of East Anglia (841–69), a shrine of national resort. A small house like Mottisfont (Hampshire) had its own special treasure, the forefinger of St John the Baptist, 'with which he had once pointed to the Saviour of mankind'.[29] Strata Florida (Cardiganshire), on the ancient pilgrim road between St David's and Bardsey Isle, had an antique mazer, exhibited by the monks with considerable success as the mysterious and elusive Holy Grail.[30]

The founder of a new monastery who neglected to endow it with a relic of this importance would be doing his monks small service. Hailes Abbey (Gloucestershire), although established in 1246 by Richard of Cornwall, the wealthiest man of his day, failed to prosper until, in 1270, Richard's son Edmund presented to the community a phial of Christ's blood, later known as the Holy Blood of Hailes. When, in the same decade, Edward I set in motion the endowment of another Cistercian community at Vale Royal (Cheshire), modelled on his uncle's Hailes and on Beaulieu, founded by his grandfather John, his unfulfilled intention to build it up into the greatest house of its order, with an establishment of no fewer than a hundred monks, stood little enough chance of success from the beginning without a relic of appropriate status. Edward, just before he became king, had fought in the Holy Land in 1271–2, taking a major role in the defence of the remaining territories against Baybars. As the chronicler of Vale Royal later told the story:

Now, while he was there the King never ceased to war against the Paynims and Saracens in the name of Christ his Lord, and, like a good soldier of Christ, he dedicated himself to death on behalf of his Master. Nor did his foot rest until he came to the place where was kept the wood of the cross on which the Saviour of the world was hung; and he violently carried off with great joy a beautiful piece of it, which he brought back with him to England with much rejoicing. By virtue thereof he overcame all those who rose up against him on all sides so utterly that there was none like unto him of the kings of all the world; nor was this to be wondered at, for in every battle round his bare neck he bore with him the most sacred ensign of Christ, whereby the devil was overcome and the world redeemed by the blood of Christ. This most sacred portion of the Holy Cross he gave with great devoutness to the abbey [Vale Royal] at its first foundation, so that it might strike terror into its persecutors and confer the gift of eternal life on those living holy lives. And besides this most precious jewel the devout King sought everywhere for relics of the saints canonically approved, and most graciously conferred them on his monastery, and endowed it most nobly moreover with hallowed vessels and whole-silk vestments and precious books.[31]

One relic alone, however prestigious, was not enough; an entire collection would have had, as quickly as possible, to be assembled.

Indeed Vale Royal, if it were ever to compete successfully with any of the great abbeys of much earlier foundation, had a lot of ground to make up from the start. In the event the king lost interest, and Vale Royal was left unfinished and only partly endowed during his reign. But even if fortune had continued to smile on the monks, it is doubtful whether they could ever have caught up with such religious as the Benedictines (formerly Cluniacs) of Reading, in Berkshire, who had been actively engaged in relic-collecting since Henry I's re-foundation of their house in 1121. Adding objects gathered from earlier pre-Conquest collections, the monks of Reading before the 1190s had put together an assemblage of some 240 relics, of which the principal treasures were twenty-nine relics of Our Lord and six of Our Lady, but which included token remains of seventy-three martyrs and fifty-one confessors, forty-nine virgins, fourteen apostles and nineteen patriarchs and prophets.[32]

At Reading, this was no casual or haphazard accumulation. Relics of the very latest and most fashionable saints rested alongside obscure Anglo-Saxon fathers, the selfsame men who Lanfranc had misdoubted, like St Haemma and St Aethelmod, St Branwalator and 'St Exaudius, archbishop'.[33] By the 1190s, Reading Abbey was fully equipped with a fine set of relics of the martyred St Thomas of Canterbury; it had something of Bernard of Clairvaux (d. 1153), of Malachy of Armagh (d. 1148), of the sixth-century Brigid of Ireland, abbess of Kildare, whose remains, with those of St Columba and St Patrick, had only recently been 'rediscovered' at Downpatrick in 1185. When Constantinople fell to the crusaders in 1204, Reading shared in the loot with a fragment of the head of St Philip, adding this to other relics from a probable Eastern Empire source, including Our Lord's swaddling-clothes, Our Lady's belt, St Veronica's shroud and the rods of Moses and Aaron.[34]

There was nothing more improbable about Reading's fragment of the bread from the Feeding of the Five Thousand than about Canterbury's 'some of the oak upon which Abraham climbed to see the Lord, and some of the clay out of which God fashioned Adam'.[35] All great relic collections of the twelfth and thirteenth centuries had their quota of curiosities of this kind. Nevertheless, it had become plain already to the 'wiser and sadder' elements in the twelfth-century Church that relic-collecting, in too many instances, had escaped from rational control. No doubt Abbot William's dislike of the clamour and publicity brought to Melrose (Roxburghshire) in the 1160s by the miracles at Waltheof's tomb was rare indeed among men in his

47 The vault, as rebuilt by Sir Gilbert Scott in the 1860s, of Henry III's remarkable polygonal chapter-house at Westminster Abbey, later to be the model for many such chapter-house rebuildings in late-thirteenth- and fourteenth-century England

48 *Opposite* The great churches of the cathedral priories at Canterbury and Durham, with Richard of Cornwall's Cistercian foundation at Hailes (Gloucestershire), showing the development in each case of elaborate east ends, their multiple chapels well suited for the veneration of relics

position, and it cost him the loyalty of his monks.[36] Yet in an earlier generation Guibert, abbot of Nogent, had thought less of the role of relics in religion than of preaching and of the practice of confession.[37] And it was precisely these priorities which in 1215, almost a full century after Guibert wrote, received emphasis at the Fourth Lateran Council. The sixty-second canon of Innocent III's great assembly was firm in its condemnation of false relics:

> Because some put up saints' relics for sale and display them indiscriminately the Christian religion is very often disparaged. So, in order that it may not be disparaged in future, we ordain by the present decree that ancient relics from now on are not to be shown outside the reliquary or put up for sale. As for newly-discovered relics, let no one venture to venerate them publicly without their having first been approved by the authority of the Roman pontiff. Neither should prelates in future allow those who come to their churches in order to venerate to be deceived by vain fictions or false documents, as has commonly happened in many places for the getting of alms.[38]

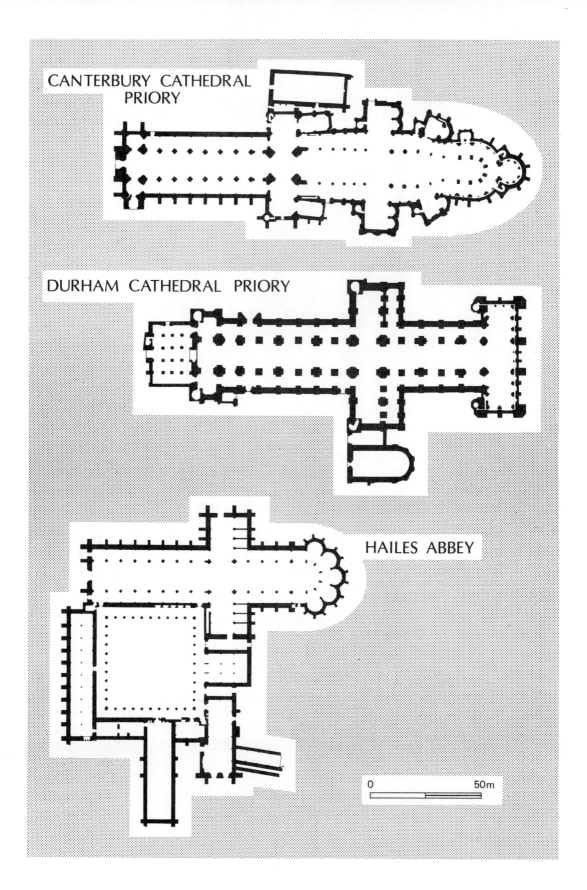

CANTERBURY CATHEDRAL PRIORY

DURHAM CATHEDRAL PRIORY

HAILES ABBEY

0   50m

49 The surviving east end of the rebuilt presbytery at Tynemouth Priory, greatly enlarged in *c.* 1200 to accommodate the cults of St Oswin and St Henry of Coquet, both popular and money-drawing saints

Others too had their more practical reasons for doubting the efficacy of the saints. 'Twice within three years,' said the chronicler of St Albans in about 1235, 'the church of St Alban was set on fire by lightning, which no one remembered to have seen before, or to have heard of. And as it is no use to rely upon the privileges or indulgences of the Saints, so the papal seal, on which is figured the Agnus Dei, which is placed on the top of our tower, did not avert the lightning, although it is said to have virtue and power to drive away such storms.'[39]

Relics might certainly be a disappointment, and even St Edmund, as Abbot Samson discovered, lacked the power to evoke generosity in King John. The king had come to Bury immediately after his coronation, in fulfilment, the monks understood, of a vow. 'We indeed believed,' wrote Jocelin, 'that he would make some great oblation; but he offered nothing save a single silken cloth which his servants had borrowed from our Sacrist – and they have not yet paid the price. And yet he received the hospitality of St Edmund at great cost to the Abbey, and when he departed he gave nothing at all to the honour or advantage of the Saint save twelve pence sterling, which he offered at his mass on the day when he left us.'[40] More seriously, Edward the Confessor, on whom the monks of Westminster had set great store, never attained the standing as a national cult figure that, in the heady days of Henry III's rebuilding of their church, they had clearly had every reason to expect.[41] But where St Edward failed, another patron might do rather better, and the virtue of a relic collection such as that built up at Westminster was that it gave the pilgrim plenty of choice. Westminster was never a pilgrimage centre on the level of Canterbury or Glastonbury, Walsingham, Bromholm, or Hailes. Yet the monks had also their own Precious Blood of Christ, given to them in 1247 by Henry III and, like the Holy Blood

50 Whitby Abbey's rebuilt presbytery of the 1220s, probably enlarged in honour of the foundress, St Hilda (d. 680), herself the centre of an active regional cult

of Hailes, authenticated by the Patriarch of Jerusalem. Another treasure, acquired much earlier from the Confessor himself, was the valuable Girdle of the Virgin.[42]

In any event, the failure of St Edward was only relative. Henry III had spent more on Westminster Abbey as a receptacle for the Confessor's shrine than on any other building project of his reign, and although the works languished after the king's death, a standard of magnificence had already been established and the status of the abbey as the tomb-church of Henry's dynasty had by then been settled beyond dispute.[43] Other monastic churches benefited likewise from their association with a single potent relic or a saint. At Hailes, the extension of the east end in its splendid *corona* of five chapels was directly the consequence of the new need felt in the 1270s to provide a fit setting for the Holy Blood.[44] And it was just these requirements – for more altar space and for an ambulatory giving room for processions round the shrine – that dictated the rebuilding of many new presbyteries as the saints were more appropriately rehoused. Canterbury provided an important model for these changes, both architecturally and in the successful promotion of St Thomas's cult. But the need was general, being as much the result of the recent major increase in the practice of pilgrimage, as of a desire to do honour to the saint. The 'loud cries and boisterous weepings' of Margery Kempe, as she knelt before the Holy Blood of Hailes, no doubt had their inspirational quality.[45] However, their intrusion on the peace of a Cistercian community was exactly what Abbot William of Melrose had tried to avoid in the promotion of the cult of Waltheof, his predecessor (above, p. 79–80), and the most practical solution to the problem of accommodating great companies of pilgrims was to build them their own extension to the east of the high altar, well clear of the choir and presbytery of the monks. At Durham, the mid-century Chapel of the Nine Altars, housing St Cuthbert's shrine with other important relics, was clearly inspired by the

51 The Chapel of the Nine
Altars at Fountains, built in
c. 1220–50 across the east
end of the abbey church to
provide a range of additional
altars where they were less
likely to interrupt the monks'
devotions in their choir.

52 Fountains: an interior view
of the Chapel of the Nine
Altars, showing the highly
decorative quality of its
stonework

53 Ornate multiple arcades in the new presbytery at Rievaulx, extended in *c.* 1230 and contrasting markedly with the deliberate austerity of the earlier twelfth-century nave

almost identical eastern transept, again with nine chapels, built at Fountains in the 1230s and 1240s. At Tynemouth (Northumberland), the great new presbytery of about 1200, considerably extending the east end of the church well beyond the original lines of the Norman choir, illustrated another more common adaptation of an existing building, too small to accommodate the burgeoning cults of St Oswin (d. 651), former king of Deira in Northumbria, and of St Henry of Coquet (d. 1127), the devout Danish hermit who had found a retreat on the priory's island cell and who, even before his death, acquired local fame as a potent worker of miracles.[46]

Other eastward extensions, usually in the form of a rectangular aisled presbytery, answered similar needs in this period. It is probable, for example, that the fine new presbytery at Whitby (North Yorkshire) with which, in the 1220s, the long-drawn-out total rebuilding of the twelfth-century abbey church began, was intended to do

54 The chapter-house entrance off the cloister at Lacock (Wiltshire), showing the high quality of the thirteenth-century work at this wealthy house, founded by Ela, countess of Salisbury (d. 1261)

honour to St Hilda (d. 680), the first abbess of the original double monastery on the site.[47] And the common tendency at the time to revive and exploit the cults of indigenous pre-Conquest saints was undoubtedly reflected in Hugh of Northwold's exceptionally lavish reconstruction of the Ely presbytery, completed in 1252, where the object once again was to accommodate the shrine of St Etheldreda (d. 679), foundress and first abbess of the double community at Ely and later one of Anglo-Saxon England's most popular saints.[48] Bishop Northwold's fostering of St Etheldreda's cult was deliberate and very successful, taking its place among a whole class of such enterprises, including the promotion of St Swithun (d. 862) at Winchester, St Wulfstan (d. 1095) at Worcester, St Hugh (d. 1200) at Lincoln, as well as Durham's St Cuthbert, Canterbury's St Thomas, and Glastonbury's spurious King Arthur. Nevertheless, important though these cults were in the frequent church rebuildings of the period, they were not the only explanation at this time for the very general surge of reconstructions. There is an obvious satisfaction in Jocelin of Brakelond's account of the preparations at Bury for Abbot Samson's renewal of the guest-house: 'Behold! at the Abbot's command, the court resounds with the noise of picks and masons' tools for the demolition of the guest-house, and it is now almost all

55 The west front of the church at Binham (Norfolk), attributed to Prior Richard de Parco (1226–44) and, even in its present mutilated condition, a work of pioneering sophistication and elegance

56 Archaeological evidence for an otherwise unrecorded collapse, early in the fourteenth century, of the north transept arch at Bordesley (Worcestershire). A block of masonry (front) had driven deeply into the church floor, at that time waterlogged as were other parts of the site, and had carried a fragment of crushed choir-stall down beneath it

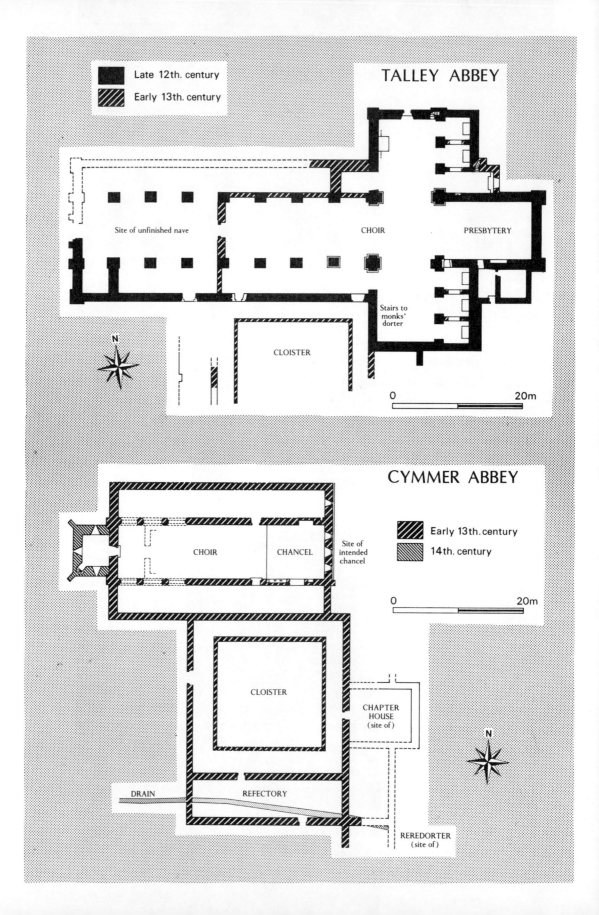

TALLEY ABBEY

Late 12th. century
Early 13th. century

Site of unfinished nave

CHOIR

PRESBYTERY

Stairs to
monks'
dorter

N

CLOISTER

0   20m

CYMMER ABBEY

Early 13th. century
14th. century

CHOIR

CHANCEL

Site of
intended
chancel

0   20m

CLOISTER

CHAPTER
HOUSE
(site of)

N

DRAIN   REFECTORY

REREDORTER
(site of)

57 *Opposite* Plans of two Welsh houses, Talley (Premonstratensian) and Cymmer (Cistercian), where originally ambitious layouts were never completed. At Talley, it was the nave that had to be cut down in size; the west range may never have been built. Cymmer similarly lacked a west range, the presbytery also being missing, although clearly intended in the first plan of the house

58 The strikingly original, but nevertheless economical, east end of Valle Crucis Abbey, another Welsh house, rebuilt with exemplary austerity in the mid-thirteenth century after a fire had destroyed the upper stages of the buildings begun soon after the Cistercians arrived on the site in 1201

pulled down'; even if he felt compelled to add, with characteristic caution, 'As for its rebuilding, may the Most High provide!'[49] And when, just a few years later, Abbot John of St Albans rebuilt the guest-house in his turn, the epithets chosen by the St Albans chronicler to record the work returned constantly to the theme of its beauty. The old hall had been 'ruinous, dark, and ugly, with walls falling from age'. In contrast, Abbot John's 'splendid' new hall 'might be called a Royal Palace, for it is two-storied and has a crypt'; its many bedchambers were 'very handsome'; its roof, formerly 'covered with shingles and weather-boarding' was now of lead 'in the best fashion'; the hall and its adjoining great chamber were 'properly painted and delightfully decorated by the hand of Richard, our monk, an excellent craftsman'.[50] Before him, Abbot William (1214–35) had completed the St Albans dormitory 'in admirable manner'; he had 'beautified the church wonderfully', re-roofing it in part and whitewashing the walls 'which the dirt and dust of ages had defiled'; he had undertaken the glazing of the windows 'so that the church, illuminated with the gift of fresh light, seemed almost like new'; he had encouraged the sacrist, Master Walter of Colchester ('an incomparable painter and sculptor'), to finish the choir-screen in the middle of the church, and had then built a feretory and altar 'most exquisitely painted', adjoining the screen, to which the relics of St Amphibalus and his companions (rediscovered in 1178) could be transferred.[51]

The quality long demanded at a great Benedictine community like St Albans had by this time spread to houses of other orders and of many different conditions. Rievaulx and Fountains, the initial bases of Cistercian expansion in the North, had started life in uncompromising austerity, exactly following the precepts of St Bernard. Yet when, early in the thirteenth century, the demand for more altar-space necessitated the rebuilding of the east end at Fountains, the work on the Chapel of the Nine Altars was both highly ornate in the style of the period and of a quality unexcelled at the time. At Rievaulx, similarly, there is no contrast more striking than between what remains of the twelfth-century nave, with its severely square columns, and the extravagant arcading and richly ornamental mouldings of the choir and presbytery, rebuilt and extended in the next century.[52] In much smaller houses, wherever conditions were favourable, the quality of the workmanship, at this period in particular, could likewise be extraordinarily high. We know nothing of the circumstances of the rebuilding of Haughmond Abbey (Shropshire) at the turn of the twelfth and thirteenth centuries. However, it is clear that the canons of this not very wealthy Augustinian house were nevertheless able to commission a new cloister which, as reconstructed recently from excavated fragments, was at the height of contemporary fashion.[53] At Lacock (Wiltshire), the personal wealth of the foundress and first abbess, Ela, countess of Salisbury, no doubt explains the quality of the vaults that survive in the east claustral range.[54] Yet Binham (Norfolk), a dependency of the Benedictines of St Albans, was never rich, and it can only have been the enterprise and ability of a single superior, Prior Richard de Parco (1226–44), that brought this diminutive community, in its remote corner of rural East Anglia, up among the architectural pioneers of the day. Richard de Parco, like other successful builders, had first secured his base by a policy of land purchase and by the recovery of previously alienated rights. He had rebuilt the cloister, roofing it in lead, and had put other buildings of the priory in good order. But the work for which Prior Richard will continue to be remembered is not the excellence of his administration, which Matthew Paris recorded, but the remarkable west front he added to the church, completing it with a great window which, in the sophistication of its tracery, anticipated by some years Henry III's work at Westminster while only slightly post-dating the first use of such bar tracery at Rheims.[55]

Richard de Parco's investment at a small priory like Binham is one indication of the optimism of the times, evidently shared by a good number of his contemporaries. Another, viewed differently, is the not uncommon failure which the less able and the over-confident of the same generation were likely to bring upon themselves in such conditions. Stories of collapses in the Middle Ages are common enough; they occurred in all countries and at most periods. There had been, for example, the catastrophe at Gloucester, soon after the Conquest, when it 'happened that the great and high tower of the church, through a defect of the foundations, suddenly crashed to the ground at the very moment that mass was completed', causing 'so dense a cloud of dust from the shattered stones and mortar' to fill the church that 'for some time no one was able to see or even to open their eyes'.[56] And other such disasters included the south aisle failure at St Albans in 1323 – 'an accident so terrible that previous misfortunes might well be considered as little or nothing compared with its magnitude' – and the collapse of the tower on the crossing at Beverley, a century earlier, blamed squarely on the soaring ambition of the workmen: 'the craftsmen who were in charge of the work were not as cautious as was necessary; not as prudent as they were cunning in their craft; they were concerned rather with beauty than with strength, rather with effect than with the need for safety'.[57]

However, miscalculations of this sort are of course still with us, and a better indication of the mood of that time was the characteristic over-optimism of its planning. Lilleshall (Shropshire) was one of those houses where a projected east extension of the church, and perhaps the addition of a north aisle as well, was quickly abandoned, but only after the foundations had been laid.[58] In Wales, second thoughts of this nature were especially common, being fostered by the uncertainties of the wars. Thus at St Dogmael's (Pembrokeshire), the otherwise extensive subsequent rebuilding of this small Tironensian house never included the completion of the nave to the plan first intended by its founders and original settlers in the twelfth century.[59] Meanwhile Talley (Carmarthenshire) and Cymmer (Merioneth) had both begun life in the 1190s on a scale they could not sustain. At Talley, a Premonstratensian house, whereas the east end of the church and its crossing were completed at full size, the nave failed to advance beyond the first four bays of the eight originally projected; it is likely that the cloister was cut down also, and the west range may never have been built.[60] Cymmer, similarly, was prevented by the wars from reaching its planned extent. Never more than the merest shadow of the great Cistercian houses upon which its first plan was based, Cymmer in its final form lacked both the presbytery and crossing of its projected cruciform church. The monks, unable to complete their buildings, worshipped in the lay brethren's choir; their refectory, breaking with Cistercian tradition, was set parallel to their small-scale cloister; without a large body of lay brethren to support, they dispensed with the west claustral range altogether.[61]

Cymmer's problem was its unrelieved poverty; it remained one of the smallest houses of the order. In contrast, St Albans suffered from the excessive wealth which might tempt its abbots into schemes that proved eventually beyond them. John de Cella (1195–1214) certainly had his successes as a builder. During his abbacy, he had demolished the 'old dark and dilapidated refectory [at St Albans] and began a new and very beautiful one, which he had the good fortune to bring to a happy conclusion in his lifetime and to feast joyfully with the brethren therein'. Similarly, he had 'caused the old dormitory, ruinous and tottering from age, to be pulled down, with its annexes, namely the necessary house, and built a new and splendid one in its place and completed it in every detail faultlessly'. But these achievements only served to underline the disaster of his abortive reconstruction of the west front of the church, originally built, as the chronicler did not fail to observe, of 'ancient tiles and enduring mortar':

He [Abbot John] began to bring together beams and to accumulate no few stones, with columns and slabs. Very many chosen masons were summoned together, over whom was Master Hugh de Goldclif – a deceitful and unreliable man, but a craftsman of great reputation; the foundations were dug out, and in a very short time a hundred marks [bequeathed by Abbot Warin (d. 1195) 'for renewing the front of the church'], and much more, not counting the daily allowances of food, were spent and yet the foundation wall had not risen to the level of the ground. It came about by the treacherous advice of the said Hugh that carved work, unnecessary, trifling, and beyond measure costly, was added; and before the middle of the work had risen as high as the water-table, the abbot was tired of it and began to weary and to be alarmed, and the work languished. And as the walls were left uncovered during the rainy season the stones, which were very soft, broke into little bits, and the wall, like the fallen and ruinous stonework, with its columns, bases and capitals, slipped and fell by its own weight; so that the wreck of images and flowers was a cause of smiles and laughter to those that saw it.[62]

A new warden of the works and fresh injection of funds were not sufficient to relieve the despair of those for whom this 'unlucky work' was the cause of constant self-reproach. Over a generation and more, the 'dead or dying work . . . scarcely achieved two feet of increase altogether'. When finished off eventually during the next abbacy under William of Trumpington (1214–35), the heart of the new abbot was no longer in the project; it was skimped, scaled down and considerably simplified as Abbot William found other things to interest him elsewhere.[63]

Chapter 5

Times of Plenty, Times of Sorrow

An abortive building project like the west front at St Albans could indeed be a serious embarrassment: a severe blow to the self-esteem of the community. But that was as far as it went. John de Cella's incompetence was forgotten in the achievements of Abbot William, his successor, nor was it ever likely that the mistakes of one superior could seriously endanger the economic health of a foundation as handsomely endowed as St Albans. Through the thirteenth century, as had been the case already in the twelfth, monastic houses were frequently in debt.[1] In the 1290s, Lewes and Reading, Rievaulx and Fountains, Kirkham, Dunstable and Guisborough were all in trouble, and the problems that had come to roost in the greater houses were certainly as well known in the smaller. Yet not one of these communities faced extinction at the time or was anywhere approaching total failure. The economy of the religious houses was still soundly based, even when their fortunes seemed as changeable as the weather.

We are probably better informed about the finances of Christ Church (Canterbury) at this time than about those of any other monastic community in England. Christ Church was wealthier even than St Albans, although not by very much; it was one of the greatest landowners in the country. But both the down-turns and the up-swings of the Christ Church economy were as startling as any in the land. Like their brethren at St Augustine's, the Benedictines of Christ Church found litigation at Rome, to which the protection of their ancient privileges rendered them especially prone, among the heaviest of their many liabilities. At the papal curia, 'great and small, they obeyed money'.[2] With these, with the recurring expenses of archiepiscopal elections, and with the increasing burden of taxation both royal and papal, the Christ Church monks before the end of the century were heavily in debt to their Italian bankers – nearly three hundred pounds to the merchants of Florence in 1285 and over a thousand to those of Pistoia. It was in that year that Henry of Eastry took office as prior. In the forty-six years of his rule, Prior Henry was to meet problems at least as great as any of those facing his predecessors; he was to embark on ambitious programmes of capital works, some of which were ill-judged in the circumstances, and would pay out large sums in taxes. Yet he left the priory, in 1331, free of debt and in very good order. He had already cleared the monks' obligations to the merchants of Pistoia within four years of his elevation to the priorate.[3]

Prior Henry's achievement was larger even than it may seem. Before his death, the problems of the monastic houses had moved into another dimension altogether, as troubles crowded in upon them from outside. At Henry of Eastry's election, the difficulties of Christ Church had been primarily, if not exclusively, of its own making. In almost every case, bad management had been the root cause of disaster.

But although the illness was easy to diagnose, there was a good deal of uncertainty about the cure. Well-intentioned reforms came to nothing. As the prior of Mont-Didier, visitor in England for the Cluniac order, remarked of Wenlock: 'I have quite come to the conclusion that it is almost impossible to elicit the truth from English monks.' He had found this Shropshire community heavily in debt in 1279, although 'one of the richest and best endowed of any'. The monks, he reported, 'perform their divine offices properly, and live honestly and according to rule', but their prior, John of Thefford, had been guilty of 'pure invention' in his own defence, and even of 'downright fraud'. This 'restless and discontented' man, with ambitions for election to a bishopric, had sold or otherwise alienated whatever he could of the priory's estates. He had run up debts in excess of 1,800 marks, and when confronted with the truth of this from his 'own papers and legal documents', he 'appeared, of course, very much astonished'. Dismissal was the only solution, for 'it is perfectly evident, and clear to any one of sense, that the priory of Wenlock will not only be liable for this debt, but still greater loss and complications will arise in respect of Bermondsey and Northampton [related Cluniac houses, similarly settled from La Charité] if the present prior remains any longer at his post . . . In all this matter we see great peril impending.'[4]

The prediction was accurate, for the houses of the Cluniac family in England were indeed in grave trouble throughout the 1280s and 1290s, from which they were lucky to escape. However, John of Thefford himself was promoted to Lewes Priory in 1285, having all but ruined Bermondsey before his elevation to Wenlock, and the uninterrupted career of a man of his duplicity is a sad comment on the continuing poverty of talent in the Church. Attempts had been made to remedy this in the past, and when, for example, the Cistercians departed from tradition in 1245 so far as to set up a Paris school of studies of their own, they had had their manifest need of good-quality administrators in mind, at least as much as the contest with heresy.[5] Nevertheless, the conflict of objectives which the Paris school exemplifies was always present in promotions in the Church, and it remained as difficult as ever in the thirteenth century to reconcile successfully the pastoral with the administrative roles of the superior. One solution, relied upon increasingly from early in the century, lay in the keeping of proper accounts. Abbot Samson at Bury had had this very much in mind from the day he took office in the community:

> At his bidding a general inventory was made, in each hundred, of leets and suits, hidages and corn-dues, payments of hens, and other customs, revenues and expenses, which had hitherto been largely concealed by the tenants: and he had all these things set down in writing, so that within four years from his election there was not one who could deceive him concerning the revenues of the Abbey to a single pennyworth, and this although he had not received anything in writing from his predecessors concerning the administration of the Abbey, save for one small sheet containing the names of the knights of St Edmund, the names of the manors and the rent due from each tenancy. Now this book, in which were also recorded the debts which he had paid off, he called his Kalendar, and consulted it almost every day, as though he could see therein the image of his own efficiency as in a mirror.[6]

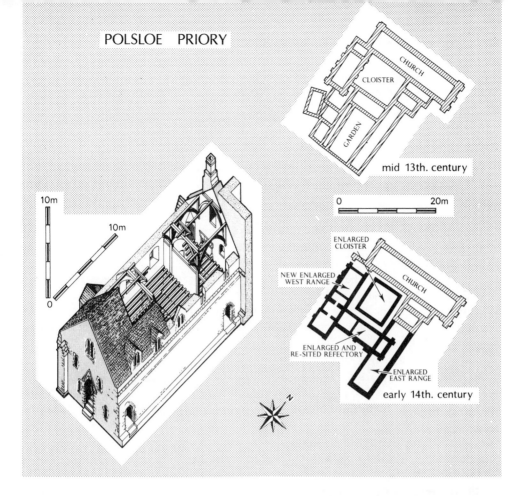

POLSLOE PRIORY

CHURCH

CLOISTER

GARDEN

mid 13th. century

0   20m

ENLARGED
CLOISTER

NEW ENLARGED
WEST RANGE

CHURCH

ENLARGED AND
RE-SITED REFECTORY

ENLARGED
EAST RANGE

early 14th. century

10m

10m

0

N

59 The nunnery at Polsloe (Devonshire) in the mid-thirteenth and the early fourteenth centuries, showing (right) the enlargement of the claustral buildings and (left) the surviving west range of that
period. Like many such houses, Polsloe experienced an expansion of numbers at just that time,
yielding to the importunities of local patrons with daughters to place in religion (Allan and Blaylock)

There were not many, of course, like Abbot Samson. Nevertheless, within a few
years the Benedictines generally had been required by the pope to prepare accounts
annually for audit, and before a century had passed it had become most uncommon
for an estate, large or small, to be without an accounting system of any kind.[7] At the
greater houses, certainly, sophisticated calculations of profit and loss were
beginning, for the first time, to influence policy decisions on the demesnes.[8] And if
there remained a divide everywhere, as was only to be expected, between the theory
and the practice of record-keeping, it was not for lack of understanding of what was
best. Without training or inclination, the nuns were especially at risk. While not all,
perhaps, as 'unversed in letters' as Dame Margaret Pole and her sisters of Langley
(Leicestershire), unable still as late as 1440 to 'understand the writings' of their own
foundation charter and other instruments,[9] a degree of simplicity remained among
the nuns to tax the expository skills of their advisers. Bishop Stapledon of Exeter
(1308–26), twice treasurer of England, evidently thought little of the current

expertise of the nuns of Polsloe and canonesses of Canonsleigh, both Devonshire houses of more than average wealth, for whom he drew up his own code of conduct:

> Item, let the accounts of all your bailiffs, reeves and receivers, both foreign and denizen, be overlooked every year, between Easter and Whitsuntide, and between the Feast of St Michael and Christmas, after final account rendered in the Priory before the Prioress, or before those whom she is pleased to put in her place, and before two or three of the most ancient and wise ladies of the said religion and house, assigned by the Convent for this purpose; and let the rolls of the accounts thus rendered remain in the common treasury, so that they may be consulted, if need shall arise by reason of the death of a Prioress, or of the death or removal of bailiffs, receivers or reeves. Item, let the Prioress each year, between Christmas and Easter, before the whole convent, or six ladies assigned by the convent for this purpose, show forth the state of the house, and its receipts and expenses, not in detail but in gross, and the debts and the names of the debtors and creditors for any sum above forty shillings. And all these things are to be put into writing and placed in the common treasury, to the intent that it may be seen each year how your goods increase or decrease.[10]

Bishop Stapledon may have had special cause to be anxious about the increase of goods at Polsloe, for the nuns of that house, like so many of their sisters, were currently engaged in an unprecedented programme of rebuilding. While they kept unchanged their comparatively modest aisleless church on the north of the cloister, they were to transform their domestic quarters at just about this time, enlarging them to accommodate greater numbers. One of their first actions was to extend the cloister by taking in the site of the original refectory to the south, and this was accompanied by the rebuilding of the claustral ranges, in each case on a more impressive scale, to the west, the south, and (lastly) the east.[11]

Contemporary rebuildings of this kind were not uncommon at the nunneries. They had occurred, for example, at the much wealthier house at Elstow (Bedfordshire) where, after continual modifications through the twelfth and thirteenth centuries, the cloister was extended during the first half of the fourteenth century, the chapter-house was rebuilt on a much larger scale, and the other claustral buildings were remodelled.[12] And what they reflected was an increase in numbers which very few nunneries were failing to experience at the time. While recruitment had stood still among the monks and canons, even registering something of a fall by the mid-thirteenth century as the competition of the friars took hold, the nuns had continued to multiply. It was the ancient pre-Conquest houses, in particular, which assembled the largest communities. But whereas a great Benedictine nunnery like Shaftesbury (Dorset) might have had as many as 120 nuns in residence in the early fourteenth century, and Romsey (Hampshire) or Wilton (Wiltshire) some eighty or ninety in all, the resources the nuns could deploy to support such numbers were always much smaller than those of equivalent-sized communities of monks.[13] Shaftesbury, although by far the richest of the Benedictine nunneries, was only half as wealthy as the great black monk houses at St Albans or Christ Church (Canterbury); Wilton was half as rich as Shaftesbury, Romsey about a third.

In the circumstances, it is not surprising that overcrowding at the nunneries quite soon became the cause of anxiety. Many houses of nuns, the Cistercians among them, had achieved full recognition only in the thirteenth century. They were useful institutions, popular among the wealthier local families as a place of resort for unmarried daughters. For the devout, they answered a genuine need. But they were poor, and the resources required to support an expansion were only rarely available when wanted. Lacock, in Wiltshire, was one of the luckier of these communities. It had had a noble and generous foundress in Ela, countess of Salisbury, and continued to attract in later years recruits from the aristocracy of the county. When the canonesses of Lacock wished to build themselves a new Lady Chapel, as many similar communities either were doing or would like to have done at the time, they were able to attract the financial support of their patron Sir John de Bluet, lord of Lacham, who could picture it as a fit place for his tomb. Yet their argument for securing the full appropriation of Lacock parish church, on which the deal at least partly depended, underlined very clearly the weaknesses they shared with other nuns as ambitious as themselves. Bishop Simon of Salisbury, granting their request in 1311 before the rest of the project was put in hand, did so 'taking note of the many burdens on the monastery which may not be supported without great costs, so that they increase daily and, with the works of charity which they exercise and are bound to exercise, may not be borne without further help; and because especially Margaret de Lacy, formerly countess of Lincoln, patron of the monastery, and other noble and powerful people who were accustomed to help the monastery effectively in its affairs with powerful help and counsel both within and without, have departed this life.'[14]

Sir John de Bluet had enjoyed the other half-interest in Lacock Church, and he was not giving it up before exacting a full price for his generosity. From the proceeds of the rectory, the canonesses agreed 'to find at their own costs a priest ... who is bound to celebrate daily for ever for the souls of Sir John and Dame Margery late his wife, and their ancestors, benefactors of the monastery, and all the faithful departed in the Lady Chapel adjoining the abbey church which is to be built at the common costs of the nuns and Sir John'. In addition, a daily mass of the Blessed Virgin was to be sung in the chapel by one of the abbey's own chaplains, and 'during these two masses four wax candles, each of two pounds weight of wax, shall burn daily at the four corners of Sir John's tomb when he has been buried in it'. To mark Sir John's obit, on the anniversary of his death, the canonesses were to distribute £5 to the poor – '$\frac{1}{2}$d each to a thousand poor people'. Finally, in a commitment that would surely be more troublesome in times to come even than those they had already undertaken, the canonesses consented 'to admit a woman into the monastery as a nun on Sir John's nomination during his life, or on that of his heirs after his death, and when she dies another one to succeed her, and so in succession, and if difficulties arise over this they are to be referred to the bishop for the time being'.[15]

This final provision, at the end of Bishop Simon's letters patent, was no doubt the fruit of bitter experience in the past. Time and again, the bishops had urged their nuns not to admit more novices to their houses than they could reasonably afford to maintain. Yet repeatedly the importunities of patrons had triumphed over caution; a superior had not known how to deny her friends, and numbers had insensibly crept up. Shaftesbury, right back in 1218, had been instructed by the pope not to allow the total in the community to rise above a hundred, for that was all that the abbey could support. But a century later, the assistance of Bishop Martival, Simon of Ghent's successor at Salisbury, was having to be invoked to establish a new maximum at 120.[16] The bishop had acted on the petition of the abbess, and it was not uncommon for the nunneries at this period to look beyond the circle of their immediate patrons for the rigour they found wanting in themselves. At Norwich, the nuns of St Mary of Carrow took their troubles direct to the pope. In 1273, Gregory X gave them the instrument they needed:

> Your petition having been expounded to us, containing a complaint that you have, at the instant requests of certain lords of England, whom you are unable to resist on account of their power, received so many nuns already into your monastery, that you may scarce be fitly sustained by its rents, we therefore, by the authority of these present letters, forbid you henceforth to receive any nun or sister to the burden of your house.[17]

Sometimes the prohibition was put less kindly. Archbishop Wickwane's rebuke to the Yorkshire Benedictines of Nunkeeling and Wilberfoss was probably well deserved. He told them to stop new admissions 'because we have learnt from public report that your monastery is sometimes burdened by the reception of nuns and by the visits of secular women and girls, at the request of great persons, to whom you foolishly and unlawfully grant easy permission'. However, these importunate 'great persons' were all too often to be found among the ranks of the episcopacy itself. John le Romeyn, next archbishop of York, asked the Cistercians of Sinningthwaite (West Yorkshire) in the late 1280s and early 1290s to admit first a novice and then a nun, only six years separating the requests.[18] It is certain that these were not the only such letters that the archbishop wrote and that the nuns would have found difficulty in ignoring.

Patrons generally, in the late thirteenth century, had lost nothing of their ancient authority. Indeed, the interference of patrons in monastic affairs was more likely to be still on the increase. Even before the great endowment controversies of the fourteenth century, founders' rights had begun to be re-stated. One of the clauses of Edward I's second Statute of Westminster (1285) had important implications for the future. It protected the patron's interest by declaring the right of the founder and his heirs to resume lands or rents either alienated or misapplied by the grantee. In effect, it opened the way to enforced forfeiture of church lands if a patron, at whatever number of removes from the original founder, felt himself seriously aggrieved.[19]

One of the clearest articulations of these feelings among lay patrons occurred early in the fourteenth century when Clement V (1305–14) roused the anger of the Norman patrons of Bec by granting its wealthy dependency at Ogbourne St George (Wiltshire) to his nephew Raymond de Got. Ogbourne, the Normans declared, had been given by their ancestors to the Benedictines of Bec to 'pray for them and for us', to maintain hospitality (of which they could take advantage), and to give alms to the poor of the locality. In the circumstances, 'we should be deeply grieved if these goods were converted to the advantage of one person [the pope's nephew]; for our ancestors gave them to the abbey and the monks there serving God for the purposes we have stated;

and if we or our heirs learned that these goods had been so converted, by the custom of the land we might take them back and hold them.'[20]

In 1289, Gilbert de Clare had gone so far as to take into his own hands the assets of another Bec dependent priory at Goldcliff (Monmouthshire), on the grounds that 'the prior and monks of the place had abused these liberties to his detriment'.[21] However, it was certainly more usual for a patron and his monks to seek common ground where advantage might come to them both. Every religious community continued to need its 'noble and powerful people . . . accustomed to help the monastery in its affairs with powerful help and counsel both within and without', as the canonesses of Lacock had found (above, p. 97). In return, the most important benefit it could confer on its patron was perpetual commemoration after death. Ewenny (Glamorgan) was never a wealthy house. However, what prosperity it enjoyed in the twelfth and thirteenth centuries was very largely owed to Maurice de Londres, founder of the priory in 1141, and to others of his family line which became extinct only with Hawise de Londres in 1274. Both are commemorated still by inscribed tomb-slabs in the church which read, in translation: 'Here lies Maurice de Londres, the Founder. God reward him for his work. Amen.' and 'Pray for the noble lady Hawise de Londres. Remember and chant for her soul two Paternosters.'[22]

Hawise de Londres was the mother of Payn de Chaworth whose interest at this time was otherwise engaged in the rebuilding of the great castle at Kidwelly, one of Maurice de Londres' original lordships. Consequently, very little was done to embellish Ewenny after Hawise's death, and the fortunes of the priory never subsequently improved before its suppression in 1540. Other communities had a longer run of luck than this. Thetford, in Norfolk, was a Bigod foundation, the burial place first of the Bigod earls and then of the Mowbray dukes of Norfolk who succeeded them. When the title passed to the Howards in 1483, they continued to regard Thetford as the best place for their tombs, striving to preserve it as such even at the Dissolution.[23] As Thomas de la Warr, the ninth of his line, said of Boxgrove (Sussex) immediately before its suppression, 'I have a poor house called Boxgrove, very near to my own poor house, whereof I am founder, and there lieth many of my ancestors, and also my wife's mother; and for because it is of my foundation, and that my parish church is under the roof of the church of the said monastery, and I have made a poor chapel to be buried in, whereof it might stand with the King's Grace's pleasure, for the poor service that I have done his highness [Henry VIII], to forebear the suppression of the same.'[24] Boxgrove survives as a fine parish church; Thomas de la Warr's chantry chapel remains where he placed it, under the south chancel arcade; its custodians, the Benedictines, had to go.

This custody of funerary monuments, while at no time the main function of a community of monks, had grown steadily more important with the years. The doctrine of Purgatory, officially recognized and defined at the Council of Lyons in 1274, quickly had the effect throughout the Western Church of increasing the standing of the memorial mass as an instrument for the relief of future suffering. Pious works and the multiplication of masses were coming to be seen as a form of investment, speeding the soul of the benefactor through the discomforts of Purgatory to the desired final resting-place in Heaven. Simultaneously, the practice of chivalry, as most obviously expressed in the elaboration of heraldry, had tightened its grip on

60 Thetford Priory from the air: one of the wealthier English Cluniac houses, owing much of its prosperity to the patronage of the earls (and their successors the dukes) of Norfolk, whose tomb-church Thetford became

61 *Left* The fine late-fourteenth-century gatehouse at Thetford, built in a style (perhaps owed to magnate patronage) characteristic of the military architecture of that period

62 *Opposite* Thomas de la Warr's 'poor' chantry chapel (1535) in the choir next to the high altar at Boxgrove Church: a fine Caen-stone monument combining Gothic and Renaissance decorative detail and inscribed – 'Of your charite pray for the souls of Thomas la Ware and Elyzabeth his wyf'. In the event, Lord de la Warr, because of a later exchange of properties, was never buried in his chapel at Boxgrove

the ruling classes, from which the bulk of monastic patrons were drawn. The effect on the architecture of the religious houses was immediate and quite frequently dramatic. When the east end of the church at Hailes (Gloucestershire) was rebuilt after 1270 to accommodate the phial of the Holy Blood which was drawing pilgrims to the abbey in such numbers, a fine new tiled floor was laid in the extension, at considerable expense and right up with the very latest fashions. Yet it was not a religious theme that occupied the tilers but the heraldry of the donor, Edmund of Cornwall, and of the families to which he was related. In the pavement at Hailes were the arms of England and of Cornwall, of the Clare earls of Gloucester and the Warenne earls of Surrey, of the Ferrers and the Beauchamps, the Maudits, the Peverils and the Staffords.[25] Together they said nothing of the power of the Holy Blood of Hailes,

England

King of the Romans

Cornwall

Clare

Warenne

Ferrers

Beauchamp

Peveril

Maudit

Stafford

Provence

von Falkenburg

63 *Opposite* Heraldic floor-tiles, commemorating the donor Edmund of Cornwall and his relatives, found in the extended east end of the church at Hailes Abbey, where they had been laid in the 1270s as part of a programme of general refurbishment associated with the housing of the Holy blood, the abbey's most celebrated relic (Eames)

64 *Above* Heraldic tiles from a floor of *c.* 1300 at Titchfield (Hampshire); note the double-headed eagle of the Holy Roman Empire (left centre), probably commemorating Richard of Cornwall, as at Hailes

while telling the story of Edmund of Cornwall and his father Richard, founders of the abbey, through their accumulated honours and titles.

Certainly the most individual of the heraldic decorations of the period was the

65 The north front of the great residential gatehouse at Butley Priory, in Suffolk, dating to the 1320s
and remarkable both for its decorative flint-work and for the heraldic panel, a roll-call of the mighty,
over the arches of the two gates

great sculptured panel of five rows of shields set over the main gate at Butley, in Suffolk, one of the wealthier of the East Anglian Augustinian communities. The Butley gatehouse is a building of distinction on several counts. It is among the first of those great residential gatehouses which, in the later Middle Ages, characterized both monasteries and castles. For the student of regional architecture, it is an early example of the decorative use of knapped flint against dressed stone to form the patterns now known as 'flushwork'. However, more than either of these it deserves particular attention for the demonstration it gives, through the choice of heraldry, of the ruling preoccupations of its builders. The unusual placing of the Hurtshelve arms on the top row of the panel, alongside those of the great Christian nations, suggests that some member of this family was the donor. William of Gayton (d. 1332) was prior at the time, and we know him to have been a figure of some importance, president of the general chapter of his order which, meeting at Northampton in 1325, made major changes in the constitution of the Augustinians of the province of Canterbury. Without question, he would himself have been expert in heraldry. Centred on the arms of the Passion, the top row of shields included those of the Holy Roman Empire, France, East Anglia (the three crowns), England (the three leopards), Leon and Castile, and Hurtshelve (three axes). The second row featured the principal officers of state, among them the de Vere earls of Oxford, hereditary great chamberlains, and the Bohun earls of Hereford and Essex, hereditary constables of England, with the Clares, stewards of Bury St Edmunds, whose line had just ended on the death of Gilbert de Clare, third of that name, at Bannockburn in 1314. Below these again was a selection of some of the great baronial families, including FitzWalter and Beaumont, Wake, Mortimer and de Ros, with the two further rows (the fourth and the fifth) recording the landowners of East Anglia.[26]

Little except the gatehouse survives at Butley. Consequently, it is less easy to recognize the essentially commemorative purpose of the heraldry at Butley than it is, for example, to see the same thing at the rather earlier gatehouse of Kirkham (East Yorkshire), itself obviously part of a more general rebuilding. De Ros heraldry occurs on both gatehouses and it seems very probable that Prior William would have known the buildings of the canons of Kirkham, whose allegiance was the same as his own. Kirkham had become, very much to its profit in the thirteenth century, the tomb-church of the de Ros lords of Helmsley. With the support of its patrons and out of the proceeds of the rich endowment it had obtained in the previous century from Walter Espec, its noble and devout founder, Kirkham had embarked on a major rebuilding from the early thirteenth century, starting with the complete reconstruction of the choir and presbytery in a new and much grander manner. De Ros family tombs occupied the positions of honour in front of the high altar and to each side, and it was entirely in character with this special relationship between the Augustinians of Kirkham and their patrons that the fine priory gatehouse put up in the late thirteenth

66 Detail of the gates at Butley and of the three lower rows of heraldry set above them; of these, the two bottom rows display the arms of important local families, among them known benefactors of the priory; above them, a third row commemorates the greater magnates of England

century should have been richly adorned with de Ros heraldry. The external treatment of the Kirkham gatehouse is of unusual quality, embellished with sculpture and with decorative tracery, with pinnacles, buttresses and ornamental panels in the court style developed at Westminster. A Crucifixion sculpture over the gate is flanked by St George and the Dragon in support on one side, by David and Goliath on the other, each in its turn being surmounted by shields – Scrope and de Ros over St George, de Ros and de Fortibus over David and Goliath. Other great families commemorated on the same façade included FitzRalph, Vaux and de Clare, associated in this way with Christ himself and with figures of St Philip and St Bartholomew.[27]

By the time that the gatehouse at Kirkham was built, a high proportion of the religious houses of medieval England had become identified more or less permanently with the interests of an important landowning family in the locality. One such alliance which yielded spectacular results, especially significant in the decades on either side of 1300, was between the lords of the rich manor of Tewkesbury (Gloucestershire) and the Benedictines of the great abbey in their town. It was the de Clare earls of Gloucester and their heirs, the Despensers, who materially assisted the already wealthy monks to rebuild their church on a magnificent scale, starting in the late thirteenth century with the reconstruction of the east end with ambulatory and chapels, and including before the middle of the following century the complete re-roofing of the nave. Yet there was a price to be paid for such munificence. If the theme of the great east window at Tewkesbury was the Last Judgement, it had also to include a donor figure of Eleanor de Clare and the heraldry of her husband, Hugh le Despenser the younger (d. 1326). In other windows to the west, also of the gift of Eleanor, there are knights in full armour, the lords of the manor – FitzHamon (the founder) and FitzRoy (his son-in-law), Clare, Despenser and

67 Kirkham Priory from the air, showing clearly the considerably enlarged choir and presbytery of the priory church, dwarfing the earlier twelfth-century nave and attributable to the patronage of the de Ros lords of Helmsley, who were buried there near the high altar

68 De Ros heraldry, with other fine stone-carving of the late thirteenth century, on the outer face of the gatehouse at Kirkham

Zouch. Ornamenting the choir, and next to the tombs and the chantries of the abbots, are the memorials of the great lay lords: Hugh le Despenser, the son of Eleanor and a particularly generous benefactor of the abbey, during whose time as lord of the manor the work on the choir was completed; Edward le Despenser, nephew of Hugh, who fought at Poitiers in 1356 and who was among the first of the knights of the Garter; Richard Beauchamp (d. 1422), Lord Abergavenny and earl of Worcester, husband of Isabella le Despenser; Guy de Brienne, another famous soldier and knight of the Garter who had carried Edward III's standard at Crecy.[28]

When the Cistercians of Neath (Glamorgan), at the high point of their prosperity between 1280 and 1330, decided to rebuild their church on a new plan altogether, they sought the assistance of the greatest landowner in their area, Gilbert de Clare, in the raising of money for the project. As completed, the chapels in the ambulatory commemorated such help with a tiled pavement bearing the arms of the local families who had no doubt played their part in the rebuilding.[29] Nor is it likely that the Augustinians of Guisborough (North Yorkshire) in 1289, after a disastrous fire had reduced their new church to ashes, could have contemplated reconstruction on such a lavish scale had they not enjoyed the support of the Brus founding family and of its later branches. Robert de Brus and his three successors in the direct Brus line had all been buried in the priory church before the fire, and when it rose again after 1289, it carried the heraldry of Brus of Skelton, with Thweng and Fauconberg, the two local families who had married into the patronage of Guisborough. Still in the sixteenth century, right through to their suppression, the canons of Guisborough continued to

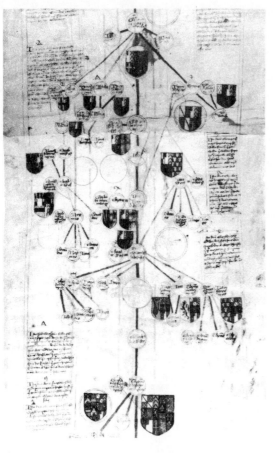

69 Part of a late-medieval pedigree
and armorial roll of the patrons
of Tewkesbury Abbey, from
Gilbert de Clare (top) to Thomas
le Despenser (bottom). English,
c. 1435

70 *Opposite* Isabella le Despenser,
kneeling before an image of the
Virgin and Child; from the
benefactors' book of
Tewkesbury Abbey. English,
early sixteenth century

draw benefit from the association. A fine table-tomb of that date, now in the parish church to which it was removed from the priory, is decorated along its length with Brus family 'weepers', of the Skelton branch on the north side, the Annandale branch on the south. They are modelled in the company of the prior and canons, of the Evangelists, the four Latin doctors and the king. The monument, known as the Brus Cenotaph, carries the rebus of Prior James Cockerell, one of the martyrs of the Pilgrimage of Grace.[30]

Vital though the contribution of their Brus patrons may have been, it was the interest and dedication of the canons themselves that had kept building in progress at Guisborough through most of the thirteenth century and that had revived it so soon after the fire. As a result of Brus and other benefactions, the priory was one of the wealthiest of the English Augustinian houses. It could afford to find work for a community of masons in the town which, permanently settled with properties of its own, could see prospects for employment so firm for the future that individual masons would themselves contribute to the priory's fabric fund, while training their children in the crafts they had imported and bringing them up as Guisborough men.[31] Similarly, the rebuilding of the church at Tintern (Monmouthshire), attributable to the support of the abbey's new patron Roger Bigod, earl of Norfolk (1270–1306), must be seen in the context of a prolonged period of general prosperity, ultimately of more

consequence to its success. Thus the Cistercians of Tintern had already rebuilt their entire claustral range before work even began on the church; after it, they reconstructed the abbot's lodgings on a scale more appropriate to the community they had just so lavishly re-housed.[32]

We know little or nothing of the circumstances of the rebuilding at this time of a great new choir and presbytery at Bayham (Sussex) for which, outside the ranks of the Premonstratensians themselves, there seems to have been no obvious patron. Nevertheless, this was work of the very highest quality in the fashionable Westminster idiom of Henry III at a house which, even after the mergers and refoundation of the early thirteenth century, had never at any time been wealthy.[33] Very likely, the canons of Bayham, like their brethren contemporaneously at Thornton (Lincolnshire), a much richer Augustinian community, had themselves become infected by that same building mania which had earlier driven the king. The

71 The presbytery at Tewkesbury, as re-modelled in the fourteenth century when it was equipped with its seven fine windows and spectacular lierne-vaulting; north of the high altar are the chantry chapels (left) of Robert FitzHamon (d. 1107), founder, and of Isabella le Despenser (for her first husband, Richard Beauchamp); the chapels were erected in *c.* 1395 and *c.* 1430 respectively

72 View of the north ambulatory at Tewkesbury, with Isabella le Despenser's Beauchamp Chapel (right) and the FitzHamon Chapel just beyond it

new east end at Bayham, thrusting out ambitiously beyond the line of the original claustral layout and greatly increasing the canons' own share of the church, was an individual masterpiece which, if it took as its beginning the developed 'court' style of Henry III's Westminster masons, yet displayed clear improvements of its own. Begun in the late 1260s, it was completed before the end of the century.[34] Just a few years later, a new chapter-house on the Westminster-influenced polygonal plan was built at Thornton as the second major element in a complete reconstruction of the abbey buildings which was to occupy the canons for as long as a century from its beginnings in the mid-1260s. One of the preconditions for this ambitious programme had been

73 Guisborough Priory: the east end of the church as rebuilt by the canons, with the help of their
Brus patrons, immediately after the great fire of 1289 had reduced all their recent work to ashes

the successful appropriation of the parish church at Kelstern, to the north of
Thornton, sanctioned in 1268. Following this, the presbytery and crossing, the
chapter-house, cloister, refectory, west range and nave were all rebuilt, only the
dormitory undercroft and adjoining warming-house in the original east range
surviving the reconstruction unaltered.[35]

74 The so-called Brus Cenotaph at the parish church of St Nicholas (Guisborough), formerly at Guisborough Priory; notable for its fine-quality stone-carving of immediately pre-Dissolution date, celebrating the long-standing lay benefactors of the priory

The canons of Thornton, rich though they were, had had to seek extra finance for the rebuilding of their church in its new 'magnificent' style, and it had been for this specifically that Bishop Gravesend of Lincoln had acceded to their request to appropriate Kelstern Church.[36] Other communities took similar initiatives when a programme of works was in prospect. We know, for example, that one of the first thoughts of the monks of Westminster, after the fire of 1298 had devastated their conventual buildings, was to set up a building fund to be supported by the revenues of four parish churches, appropriated especially for this purpose. And while these processes of appropriation were both expensive and prolonged, they were ultimately very worth while.[37] At St Augustine's, Canterbury, in 1325, 'a collection was granted by the whole convent for the building of the new chapter-house, viz. from the accounts and from the pittance wine, from wax and spices, from the wardens, the sacristy, the almonry and from anniversaries. And this collection for the above-named work lasted for eight years and more: and the total of the collection made for expenses by brothers Ralph Gatewick and J. Masonn was £277 4s. 8d.'[38] Very much the same emphasis on the community's own resources is clearly present again in the list of those who, in 1323–4, made some contribution towards the cost of Alan of Walsingham's 'new work' at Ely. The list included the prior himself, the almoner, the infirmarer, the precentor and other obedientiaries of Ely, with a very substantial levy on the pittances of the monks, with individual gifts and legacies, and with subsidies from John Salmon, bishop of Norwich (1299–1325), and John Hotham, bishop of Ely (1316–37), himself then becoming very actively engaged in another programme of works at the cathedral priory.[39]

75 Tintern Abbey from the air, showing the great church that the monks were able to reconstruct in *c.* 1300 with the help of their new patron, Roger Bigod, earl of Norfolk (*British Crown copyright reserved*)

76 Tintern from the west, seen in its typically Cistercian valley setting, with wooded hills beyond

Ely at that time was the scene of exceptional building activity, where contemporary but distinct projects were each to be associated with men of unusual ability. To Alan of Walsingham, sacrist of Ely, had fallen the task of reconstructing the crossing of the priory church after the collapse of the central tower in February 1322 had left him 'not knowing whither to turn himself or what to do'.[40] His solution, the construction of a huge timber lantern resting on a stone octagon itself carried on eight newly fashioned columns – an 'ingenious wooden structure . . . designed with great and astonishing subtlety' – has remained to us still as one of the principal architectural marvels of the later Middle Ages in England.[41] In the meantime, Bishop Hotham was finding the funds for a rebuilding of the presbytery which had lost its four western bays in the collapse; Prior Crauden (1321–41) was active in the reconstruction of the conventual buildings, his chief surviving monument being the fine chapel he built there for his own lodgings; and John of Wisbech, 'a simple monk of Ely', was devoting his life to the completion of the new Lady Chapel – 'And when he had with the greatest enthusiasm continued the work for 28 years and 13 weeks, and had completed the stonework, with the images within and without the chapel, 147 in number, not counting the small images on the reredos above the altar and the images at the entrance door, and the wooden roof covered with lead, and the east gable with two windows on either side of the chapel beautifully finished with iron and glass, on 16 June 1349, at the time of the widespread pestilence, he died, and left the control of his work to his successor free of all debt.'[42]

John of Wisbech's enthusiasm and his dedicated labour were to leave behind him a

77 Remains of the choir and presbytery at Bayham (Sussex), both greatly extended in the late thirteenth century despite the relative poverty of the community

78 Detail of part of the north transept at Bayham Abbey, showing the high quality of the stonework

79 Thornton Priory from the air: in the
foreground, the foundations of the great
church rebuilt entirely in the late
thirteenth and early fourteenth
centuries; to the left, the octagonal
chapter-house; at the top, the imposing
gatehouse built in the 1380s

work as ornate as any of its period in England. And it is this quality in particular, of decorative richness achieved regardless of cost, that characterizes the rebuilding of Ely, as elsewhere, in the half-century preceding the Black Death. The Ely Lady Chapel is noted especially for the luxuriant sculptures that the priory's chronicler himself so much admired. At Prior Crauden's private chapel, it is the remarkable tile mosaics that immediately claim attention, and these, it has been suggested, may originally have been designed for an even grander pavement in John of Wisbech's Lady Chapel before work on that project, after the collapse of 1322, had had to be resumed more soberly.[43]

Tile mosaics of this kind, although more elaborate than most and already subject to cheaper imitations, had a long history of use in monastic building. One of their earliest appearances, and perhaps their first, had been in the pavement of Thomas Becket's Canterbury shrine, datable not later than 1220. By the mid-thirteenth century mosaic pavements had been laid in many of the greater Cistercian churches in the North of England, and the desire for such floors had begun to spread more widely.[44] Tile mosaics were never cheap. In the degree of elaboration that, for example, they reached at Warden (Bedfordshire) or Norton (Cheshire), in each case during an early-fourteenth-century rebuilding, they could be very expensive indeed.[45] But that was at least part of their attraction. At neither Warden nor Norton is there any reason to think that the finest tile mosaics were ever laid down in those areas of the buildings not reserved to the monks or the canons; they occurred in the presbyteries and choirs of the churches, in chapter-houses, abbots' lodgings, and perhaps refectories. Similarly, when tile pavements were put down in the church at Strata Florida (Cardiganshire), they were restricted to the more sacred areas of the building, to the monks' east end and to the choir of the *conversi*, leaving the rest to be floored more cheaply in the local slate.[46]

A fine tiled floor had come to be, in these pre-plague decades, as satisfactory a memorial as any building work by which an abbot might choose to leave his mark. The most talented tilers of the day were those who had worked at Chertsey (Surrey) on the pavements of that rich Benedictine house and on such other major projects, dear to the king, as the Westminster chapter-house, floored in the 1250s, or the new ambulatory and chapels at Hailes (above, p. 101). Accordingly, when Abbot Nicholas of Halesowen (Worcestershire), superior in the late thirteenth century of one of the more prosperous of the Premonstratensian communities, wished to commission a pavement of his own, he naturally turned to craftsmen in this tradition to do the work for him. At Halesowen, they were to re-use designs they had perfected already on the pavements at Chertsey and at Hailes. But they added to these patterns a new series to order, depicting monks and former abbots of the house. Among the more impressive of the decorative roundels characteristic of the work of the Chertsey tilers thus came to be a portrait tile of Abbot Nicholas himself, seated in a pose of authority. On it, the abbot is surrounded by an inscription recording the donation of the pavement to Halesowen and its dedication to the Mother of Christ.[47]

In another expression of commemorative piety, characteristic of these prosperous years, the many shrines of medieval England were everywhere refurbished or renewed. In this, as in the commissioning of fine tiled pavements, the example of the king was infectious, both Henry III and Edward I being known as energetic visitors

80 Fine ornamental detail in the two surviving walls of the late-thirteenth-century octagonal chapter-house at Thornton, probably modelled originally on Henry III's even grander work at Westminster

81 Alan of Walsingham's timber lantern over the crossing at Ely, built to replace an earlier central
tower which collapsed in 1322

82 Detail of the timber framing supporting the lantern at Ely

83 The east end at Ely, showing John of Wisbech's Lady Chapel (right), built just to the north of Bishop Hotham's expensively restored choir, both being contemporary with Alan of Walsingham's reconstruction of the crossing

to shrines.[48] Yet the re-housing of relics was also naturally a part of that improving environment which the monks and canons of the late thirteenth century had come to expect for themselves. The greatly enlarged east end of Battle, with its fine ambulatory and *corona* of radiating chapels, was of course intended to accommodate appropriately the monks' notable collection of relics. However, the extension enabled them also to resite their choir away from the crossing, where it had previously been, in the greater comfort and more spacious setting of a new eastern arm almost as long as the nave.[49] Contemporaneously, in the first decades of the fourteenth century, the canons of the much smaller Augustinian house at Bicester (Oxfordshire) were engaged in a rebuilding of the east end of their own priory church, one purpose of which was undoubtedly the re-housing of the shrine of Edburga, said to have been the daughter of Penda of Mercia and one of those Anglo-Saxon saints whose cult had been revived in the late twelfth century to the considerable advantage of the canons. St Edburga's shrine base, entirely rebuilt for the move and highly carved in the fashion of the day, later escaped the attention of Henry VIII's Commissioners for the Destruction of Shrines, to be translated to the parish church of Stanton Harcourt, where it remains. With the contemporary and very similar shrine of St Alban, also of Purbeck marble, it is one of the very few such renewed bases to have come down to us.[50]

84 Detail of the stone-carving in the Lady Chapel at Ely, to which John of Wisbech devoted so much of his working life

Grand new presbyteries were of course desirable; and all the more so with the handsome tile-mosaic pavements and re-carved shrines with which they were frequently equipped. Many religious communities believed themselves still perfectly able to afford them. But they spelled trouble for the financially insecure. In the past, a number of solutions remained open to the monks. They might tighten their administration to recover lost rents, they might sell corrodies and appropriate churches, they might manumit (free) serfs in return for cash payments. Each of these measures was resorted to by Wolstan de Bransford during the twenty-one years of his priorate of Worcester before his election in 1339 to the see.[51] In extreme and sudden difficulty such as might be caused by an unanticipated demand for taxes, the programme of economies, as at Dunstable Priory in 1294, could affect every aspect of life in the community:

The same year because of the aforesaid payment to the king and to further the affairs of our monastery we granted on a lease our tithes at Newbottle for five years, namely in return for 15 marks p.a., of which we received 45 marks in advance. We also sold for the same reasons William of Marston a corrody of one free servant, in return for which we received 24 marks. For the same reason we also sold Walter de Cobilingtone many corrodies for a year and the great solar and the little stable by the almonry; and we received 60 marks from him. The nature of the corrodies is contained in his charter. Also for the same reason we provided at Michaelmas for certain economies to be made and adhered to until we thought fit to revoke them when the payments to the king stopped and the finances of our monastery were relieved. The consumption of small white loaves we reduced by the weight of 10s. We decided that one portion of conventual dishes of every kind should be set before two brothers. Of the other economies made at that time, as regards the number of dishes in the convent, as regards the almonry, the reception

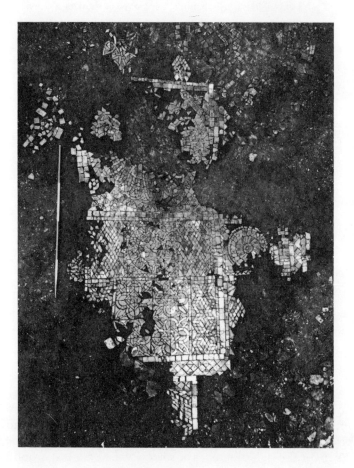

85 A tile mosaic pavement excavated at Warden Abbey, in Bedford-
    shire, dating to the early fourteenth century

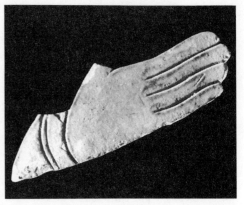

86 Individual elements from another pavement
at Warden, similar in date but of a more
naturalistic style:
(a) head, possibly of an abbot
(b) hand, either gloved or showing a sleeve
at the wrist, approximately life-sized in the
original
(c) laying instructions on a fragment of tile,
giving its relationship to another – *sup(er)
tibia equ(um)* (over the leg of the horse):
scale in centimetres

of guests, and the management of the household, you will find the particulars
entered in the old book of obits.[52]

Within limits such devices could work well enough, and Dunstable Priory, always a
rich house by Augustinian standards, certainly passed through its temporary
embarrassment. However, the king's high taxes and the 'dearth of corn', which had
been the cause of the priory's difficulties in 1294, were not as short-lived as the
canons' personal crisis. Even for the rich, the times of sorrow were only just around
the corner by 1300; for many others, they had arrived and had come to stay.

87 Detail of a tile mosaic pavement of *c.* 1300, recently excavated at Norton Priory, in Cheshire

One reason especially for this new vulnerability to crisis was that, for most religious houses of the older-established orders, the springs of lay generosity had run dry. Fashions change, in religion as in anything else. Everywhere, a more personal faith, bringing God and Man into direct confrontation, had eroded the intercessory functions of the monks. And in the towns particularly, which they had made their base, the mendicant friars – first the Dominicans (Black Friars, or Friars Preacher) and Franciscans (Grey Friars, or Minorites), then the Carmelites (White Friars) and Austins (Hermit Friars of St Augustine) – offered a service which was at once more personal and, because of the relative austerity of their Rules, seemingly more likely to draw down the benevolence of God. Both Worcester and Dunstable were urban houses, and they had each felt the chill of this competition. Within a decade of the first arrival of the Franciscans in England, 'Walter, a canon of Dunstable who had taken the vows, and John, one who had not, went without permission by a broken window and leapt over the wall of the monastery and took the habit of the Friars Minor at Oxford'. In 1259, by exploiting their favour with the king, 'the Friars Preacher by very great industry and deceit entered Dunstable against our will'. It was not until 1277 that the prior of Dunstable 'ate with the Friars Preacher in the vill for the first time', and ten years later the two communities were again in dispute, at heavy cost to the finances of the Augustinians: in 1287, 'to forestall the machinations and evil deeds of the Preaching Friars in Dunstable we caused Thomas our doorkeeper to buy a messuage, once Robert Francis's, in Dunstable next to the

88 St Edburga's shrine base, of Purbeck marble formerly painted and gilded, once at Bicester Priory and now in the chancel of the parish church at Stanton Harcourt; early fourteenth century

ground of the said friars; and by the said Thomas we were enfeoffed with the said messuage, lest the said friars enlarged their bounds against our will . . . And as a result of that transaction we were heavily burdened with yearly corrodies and other things.'[53]

Indeed, few crimes between religious would be considered more serious than the poaching by one house of another's principal benefactor. Yet in 1298, as the Worcester chronicler complained, the Franciscans of his city had been guilty of just that offence in the death-bed persuasion of William Beauchamp, earl of Warwick, to seek burial, not in the cathedral priory where his ancestors were interred, but with the friars in their thoroughly inferior burial ground, little better than a bog in the winter; they had then made the capture much worse by holding a triumphal procession through the streets of Worcester, designed to show off their trophy to the citizens.[54] Fear of such a loss, not unjustified in the event, was to drive the canons of Walsingham in the mid-1340s to address a petition to their patron, Elizabeth de Clare, attempting to dissuade her from continuing in her project to settle Franciscans in the town. Elizabeth was a very great lady, sister of Eleanor de Clare, benefactress of Tewkesbury, and daughter of Gilbert, builder of Caerphilly. She dismissed the petition, and from 1347 there were Franciscans resident at Walsingham, running a successful hospice for poor pilgrims to the shrine of Our Lady, very much as the canons had anticipated. Yet the document presented to Dame Elizabeth had voiced exactly those anxieties that the so-called 'possessioner' houses, well before this date, had learnt to feel on hearing of the approach of the Mendicants. Addressing themselves to the 'egregious and noble Lady de Clare', her 'humble chaplains', the prior and canons of her priory at Walsingham, pointed out as best they could the dangers of the projected Franciscan settlement. Their receipts from tithes, repeatedly guaranteed to them by the Clare earls of Hertford since the foundation of the priory in the 1160s, would be diminished just as soon as the friars, claiming exemption from tithes, began to build up their properties in the parish; such properties were not permitted by their Rule, yet the friars would increase them by attracting to themselves the oblations of the faithful as well as collecting together all those customary dues, on the occasions of birth, marriage and death, which would rightly have fallen to the canons. One particular fear, peculiar to Walsingham, was given a prominent place. It had become necessary for the canons, as custodians of the shrine and of the many precious objects bestowed on it by Elizabeth de Clare among others, to lock their gates at night against robbers and other ill-disposed persons. Pilgrims, arriving at Walsingham after the chapel was closed, had hitherto customarily reserved their offerings till the morning, which they might not now do if intercepted beforehand by the friars.[55]

The canons, it may be, deserved to fail in their petition; indeed they seem, from its phrasing, to have had little hope that it would succeed. Nevertheless, what they predicted about their receipts had much truth in it, already anticipated in earlier very similar contexts as much as a century before. Matthew Paris (d. 1259), a monk of St Albans and the most celebrated chronicler of his day, had at first written kindly of St Francis and his followers. By the 1240s, no more than a couple of decades after the first Minorite settlements in England, with the tide of mendicant expansion in full flood, he had had cause to change his mind. He tells the story of the quarrels and rivalries that had already arisen between the Minorites and their nearest rivals, the Friars Preacher, 'a great and scandalous strife' which he compares to the trouble between the military orders (the Hospitallers and the Templars) in the Holy Land. Then he points out the disparity, evident so soon, between what the friars preached and what they did:

And what is terrible, and a sad presage, for three or four hundred years or more, the monastic order did not hasten to destruction so quickly as their order, of whom now the brothers, twenty-four years having scarcely elapsed [since their arrival], had first built in England dwellings which rivalled regal palaces in height. These are they who daily expose to view their inestimable treasures, in enlarging their sumptuous edifices and erecting lofty walls, thereby impudently transgressing the limits of their original poverty, and violating the basis of their religion . . . When noblemen and rich men are at the point of death, whom they know to be possessed of great riches, they in their love of gain diligently urge them, to the injury and loss of the ordinary pastors, and extort confessions and hidden wills, lauding themselves and their own order only, and placing themselves before all others. So no faithful man now believes he can be saved, except he is directed by the counsels of the Preachers and Minorites. Desirous of obtaining privileges in the courts of kings and potentates, they act the parts of councillors, chamberlains, treasurers, groomsmen, and mediators for marriages; they are the executors of the papal extortions; in their sermons, they either are flatterers or most cutting reprovers, revealers of confessions or impudent accusers. Despising also the authentic orders which were instituted by the holy fathers, namely by St Benedict and St Augustine . . . they set their own community before the rest. They look upon the Cistercian monks as clownish, harmless, half-bred, or rather ill-bred, priests; and the monks of the Black order as proud epicures.[56]

Matthew Paris was himself a monk 'of the Black order'. As a prominent member of one of the richest Benedictine communities in England, he was not likely to take an unprejudiced view of his own accusers. But biased in general though his diatribe may have been, it was accurate enough in the delineation of the threats which the Benedictines now perceived to themselves. In the thirteenth century, undisguised attacks on the wealth of the monks, although present already in the preaching of the friars, were still comparatively rare. However, an erosion of confidence had begun. Ultimately, it was the very affluence of the 'possessioners' that would prove their undoing, although they were to carry their accusers, the friars, down with them.

The expansion of the friars was exceptionally rapid, being concentrated largely within a couple of generations and, by 1300, virtually complete. In effect, when a down-turn in the economy finally gripped the monastic houses, in the early fourteenth century or a little before, few were without friars as near-neighbours. The competition had peaked at a particularly unfortunate time. We cannot be certain that it was the rivalry of the friars that checked new endowment of the little Augustinian priory of St Denys. Yet this Southampton house had clearly lost its attraction to donors by 1300, whereas the Franciscans in the town remained popular with the burgesses for another two centuries at least.[57] It was a failure the community could ill afford. The fourteenth century brought war and plague to Southampton, and St Denys was seldom out of trouble. It may have recovered a little in the fifteenth century, when the fortunes of the adjoining borough picked up. But on its suppression in 1536 among the poorer houses, it was well below the income limit that might have given it some temporary protection. Whereas its canons were reported to be of 'good conversation', the conventual buildings of St Denys were derelict at the time and its other properties poorly maintained.[58]

There were, of course, still those religious houses which, under exceptional management, could get along well enough without new donors. One of them was Tavistock (Devonshire) under Robert Champeaux (1285–1324), remembered as a great builder and as the restorer of the fortunes of his abbey.[59] Another was Bolton (West Yorkshire) which, during much of the long priorate of Robert's contemporary, John of Laund (c. 1285–1331), had never known better days. However, at both this prosperity was soon checked. Robert Champeaux was succeeded at Tavistock, after a costly disputed election, by a papal appointee, Bonus, formerly abbot of St Orientius at Larreule (Bigorre). Unfamiliar with English customs, thwarted at every turn by his resentful and rebellious community, and no doubt driven to despair by Devon's heavy grey skies, Abbot Bonus took to the bottle. In the six years of his luckless rule,

Tavistock lost many of the benefits of Robert Champeaux's abbacy, to be described as nearly bankrupt in 1333 when Bonus was eventually sent home.[60]

Tavistock's troubles did not end there, but although successive abbots were afterwards called to task for the community's repeated insolvency, their part in these difficulties was merely secondary. Tavistock is next to Dartmoor, in South Devon. Like Bolton, in Wharfedale on the Pennines, it held much property in the upland moors, on the very frontier of viable cultivation. In each case, the first major expansion of the community's lands had occurred during the climatically favourable conditions of the warm epoch now known to have lasted for about a century from its onset in approximately 1150. Well before 1300, the warm dry summers and mild wet winters of this exceptional climatic optimum were a thing of the past. They had been succeeded characteristically by cool wet summers and cold dry winters in a general cooling phase which, while not as pronounced as it would be much later in the nadirs of the late sixteenth and late seventeenth centuries, was yet quite sufficient to destroy, in the long term, the viability of cereal cultivation on the more exposed and marginal uplands; in the short term, a succession of spoilt harvests in unusually wet summers could trigger off, again especially on the frontiers of settlement, a crisis of epic proportions.[61]

It was exactly such a crisis, induced by the harvest failures of 1315–16 and 1320–21, that was at least as important in the ruin of Prior Laund's work at Bolton as the notorious raids of the Scots. John of Laund, like Robert Champeaux of Tavistock or like the still more remarkable Prior Henry of Canterbury with whom he has since been compared, was a great builder. Despite the relative poverty of this remote Augustinian house, Prior Laund built himself new lodgings there on a magnificent scale; he was probably responsible for the splendid new octagonal chapter-house in the Westminster style, and at least began on the major reconstruction of the priory church which was to leave it with new transepts and a much extended presbytery, more ambitious than the income of his house would seem to warrant. All of this he paid for out of shrewd investments, including the purchase of two manors at Appletreewick (1300) and Holmpton (1307) and the appropriation, even more profitable in the long term although expensive at the time, of the parish churches of Carleton (1292) and Long Preston (1304).[62] In the best period of his priorate, between 1305 and 1315, when these investments had begun to yield a good return, John of Laund succeeded in doubling the income of his community.[63] Yet Bolton would never do better, for in 1315 the rains came, the crops failed, and the priory's flocks of sheep, within the next two years, had been cut back by as much as two-thirds. The canons, who had eaten so well in the days of plenty – better than ever before – found themselves, during the worst of the famine years in 1315–16, short of bread and stinted in ale. They were only just recovering in 1318, after the bountiful harvest of the previous summer, when the Scots arrived to plunder their lands, first in a raid through Wharfedale in the spring of that year, then again during the 1319 cropping season. By 1322, after the further harvest failures of the previous two years, the priory's rental income had fallen by almost a third; the receipts from tithes and spiritualities were down by between a third and a quarter; the community itself had been dispersed since the late autumn of 1320, 'devastated and subject to such loss and collapse that its own resources are no longer sufficient to provide for the maintenance of the college of canons serving God there and for the support of the usual burdens of hospitality'.[64]

Bolton shared its miseries with others. Unlike the Anglo-Welsh houses which, as at Ewenny Priory in coastal Glamorgan, had become accustomed to make some provision for their own defence, the monasteries and nunneries of the Northern Marches were entirely unprepared for what had come upon them. Fortified enclosures such as that at Ewenny were indeed to be supplied in later years at the Northumberland houses at Hulne (Carmelite) and Alnwick (Premonstratensian), both sheltering under the shadow of the great Percy fortress that was rising at Alnwick itself.[65] But these followed as a consequence of the Scottish raids, as did other fortifications of their kind on both sides of the Pennines and north of the border as well as south; they did not anywhere anticipate them. The Augustinian canonesses of Holystone (Northumberland), right up against the border, had once been prosperous. They were ruined by the Anglo-Scottish wars. Already in 1313, Bishop Kellaw of Durham was writing of the miseries of their condition:

> The house of the said nuns [Holystone], situated in the March of England and Scotland, by reason of the hostile incursions which daily and continually increase in the March, is frequently despoiled of its goods and the nuns themselves are often attacked by the marauders, harmed and pursued and, put to flight and driven from their home, are constrained miserably to experience bitter suffering.[66]

Twenty-seven in number in 1291, just before war began, there were only five canonesses at Holystone in 1379 and the community seems never to have recovered much beyond this.[67]

Egglestone and Coverham, both Premonstratensian houses of no more than moderate means situated in the North Yorkshire Pennines, had suffered equally with Bolton in the raids; in 1327, the community of Egglestone was still dispersed and its lands and goods had been so 'destroyed, burned and wasted by frequent invasions of the Scots' that 'nothing taxable is found in this place from which any tenth can be demanded or raised'.[68] However Coverham, when it obtained a licence in 1333 to appropriate the parish church at Sedbergh (east of Kendal, on the other side of the Pennines), did so not only by reason of its losses in the raids but because the abbey itself was 'situated in a barren and desert land', immediately to the west of the great castle at Middleham and very similar, in point of fact, to the placing of Egglestone, hard by Barnard Castle to the north. As at Bolton again, it had not been the war alone that had bankrupted these houses, for the growing inhospitality of their upland settings, especially exposed to the contemporary deterioration in climate, had converted productive land into barren waste, opening all three communities to calamity.

In one of the western dioceses at just this time, Adam Orleton, bishop of Worcester (1327–33), was having to listen to petitions for appropriations which, while naturally free from complaints about the Scots, listed unceasingly the whole round of disasters which together had caused, between 1315 and 1322, the great famine and agrarian crisis.[69] One of the more affecting of these petitions originated in 1331 from the Cistercian nuns of the little house at Cook Hill (Worcestershire), seeking to appropriate, and thus lay hands on, the revenues of the nearby parish

89 Bolton Priory from the east, showing the extended presbytery and transepts which the church probably owed to John of Laund (d. 1331), one of Bolton's most notable building priors

church of Bishampton. Bishop Orleton, who granted their request, had understood from their 'tearful plaint' that they feared that without such assistance their nunnery would be brought to 'the irredeemable shame of dissolution'. What had reduced them to poverty had been the 'sterility of their lands, the destruction of woods, murrain of animals, and the withdrawal of alms which they were wont to receive from certain great men', the latter perhaps as oppressed as themselves.[70] The bishop found the nuns' allegations 'so notorious as to defy concealment'. He would have heard the same story just two years before from their brothers in religion, the Cistercians of Abbey Dore (Herefordshire), whose reasons for the appropriation of Duntisborne Militis were the now familiar ones of sterility of lands and murrain of animals, in addition to the 'wars and other external disturbances of the times'.[71]

At Abbey Dore, in 1329, the situation of the monks was said to be deteriorating daily, nor need this have been far from the truth. Certainly, the worst of the agrarian crisis was already over. The livestock murrains – sheep in 1315–17, cattle in 1319–21 – were no more than a memory; the rains had let up, and the harvests had been brought in without difficulty. However, the crisis-inducing sterility of the soil, of which both the nuns and the monks complained, had as yet to be found a cure. With the weather, it had followed from exhaustion of the soil, from the over-crowding of the men who worked it, and from chronically 'dirty' (weed-infested) lands. By modern standards, cereal yields in medieval England were absurdly low. Only a demographic catastrophe on a major scale could set right the balance between land and men: between a declining and exhausted arable acreage, eroded at the margins by the deterioration of the weather, and the population it was called upon to support.[72]

Over-crowding had had other unfortunate consequences. Crime levels had touched new heights in the famine years, but they had been rising already before that, and the civil commotions of Edward II's reign had more than one grievance to promote them. In the great monastic boroughs, tension between the monks and their tenants, the townspeople, had long been rising. In 1327, closely following the deposition of Edward II and throughout the near anarchy of Isabella and Mortimer's regime, not at an end before the autumn of 1330, resentments flowed over into riots. There were ferocious scenes at St Albans, at Bury St Edmunds and at Abingdon in 1327, in each case including an armed assault on the abbey and the burning of at least part of its buildings.[73] On the abbey manors, the better-off peasants made common cause with the townspeople, and there was trouble, for as long as the central government was weak, on many monastic estates. It was not until 1332 that the abbot of St Albans forced surrender on his burgesses, recovering all that, ostensibly, he had lost. But there was nothing that even Abbot Richard could do that would make good the more permanent damage. On the St Albans estates, and probably elsewhere, opposition to the abbot had become hereditary by the fourteenth century, rent-strikes and other rejections of authority being passed from father to son.[74] Hardly surprisingly, during the Peasants' Revolt in 1381, the riots in the borough were at least as painful; in the countryside, they were even more severe.[75]

The advantage, in any event, had begun to slip from the hands of the wealthier landowners. Wages on many monastic estates had been allowed to rise during the serious inflation of the English currency in 1304–14. However, the high prices of the period, although contributing most materially to the sufferings of the landless, had suited the possessioners very well, as they continued to do for at least another decade when the first signs of a permanent descent became apparent. In 1325–30, the receipts from the Christ Church (Canterbury) estates, some of the best managed in the kingdom, were lower on average than they had been since before the 1290s. Through stringent economies and as a result of their savings on the prices of the wine and other foodstuffs bought in, the treasurers of Christ Church succeeded in keeping the cathedral priory solvent.[76] Yet for them, as for others in their position, salaries and pensions remained a fixed charge, and the relative security of many religious houses from this date depended chiefly on the size of their wage bills. In effect, the prolonged deflation of the 1330s and 1340s had as serious consequences, in its own way, for the greater monasteries as had the inflation of the previous decades for their dependants. Their barns were full of unsaleable foodstuffs, their markets crowded with unwanted goods.[77]

Many, in the better times that were only just behind them, had committed themselves to ambitious programmes of new works. Sempringham Priory, in Lincolnshire, was one of these, where a new church, begun in the grandest manner in the first years of the fourteenth century, was still unfinished in the 1390s because of

90 Egglestone (North Yorkshire), one of the poorest of the Premonstratensian houses, in the remote Pennine setting that exposed it to the raids of the Scots

the canons' poverty and the acknowledged 'malignity' of the times. The Gilbertines of Sempringham were not a poor community; after Watton, in East Yorkshire, their house was the richest in the order. Nevertheless, the church that the canons had laid out for themselves in 1301 – of 'marvellous greatness' and 'a most costly undertaking' – was to be as big as were many cathedrals. Edward II spoke from his own experience of such works when he advised the pope in 1317 that the canons of Sempringham were in need of his help, for they had taken on something which, even at that time, they were in no position to complete on their own.[78]

Nothing remains of Sempringham now, and we have no means of knowing whether the canons' new church was ever finished on the scale first projected. At Milton, in Dorset, an even wealthier community failed utterly to achieve its ambitions. On the night of 2 September 1309 lightning struck the church; the fire had spread rapidly, and both the building and its contents (including the church plate and vestments, the books and relics, the estate records and common seal of the community) had been consumed.[79] Although work on the reconstruction began quickly enough, with a fine new presbytery and choir soon completed as far as the crossing, the nave allowed for in the original plan, and certainly started at this period, was never built. It was not until towards the end of the fifteenth century that the central tower on the crossing was finished, nor were either of the transepts ready until much later. Incomplete as it remained, the church at Milton Abbas is still today one of the finest and most expensively detailed in Dorset. Like Sempringham, it could have been a building of a very different sort, comparable to some of the greatest in the land, had the monks been able to finish their church and had harsher times not stunted its growth.[80]

A major element in these harsher times was, of course, the onset of plague. Late in 1348, the Black Death reached England. The plague was at its most deadly in the spring and summer of 1349, when it carried off fully half the community at Westminster Abbey, taking the abbot and most of his monks at the great house of St Albans, and reducing many of the smaller communities to near-ruin.[81] Few religious houses were extinguished utterly at this time, Wothorpe (Northamptonshire) being almost alone as a well-documented example of such collapse.[82] But for a good number, among them the Augustinian priories of Sandleford (Berkshire) and Ivy Church (Wiltshire), religious life was brought at least temporarily to a halt,[83] while for perhaps the majority of the communities in England after this date, any recovery to pre-plague enrolments became impossible.

As serious to the communities as the gaps in their own numbers were the losses they suffered on their manors. On the Titchfield estates in 1348–9, the tenants of this Hampshire Premonstratensian house lost almost sixty per cent of their number, or 305 out of an original 515; when the plague struck again in 1361–2, another 92 were removed.[84] Between May and July 1349, on the Cambridgeshire manors of Crowland Abbey, sixteen land-holders died at Cottenham, twenty-three at Oakington, and eleven at Dry Drayton. Taking the period of the plague as a whole, from October 1348 until January 1350, some fifty-seven per cent of the tenants at Cottenham died, as many as seventy per cent of those at Oakington, and forty-eight per cent at Dry Drayton.[85]

It is now sometimes held that both the mortalities in the Black Death and the plague's immediate impact on the English economy have been exaggerated. Certainly, with over-population as the major social problem of the pre-plague years, there was a good deal of slack to be taken up.[86] But the notorious pestilence of 1348–9 was only the first of many. For a century and more, bubonic plague was endemic in England. With other infectious killer diseases, scarcely better understood or controlled, recurring plague epidemics delayed the full recovery of the English population until well into the sixteenth century. After the Black Death itself, plague returned as a nation-wide catastrophe in 1361 and 1368–9, while from that time forward there was scarcely a decade in the later Middle Ages when the greater part of the country was free of it.[87] Christ Church (Canterbury), one of the communities least affected by the first outbreak of plague in 1348–9, was nevertheless the victim of repeated epidemics in every decade of the fifteenth century, only the 1490s being free of them. On the evidence of the Christ Church obituary lists for the period, at least sixteen per cent of the monks died of plague, while others of their community

91 The abbey church at Milton (Dorset) from the west; after the fire of 1309, reconstruction began on the church at Milton but never got beyond the crossing; the nave, although planned and started at foundation level, was abandoned; of the transepts, neither was completed before the abbacy of William Middleton (1481–1521); the porch in the blocked crossing arch is Victorian

were carried off by diseases of comparable virulence, including the sweating sickness of 1485 which killed as many as nine monks in somewhat less than that number of days.[88]

In these conditions, recruitment continued to be a worry, not least in the care of estates. Battle Abbey, we know, was between a third and a quarter down on its pre-plague income by the 1380s, and much of this loss was permanent.[89] At other houses, with less fat to live on during the crisis years, each new onset of disease threatened disbandment. Particularly exposed, as always, to economic disaster were the ill-endowed communities of nuns. In the 1390s in Lincolnshire and the 1400s in Sussex, on both occasions following outbreaks of the plague, the complaints of the nuns were the same. Legbourne (Lincolnshire) was a small house of Cistercian nuns, unable to keep its land in good condition 'on account of the dearth of cultivators and rarity of men, arising out of unwonted pestilences and epidemics'. At Easebourne (Sussex), in the following decade, an even poorer community of Augustinian canonesses found itself driven to appeal for help as a consequence of 'epidemics, death of men and of servants'. Easebourne's property was already so ill-maintained that 'few tenants can be found willing to occupy the lands in these days, and the said lands, ever falling into a worse state, are so poor that they cannot supply the religious women with sufficient support for themselves or for the repair of their ruinous buildings'.[90]

Both nunneries survived, to be dissolved with the lesser houses in 1536 but to last at least until then. However, these were by no means easy times for any religious

community, and the principal losses were not always, even so, the most obvious ones. Low morale and fading ideals were to become, as we shall see, major problems in many houses during the later Middle Ages. But neither there nor on the estates were the failures of the time necessarily related to money. The search for recruits and new tenants after the Black Death inevitably resulted in a temporary lowering of standards. When Abbot William of Bury, in 1351, obtained permission from the pope to have ten of his monks ordained as priests before reaching the statutory age, he was responding to a crisis 'because of the lack of monks who were also priests, at the time of the plague or epidemic, which in time past was raging in these parts, because of those who are missing, this monastery is known to be in need of monks who are also priests, who can celebrate mass and other divine services'.[91] Yet the chaplains prematurely ordained in these difficult times had a long life ahead of them in the community, and the quality of the religious life at Bury, as elsewhere, could not fail to be reduced by such conditions.

On the estates, similarly, old relationships built up successfully over the years and shattered by the great pestilence and its successors, were everywhere hard to recover. Tenants, although still not difficult to find for the better lands, were not of the same breed as before. On the Ramsey manors, on those of Westminster or of Crowland, the same phenomenon was observable. Tenants in these times were more captious than before, less well-disciplined and more inclined to make trouble.[92] If this kind of restlessness and these discontents were to spill over into the politics of the nation, as in time they would, the consequences might indeed become serious.

92 *Opposite* St Albans: one of the greater abbeys, known to have suffered especially severely in the Black Death (1349), which carried off the abbot and most of his monks

Chapter 6

Bending the Rule

St Benedict composed his Rule in A.D. 530–40. Almost exactly a thousand years later, when confronted by a programme of reforms, the English Benedictines had to tell their critics that they could no longer insist on the literal observance of the Rule, for such austerity would depopulate their abbeys.[1] How, and at what period in particular, had things begun to go so badly adrift?

Of course, the Benedictines had been under attack since before the twelfth century. Moderate though St Benedict's Rule had been intended to be – a rule for beginners, teaching the merest 'rudiments' of monastic observance and attuned to the weakness of the 'faint-hearted'[2] – it had not been drawn up for the monks of the North. The winter at Monte Cassino is severe enough, but the climate is not that of North Yorkshire. The earliest surviving series of English visitation records, preserved in the archbishop's archives at York from the late thirteenth century, is enough to show that the monks and nuns of this northern province were already guilty of most of the misdemeanours of which they would later be so freely accused. At the midnight hour, monks were failing to rise for matins, or were gabbling the office if they did. St Benedict, as always, had foreseen the difficulty. 'When they [the brethren] rise for the Work of God,' he had said, 'let them gently encourage one another, on account of the excuses to which the sleepy are addicted.'[3] But he had not known what it was like to live in the North, and rising for the night office, even with the customary relaxations for the winter, remained a singular trial. At Kirkham (East Yorkshire), the canons had lightened the moment by shouting each other down in the responses. Those of Bridlington, of Bolton and of Healaugh Park, all Yorkshire Augustinian communities, had kept themselves fit by hunting. Social drinking after compline, the last office before bedtime, was common; conversation was excessive; strangers made themselves too much at home within the precincts. Private property of which St Anselm, we are told, had had a horror of the mere words, and which St Benedict adjudged to be the vice which should especially 'be utterly rooted out of the monastery', was already openly tolerated.[4] Although not the abuse it would come to be in later years, when the least desirable characteristics of most religious houses seem to have stemmed from it, private property had arrived to stay. The monks kept possessions of their own in their studies (carrells) in the cloister; at Swine and Nun Appleton, medium-sized Yorkshire nunneries of the Cistercian family, the nuns had kept their things in locked private boxes which the archbishop subsequently required them to leave open.[5]

Misbehaviour of this order was certainly no novelty in thirteenth-century monasticism. We must be on our guard, furthermore, against assuming too readily that it ever got markedly worse. Nevertheless, there are reasons for thinking that

93 The Wheel of the Religious Life: the abbot (top), with monks ascending and descending on either side. English, mid-thirteenth century

even if the individual monk in the Late Middle Ages was no more prone to vice than his predecessors, at least the discipline under which he lived had been relaxed. St Benedict had acknowledged that there might, on occasion, be commands too 'hard and impossible' for a monk to accept from his superior. But his solution to such oppressions was reasoned objection, to be followed by obedience if that failed: 'If after his representations the superior still persists in his decision and command, let the subject know that it is expedient for him, and let him obey out of love, trusting in the assistance of God.'[6] Many centuries later, monks continued to behave in this way, but obedience by this time had been made so much the easier as superiors were satisfied with less. There had come to be, in the formerly strict orders as well as in those traditionally more lax, what one recent student of the late-medieval Cistercian abbots has described as 'too easy an acquiescence in the fallibility of human nature, too optimistic an assessment of man's power to reclaim himself after a serious lapse . . . critical judgement in high places had been dulled'.[7]

Part of the blame for this could be laid at the door of the most highly placed authorities in the Church. Stability and obedience, from the very beginning, had been the two first essentials of monasticism. Yet Clement VI (1342–52), for the purpose of the papal Jubilee in 1350, had exempted all religious wanting to come to Rome from the obligation to obtain first the permission of their superiors. As the Cistercian abbots were then sourly to observe, if those who flocked to Rome in such numbers under this licence were not already sinners when they entered the city, they had certainly become so before they left it.[8] In point of fact, monastic apostasy – 'abandoning Israel to return to Egypt' – was never practised on a large scale in late-

94 Nuns being wheeled home in a barrow by a naked man. Flemish, fourteenth century

medieval England. Both monks and nuns were too comfortable where they were, and the fugitive religious, whatever his reasons for leaping the wall, was usually back home within weeks.[9] However, the warmth of the welcome so often accorded to the returned apostate was yet another indication of the enfeebling tolerance of the times. When successive rival popes at Rome and Avignon, competing for support during the Great Schism of 1378 to 1417, granted every kind of privilege to those wealthy or powerful enough to demand it, the main principles of Benedict's Rule were so often flouted that its worth was set at naught.[10] Markby, in Lincolnshire, was an Augustinian house, and its shameful condition in 1438 was certainly not typical of all communities of canons even within this least rigorous of orders. But how could the system have slipped so far that a canon of Markby should himself agree that 'religious discipline is observed in naught', adding that 'religion is almost utterly and in all things dead' in his house? In correcting the prior, whose resignation he obtained, Bishop Alnwick of Lincoln did not mince his words in criticism:

> In our actual visitation of the said your priory, and by our anxious inquiry concerning and touching the premises, we found it clearly apparent to the eye, not only by such inquiry, but also by the report that is current in the whole neighbourhood touching this, that the said monastery, by carelessness and negligence, and by the dilapidation and wasting of property, goods and woods, and by occasion of disorderliness, is suffering, which is a grievous thing, almost irrecoverable damage; that in the said priory there is no religion or regular observances, but hardly even so much as the outward form of religion, save only the sign whereto that which is marked with it answers not. There, to wit, is all manner of laxness; there is no obedience there; all manner of wilful gadding about, haunting of public taverns, drinking, messes, and every sort of surfeit; wilful, nay, undue wastefulness of the things temporal without which this present life cannot be passed; we do not say fleshly concupiscence, but in short all things that are contrary to the purity of religion flourish there.[11]

Everything was wrong. But the prior, whose neglect of his responsibilities had contributed most to the decline of the house in his charge, was pensioned off generously at the expense of his impoverished community. He was to have a good clothing allowance, free fuel and a personal servant. Within the priory precinct, he was to be found 'an honest lodging with a fireplace and a privy, and, whenever he shall eat in his lodging, he shall receive of bread and beer and from the kitchen as much as two canons of the house receive'.[12] John Alford, the notorious pederast, and his companion canons at Markby whose evening drinking bouts had left them so 'heavy' that 'they do not come to matins, and, if they come, they are so sleepy that they profit not', were given another chance to make amends. William Alnwick of Lincoln was a zealous visitor and a conscientious corrector of the faults of the religious communities in his diocese. But the bishop's bark, as the monks can scarcely have failed to observe in their turn, was very much worse than his bite.

Discipline, in any event, might not be the only problem – or the worst. Earlier in the same decade, William Alnwick's predecessor, Bishop Gray (1431–6), had already

95 A soul is carried off to Hell by devils, while monks watch helpless from a boat. Flemish, late fifteenth century

96 A monk and a nun play a ball game together, watched by a group of spectators. Flemish, fourteenth century

97 The great church at Durham, focus of a rich and busy community

written in similar terms to the Benedictines of Bradwell Priory, in Buckinghamshire, where his commissary had found 'the same rule of religion which you have professed not observed therein, but only as it were the shadow or counterfeit of religion'. But Bradwell was a poor house, among the poorest of its order in England, and the main difficulty it continued to face until its premature dissolution in 1524–5 with the other lesser houses suppressed by Cardinal Wolsey, was in maintaining a community sufficiently large to keep a life of religion in being. Not for them the 'high crying' and 'vain trilling' which John Wyclif had found so objectionable in what he saw as the over-elaborate devotions of the 'many proud good-for-nothings' of their order.[13] At Bradwell, 'seeing that the scanty number of monks is not sufficient for this purpose', the members of the community were to recite matins without music, 'nevertheless together and in a low voice, devoutly and clearly and with pauses; and when the number of singers is increased, you shall sing and chant them devoutly and clearly by note'. Again by reason of their small numbers, the Benedictines of Bradwell had not been eating together regularly in their refectory (keeping frater) in accordance with the Rule; they had not held a chapter, or general meeting, every day; they had not observed correct routine in daily meditation and reading in their cloister. Obviously, the first priority, fully recognized by the bishop, was to restore the community to full size:

98 Durham's seyney-house at the near-by dependent priory of Finchale. In the later Middle Ages, the residential buildings to the south of the cloister (right) and south-east of the church (top right) at Finchale became exceptionally extensive, having to provide for the needs of holidaying monks from the cathedral priory just up-river

> We enjoin upon you, the prior . . . that with all the speed you can, you cause more monks, so far as your resources are sufficient, to receive the tonsure in the priory, and some teachable children to be maintained on the broken meat of your tables and instructed in reading, song and the other elementary branches of knowledge, that they may serve the monks at the celebration of masses and be admitted as brethren and fellow-monks of the said priory according to their manners and deserts.[14]

How successful the prior could be in recruitment, with the limited means at his disposal, must always have lain in doubt. On Bradwell's suppression in the 1520s, there were no more than three or four monks resident at the priory, and this had probably been the case for many years.

One of St Benedict's chief purposes in laying down a routine was to avoid that idleness (*otiositas*) which he saw as 'the enemy of the soul'.[15] And of course it was in the very smallest communities, where routines were broken or ignored, that the deadly lethargy of 'accidie', or spiritual and intellectual sloth, was always most likely to prevail. *Accidia*, part ennui and part melancholia, has rightly been identified as 'the peculiar menace of the cloister', being a rejection of routine by those 'in whom Nature, expelled by a pitchfork, had returned a thousand times more strong'.[16] In a rich and busy community like the great cathedral priory at Durham, idleness was kept at bay by the many tasks, both secular and religious, that every monk might be called upon to perform. More than half the community, at any time, had been assigned some regular employment in the priory's affairs; lists were kept of responsibilities in the church, and monthly rotas were observed, one consequence being that the life of religion at Durham, supported by discipline and by communal endeavour, was arguably both happy and fruitful to the end.[17]

Other communities had remedies of their own. At Ulvescroft (Leicestershire), just before its dissolution, there was 'not one religious person there but that they can and doth use either embroidering, writing books with very fair hand, making their own garments, carving, painting, or engraving'.[18] At Hailes (Gloucestershire), it was allowed at the visitation of 1442 that 'twice or three times a week, if the abbot granted permission, the prior or one deputed by him might lead the convent out into the fields, where the monks might take recreation in a manner seemly for religious, but nobody should separate himself from the main body, and especially they should not enter taverns or the town'.[19] The monks of St Augustine's, Bristol, saw their regular walks in the hills and fields as a means, their abbot once explained, 'to recreate their minds and to lax their veins, whereby they may be more apt to continue both night and day in the service of God'.[20]

Not unaware of the effect on their health of a sedentary life in cloister, refectory and choir, the monks of all orders had long practised periodic blood-letting, followed by a recreational break (seyney or *minutio*) during which the monks under treatment (the *minuti*) enjoyed a more nourishing diet. Originally, this had taken place in the infirmary, with little relaxation of discipline.[21] However, the custom had grown up over the years of allowing regular breaks at a country manor-house away from the monastery, many of the greater houses designating one of their more congenial rural properties for this purpose. Still, as late as 1329, Bishop Orleton of Worcester would find it in his heart to condemn the monks of Winchcombe (Gloucestershire) for their 'corruption of blood-letting at Corndean', where they had indulged in unduly lax behaviour and idle gossiping. They were to be bled, he provided, in an 'honest and convenient place', with no more than moderate amendments of diet and routine.[22] But the bishop's rigour, at this period, was unusual. Three years before, Adam Orleton's own metropolitan, Archbishop Reynolds of Canterbury (1313–27), himself a former bishop of Worcester, had made over to the monks of his cathedral priory of Christ Church the manor at Caldicote, east of Canterbury, where they might breathe the fresh country air after blood-letting.[23] How they might be expected to comport themselves there is set out plainly in the regulations later devised by Archbishop Courtenay (1381–96) for the *minuti* of Spalding (Lincolnshire), taking their seyneys at the priory's grange at Wickham. It was the archbishop's intention, he said, to increase the value of these periodic leaves, for he understood very well the worth of recreation in a well-ordered life of religion. To this end, the *minuti* were to leave the priory after the solemn procession on Sunday, returning the following Saturday. They were to maintain a limited religious routine, including prayers for the foundress and other benefactors, with a mass for the health of the archbishop himself and for the security of his soul after death. While at Wickham, each recuperating monk was to have a gallon and a half of beer daily, with two good-quality loaves of bread and such other victuals as he would normally have enjoyed at the priory; adequate fuel would be provided for his needs and for those of the servants who attended him.[24] So attractive was the regime at Redburn Priory, the Hertfordshire seyney-house of the great abbey of St Albans, that Thomas de la Mare (1349–96), who has been described as 'the outstanding abbot of his day', was a frequent visitor there, appearing very much more approachable and relaxed in such surroundings. He loved to rise early, before anybody else was up, and would himself ring the bell for office. Although disapproving of those who were late for meals, he was never as sharp as he would have been in comparable circumstances at home.[25]

99 The rich and populous cathedral priory at Worcester, disturbed in 1317 by the 'noisy lips and braggart tongue' of an ill-mannered monk who had then to be sent away for disciplining (*British Crown copyright reserved*)

Thomas de la Mare was a busy man, and it was not monotony that he came to Redburn to avoid. Yet for others the daily routine of a religious community could indeed be oppressive, requiring relief in many different ways. One of the more ingenious of these was the elaborate sign language, certainly in use in the thirteenth century, by which regulations about silence might be circumvented. A code of such signs, as used by the Victorines of Dublin, is headed generally 'Of signs of certain things' and begins 'Of those that specially appertain to the divine office'. It includes 'For the general sign of a book, extend the hand, and move it as the leaf is usually turned . . . For the sign of allelujah, raise the hand and the tops of the fingers bent; move as if to fly, on account of the angels, because it is called their song . . . For the sign of the antiphonary, having first made the sign of a book, in addition bend the thumb, on account of the curves of the notes – the "neumae", which are so bent . . . For the sign of the psalter, in addition place the hollowed hand on the head, on account of the similitude of a crown which a king usually wears.' The next and longer section of the Victorines' code, although introduced simply as 'Of those [signs] which appertain to food', was clearly designed to cover most contingencies of domestic life in their community. Thus:

> For the sign of bread, make a circle with both thumbs and the two next fingers . . . For the sign of pottage cooked with herbs, draw one finger over another, as one does who cuts up herbs for cooking . . . For the sign of an eel, shut up each hand as one who holds and presses an eel slipping away . . . For the sign of honey, make the tongue appear for a little, and apply the fingers as though you wanted to lick them

. . . For the sign of garlic or radish, extend the finger across the mouth a little opened, on account of the savour which is perceived from them . . . For the sign of a bolster or pillow, lift the hand and the tops of the fingers bent, move as if to fly, afterwards place on the cheek as one is accustomed to do when sleeping . . . For the sign of a needle, having first made the sign of metal [strike the fist roughly with the fist] feign as though you held the needle in one hand and the thread in the other, and that you wanted to put the thread through the eye of the needle . . . For the sign of a comb, draw three fingers through the hair, as one who combs it . . . For the sign of a martyr, place the right hand on the neck, as though you wanted to cut something . . . For the sign of speaking, hold the hand against the mouth, and so move it. For the sign of silence, place a finger upon the closed mouth . . . etc.[26]

These signs, when used to excess, had attracted critics, among them Gerald of Wales who, in the late twelfth century, had found the gesticulations of his enemies, the Cluniacs, needlessly histrionic, or actor-like.[27] But they were scarcely worse than the 'noisy lips and braggart tongue' of the monk of Worcester who, in 1317, had so 'greatly disturbed the peace and the quiet intercourse of the brethren' that he had to be sent away, by general agreement, to another community for disciplining.[28] And they were one way of limiting, within the spirit of the Rule, those unlawful meetings and discussions – the 'parliaments' held in church and cloister – with which the Benedictines of Winchcombe (Gloucestershire) in 1329 were so exhausting themselves 'that both heart and tongue are withdrawn from divine matters'.[29]

Other things, too, could seduce the heart and tongue, not least the appeal of fashionable clothing to which the religious, both monks and nuns, were always liable to fall victim. One of the ways in which the wealthy Benedictine nuns of Elstow (Bedfordshire) held ennui at arm's length was by keeping themselves up to date with the latest modes, displaying great virtuosity in that pursuit. John Longland, bishop of Lincoln over the period of their final demise, had earlier corrected them in 1531 in such a way as to show himself no mean student, in his own right, of the fashions:

We ordeyne . . . that no ladye ne any religious suster within the said monasterye presume to were ther apparells upon ther hedes undre suche lay fashion as they have now of late doon with cornered crests, nether undre suche manour of hight shewing ther forhedes moore like lay people than religious, butt that they use them without suche crestes or secular fashions and off a lower sort and that ther vayle come as lowe as ther yye ledes . . . And undre like payne inoyne that noon of the said religious susters doo use or were hereafter eny such voyded shoys, nether crested as they have of late ther used, butt that they be of suche honeste fashion as other religious places doth use and that ther gownes and kyrtells be closse afore and nott so depe voyded at the breste and noo more to use rede stomachers but other sadder colers in the same.[30]

They had had their example earlier in the golden rings, silvered girdles, silken veils and shifts of 'cloth of Rennes' of Dame Clemence Medforde, prioress in 1441 of the nunnery at Ankerwyke (Buckinghamshire); or in the silken veils, high at the forehead, and long flowing robes of Dame Clemence's contemporary rivals in fashion, the Benedictine nuns of the small community at Langley, in Leicestershire.[31] At

100 A truncated fragment of the eastern block of the late-fifteenth-century gatehouse at Ramsey Abbey, its rich mouldings being among the few remaining material indications of the wealth of this once great monastery

another Leicestershire house in the same period, the Augustinian canons of Kirby Bellars were evidently accustomed to cut quite a dash. They wore clasps in their boots, one of their number complained to the bishop, 'and now of late the young canons do carry purses adorned with orphreys [embroidery] and silk, that hang down from their belts to their knees, to the stain of their religion and the overturning of their ancient habit'. Bishop Alnwick's injunctions, delivered in 1440, included the requirement to 'refrain from all these things in every way'.[32]

In William Alnwick's time, the war continued against private property in the religious houses: a vice not confined to fine dress. At Ramsey Abbey, for example, the bishop had found the monks engaged in 'bargaining and private gain', hiring fields and sowing them with woad and other crops, 'and so, taking opportunities of withdrawing themselves from divine service and from attendance in quire and from the other regular observances, [they] roam abroad among secular folk and women of ill fame also whom out of their liking they hire to till the aforesaid places, and, contrary to the doctrine of the apostle, do intermeddle with such worldly businesses and employments, not without suspicion of evil'.[33] But whereas in the old days

101 The abbot's kitchen at Glastonbury Abbey, built in the second half of the fourteenth century and equipped with ranges across each of its four corners to create an octagonal interior plan under the impressive central smoke flue and lantern

Bishop Alnwick's predecessors would have found such practices utterly abhorrent and Alnwick himself continued formally to condemn them, it is abundantly clear that what was now most likely to cause disquiet at a house like Ramsey was no longer the very existence of private means among the monks but rather the abuse of such means by the incompetent or, worse, by the dishonest. 'To every monk,' the bishop provided, 'who is so given to fine living that he cannot control himself with prudence there shall be appointed a guardian, who shall receive his pay and furnish him with things needful, and at the end of the year shall give an account of his ministry to the lord abbot.'[34] In an earlier generation, among the Benedictines of Ramsey as for every other order, such individual stipends would have been unheard of; for Bishop Alnwick, they had become an institution it was one of his duties to protect.

In point of fact, the *peculium*, being an annual allowance of pocket money in lieu of free distributions of clothing and other necessities, was still a comparative novelty in many houses. Distributions of this kind, in breach of both the spirit and the letter of St Benedict's Rule, had always been forbidden before the thirteenth century, and even then, as they became more common, were habitually roundly condemned. Yet it could be argued that private property was not in question so long as the *peculium* was found, in each case, out of the common fund. By the early sixteenth century, when a return was attempted at Faversham (Kent) to the once traditional issues of goods from the common store, the complaints of the community were bitter. Few liked having to go to the abbot for their clothes and shoes; not having any spending money to call their own, they felt helpless and oppressed; although the value of the issues was generally agreed to be higher than the cash receipts of the monks in the past, most found the exchange unsatisfactory, noticing also how it was putting off potential recruits to the community.[35]

The system of cash doles was not altogether a happy one. It reduced the monk to the status and condition of a pensioner.[36] But this did not make it any the less popular among religious of every persuasion. At Glastonbury, for example, the proportion of the abbey's revenues given over to cash doles rose steadily through the fourteenth century, to be augmented on occasion by such additional receipts as the revenues of an appropriated church.[37] The nuns of Shaftesbury, allowed 2d weekly out of the profits of their house by the order of Bishop Ralph Erghum in 1380, complained promptly to his successors if the payments were ever in arrears.[38] At St Albans, one of the works of Abbot John Whethamstede (d. 1465) to be remembered with most affection by his monks was the increase he assigned them in their dole:

> Also, so that the labourer in the vineyard of the Lord from morning till evening might find the work easier, and the period of working shorter, the said abbot added a wage of 6s 8d to each of the monk priests, lawfully labouring in this vineyard; and ordered the payment of that money to be divided into three parts, to be paid three times a year, in the form which is stated elsewhere in the register.[39]

For a tiny minority, the receipt of cash doles might provide an opportunity for the exercise of entrepreneurial talents. John Rysley of Dunstable (Bedfordshire) was a bee-keeper; as reported in 1442, he 'has nineteen hives of bees and applies them wholly for himself to his own uses, nor in aught does he make known to the prior what he does with them'. His associate, Thomas Alstone, had twenty hives which he likewise maintained for private gain.[40] But for most religious, the purpose of pocket money was much as it is now, to round off the edges of austerity. Dom William Ingram, a monk of Christ Church (Canterbury) in the early sixteenth century and the custodian of important relics of Thomas Becket, showed instincts of both kinds in his make-up. In the book of accounts which he began in 1504 and which he kept for another two decades, William Ingram recorded an income in fees and other emoluments that made him, by the standards of his day and his profession, a man of

102 A monk at prayer (left) and receiving divine guidance (right) in his spacious and comfortably
   furnished cell. Flemish, late fifteenth century

considerable substance. Like the monks of Ramsey, he appears to have had interests
in property outside the priory for which he bought furniture and other equipment,
some of it for the house which he rented for his mother in the suburbs on the road out
to Sturry. At the priory itself, Ingram kept a garden to the south of the cathedral in
which he built himself a gazebo to catch the sun, denied to the great cloister on the
north. When a friend came to dinner, as once did John Whatlyngton, a monk of
Battle, Ingram was happy to lay on a feast.[41]

Sometimes, of course, the possession of at least some private means, with the
comforts that inevitably went with them, became the understood precondition for
successful entry to a life of religion. Among the so-called 'brides of Christ', the dowry
on admission had never been favoured by the Church. Yet already in 1215, at the
very peak of their expansion, 'the stain of simony has discoloured many nuns to such
an extent that they admit scarcely any as sisters without payment – wishing to cover
this vice with the pretext of poverty'.[42] Moreover, although the bishops long continued the struggle against such dowries, as against every other manifestation of private
privilege in the religious orders, certain constituents of the practice had come to stay.
More acceptable than most was the provision of the nun's habit on admission to the
community: a trousseau which varied in value with the wealth of the nunnery and
which often included items of private furniture as well. Of this last, we know that
Dame Agnes Davye, when admitted as a canoness of St Sexburga at Minster (Kent),
'browghte with her' painted hangings for her chamber, three pairs of sheets, a
counterpane, a chest and cupboard, two andirons, a pair of tongs and a firepan. Her
contemporary, Agnes Browne, had many other comforts 'given her by her friends',
among them a nice collection of silver and pewter, with the usual painted hangings

103 The fine fifteenth-century cloister of the canonesses of Lacock, its walks well protected against the elements

and bedclothes, all of which were counted as this lady's private property and were therefore exempt from confiscation by the king's officers at the Dissolution.[43] Rather over a century before, at the similarly wealthy and exclusive house of Lacock (Wiltshire), recruiting largely from among the daughters of the local gentry, Joan Samborne took the veil in 1395/6 at the cost, we must assume, of her father. A note was kept of the expenses he incurred on that occasion, and even these, it seems likely, are incomplete:

Inprimis, paid to the abbess for her fee 20s. Item to the convent 40s., to each of them 2s. Item paid to John Bartelot for veils and linen cloth, 102s. Item to a certain woman for the veil 40d. Item for a mattress 5s. Item for a coverlet and a tester 12s.

104 The great cloister at Gloucester Abbey, rebuilt in the second half of the fourteenth century and noted especially for its unusually early fan vault

Item for a mantle 10s. Item for a furring of shankes [rabbit fur] for another mantle 16s. Item for white cloth for lining the first mantle 6s. 8d. Item for white cloth for a tunic 10s. Item a furring for the pilch [a fur-lined undergarment] aforesaid 20s. Item for a mazer [a cup, often with silver brim and base] 10s. Item for a silver spoon 2s. 6d. Item for blankets 6s. 8d. Item in canvas for the bed 2s. Item for another mantle of worsted bought 20s. Item paid at the time of profession at one time 20s. Item for a new bed 20s. Item for other necessaries 20s. Item paid by the abbess of the debt due to me besides 20l. and 40d. still due to me. Item paid to the said Joan by order of the abbess 40s.[44]

In placing his daughter with the canonesses of Lacock, Nicholas Samborne had done

105 The monks' wash-place (*lavatorium*) in the north walk of the cloister at Gloucester;
running water was originally available at the trough and there was provision for
towels in a wall-cupboard (almery) near by

106 *Opposite* A reconstruction, from excavated fragments, of the fifteenth-century
cloister arcade at Bordesley (Worcestershire); fully glazed cloisters in this more
comfortable style were a common late-medieval improvement at the wealthier
houses, where they replaced (as here) an earlier, less weather-proof arcade (Walsh)

well both for her and for himself. But her entry-fee or 'dowry' – call it what you will –
had been substantial.

Lacock was a house of gentlefolk, accustomed to their comforts. Like many of its
equivalents, up and down the country, it was being transformed at just about this
time into a mansion where a certain 'ease and state' might reasonably be maintained,

108 The inner face of the refectory entrance at Hailes, with adjoining cupboards; beyond and on the left is the fifteenth-century west cloister arcade, of which only three arches survive

every year, using the best stone to do it and working throughout to the patterns already agreed in discussions between himself and the community.[49]

The rebuilding of a cloister, although sometimes conceived as a separate enterprise as at Boxley, was very often accompanied by the modernization of the adjoining domestic ranges. Foremost in such thinking was an improvement in the community's comfort and amenities, and both dormitories and refectories were likely to be modified at this time. But for a Cistercian community like Hailes – and probably for Boxley too – another opportunity had recently presented itself in the final vacating of the west claustral range by the formerly large class of lay brethren. These 'pious

109 A nun receives spiritual instruction in a cell off the cloister. Flemish, late fifteenth century

110 The *capella ante portas*, or lay persons' chapel, of the former Cistercian abbey at Kirkstead; it was not Cistercian practice to allow laymen to worship in the abbey church itself

112 *Opposite* Sawley Abbey from the air: a blocking wall (centre) crosses the church, where it had to be inserted in the fourteenth century to cut off the disused nave west of the monks' choir, once the departure of the lay brethren had made it surplus; note also the great size of the presbytery at Sawley, extended when the community, in the thirteenth century, had been enjoying more fortunate times (*British Crown copyright reserved*)

draught oxen of Christ', as Abbot Huby was later to describe them,[50] had almost disappeared at most Cistercian houses before the end of the fourteenth century. At Bordesley, for example, there was only one lay brother in 1380/81, alongside a community of fourteen monks, nor would there have been anything unusual about such numbers.[51] West ranges stood empty; in the church, the lay brothers' choir-

111 Interior of the chapel at Kirkstead, showing the high quality of the vaulting and other decorative stonework in this building of *c.* 1240

stalls, which had been sited in the nave, became redundant and were usually removed. At Hailes, the conversion of the west range into a fine new suite of lodgings for the abbot was among the expedients most commonly adopted at houses of all conditions in the order. But whereas Hailes had no problem in preserving its great church as a pilgrimage centre and as the abode of the miraculous Holy Blood, other Cistercian communities now found themselves with churches that were cavernous and draughty, expensive to maintain and very much too large for their needs. Unlike other orders, the Cistercians had no tradition of opening their churches to the laity; travellers and other laymen worshipped at the chapels they built at their gates, a fine example of which, at Kirkstead (Lincolnshire), is the only major surviving monument of this formerly prosperous community. Accordingly, when the lay brethren withdrew, a small house like Sawley, in Lancashire, might find itself having to demolish the nave, while re-using the lay brothers' quarters, now stranded to the west of an over-large cloister, as accommodation for corrodians or for guests. Where the monks' choir ended, just west of the crossing, a blocking-wall cut off the rest of the nave, which then became wholly disused. The community at Sawley had more than enough liturgical space in the great aisled presbytery of thirteenth-century build, into which it had expanded when fortune had smiled upon it more sweetly.[52]

Enforced shrinkage was not always, as it turned out, the worst fate that could befall a community. Cleeve Abbey, in Somerset, was another small Cistercian house, better situated than Sawley but in other ways no more lavishly endowed. Yet the last century of Cleeve's existence was to be characterized by a building programme that transformed it from the comfortless shell of St Bernard's original prescription into a mansion appropriate to men of dignity and affluence, the fortunate inheritors of a generous sufficiency which they could apply in almost any way they chose. Cleeve, although one of the later Cistercian foundations not settled before 1198, had begun life, as every other house of its order and generation would do, with a double community – the monks to the east and the south of the cloister, the lay brethren in their customary position to the west. As was usual by that time, the monks' refectory had been laid out on a north-south axis, perpendicular to the cloister, and it was the

113 Cleeve Abbey (Somerset), seen from the north, looking across the foundations of the demolished church to the north gable end of the dormitory range (left) and beyond to the rebuilt first-floor refectory south of the cloister

re-siting and total rebuilding of this refectory (frater) range that was the most significant alteration at fifteenth-century Cleeve, as the choir monks took possession of the entire cloister. By the 1530s, when the abbot's quarters in the west range were remodelled, Cleeve had come to resemble a fine country house of courtyard plan such as any gentleman of the period might have envied. The frater, now a handsome first-floor hall parallel to the cloister, was an apartment of exceptional dignity, well lit and magnificently roofed. Below it, there were two sets of lodgings, each with its bedchamber, its living-room, and independent garderobe, or lavatory. The abbot's quarters, with further lodgings, offices and stores, occupied the former cellarer's range to the west. On the opposite side of the cloister, over the unchanged thirteenth-century chapter-house, the monks' dormitory had been remodelled within as a set of private bedchambers, each with its window, separated from the next by partitions.[53]

At Cleeve, very little has survived of the abbot's lodgings. Adapted for lay use following the Dissolution, they were subsequently so transformed by later rebuildings as to make their plan unrecognizable today. However, it is certain that the splendour of the frater at Cleeve would have been matched, and probably exceeded, by that of the superior's apartments, as we know to have been the case at other communities of this size where the remains are more readily interpretable. Castle Acre (Norfolk) and Much Wenlock (Shropshire) were Cluniac houses, and each had been originally more populous than Cleeve. Nevertheless, before their suppression in the late 1530s, both communities had shrunk below the numbers of the Cistercians of Cleeve, although they remained just as handsomely accommodated. Today, the most impressive survival among the ruins of Castle Acre is the prior's separate mansion, adjoining the west door of the church. It is a many-phased rebuilding of the twelfth-century west claustral range to include not only a fine study (with bay window), chapel and bedchamber for the prior, but generous accommodation for his guests in addition. The prior's lodgings, through successive transformations in the fourteenth and fifteenth centuries, had become what they still give every impression of being – a large secular mansion, appropriate to the great landowner that the prior had become but very far removed from the modest separation of households which was all that, in the twelfth century, had been permitted to superiors and to which later reformers would return.[54]

114 Cleeve's comfortable fifteenth-century refectory, notable especially for the great windows in both side walls and for the fine (unfinished) waggon ceiling, expensively carved in the West Country manner

115 The Cluniac priory at Castle Acre (Norfolk), seen from the air: the prior's lodging (left) adjoins the west front of the church; east of the cloister, the monks' dormitory runs south to the rere-dorter, still straddling the drain which bisects the priory's kitchen (bottom left) (*British Crown copyright reserved*)

117 *Opposite* The west front of Castle Acre as it is today; on the right, a great bay window lights the room formerly used by the prior as his study

Henry V, in just such a reforming mood, had urged the Benedictine heads of houses in 1421 to set a better example to their communities, to officiate more often at divine service in their churches, and to be more active in their pastoral roles; 'Also let the costly and excessively scandalous cavalcades of the abbots be moderated, as well in the varied and irregular array of servants as in the adornment of the horses; and let not even the greater abbots amongst them presume to ride with more than twenty horses, including baggage horses, under pain of grave temporal penalty by the Apostolic See.'[55] Yet the response among the black monks had been no more than muted, and there is certainly little material indication in the prior's lodgings at Castle

116 Castle Acre: a model of the priory as it might have looked shortly before its suppression, showing the west end of the church and the prior's lodging (right), more like a secular manor-house than a building suitable for monks

Acre, or in those of Much Wenlock, of an austere or reforming temper. Prior Richard Singer (1486–1521), during whose priorate Much Wenlock shrugged off the last ties that had bound it to Cluny and to La Charité-sur-Loire, was a great builder. He restored the church at considerable expense, adding a new hexagonal sacristy south of the choir, and was probably responsible for the magnificent east range of the infirmary court which remains still today one of the most intriguing survivals of the domestic architecture of its period. Prior Richard's south-east range, set apart from the main conventual complex round the great cloister, was wholly secular in both appearance and function. At its north end, adjoining the infirmary hall to which it was attached on the west, the range included what was probably the infirmary chapel, and there may have been lodgings within the range for the master of the infirmary or herbalist. However, the bulk of this great building, with its huge steep roof and sophisticated fenestration, was given over to the prior himself, to the men and boys of his suite, and to his guests.[56] In 1523, only two years after Prior Richard's death, the troubles that had attended the election of his successor resulted in a formal visitation of the priory. The monks, it was found, were given to fine clothes, they drank and gossiped after compline, kept hounds and gabbled the divine office. Among the recommendations, or 'counsels', left with them by Dr Allen, their visitor, was the sensible advice to practise useful crafts; ritual processions – seductive occasions for display – were to be reduced in number; there were to be fewer servants, the cuts falling in particular on those who had been employed to make a show.[57]

The disease, though, was deep-seated and probably ineradicable by this period. Among the 'greater' abbots, multi-department households had long been familiar; to operate them, the abbot kept many in his livery; when he rode abroad, his retinue (the 'riding household') might be as large as that of a lay magnate.[58] In practice, the status of the monastic superior had been continually on the increase, and the 'fathers and heads of houses' whom Henry V addressed and whose 'acts and lives', in the king's

118 Wenlock Priory (Shropshire) from the air: on the right are the two surviving ranges of the infirmary court, south of the presbytery (top) and south-east of the great cloister (centre)

view, were to be a model to the monks they directed, were precisely those least equipped by his day to return to the austerities of the past. One of the methods by which late-medieval superiors frequently sought to enhance their status, both within the Church and outside it, was by winning the right to use the pontificalia (the mitre, ring and staff, and vestments of a bishop) by personal application to the pope. The privilege meant little enough in truth, resulting in no increase in power within the community. Nevertheless, both abbots and priors in the late fourteenth century, when such privileges during the Schism were relatively easy to obtain, applied for them regularly, as they did also for other more valuable promotions and exemptions. Norton Priory (Cheshire), one of the better-off Augustinian communities, was well placed to take advantage of Boniface IX's special difficulties. It was this pope who, to raise revenue for the struggle against the anti-pope Benedict XIII, awarded the pontifical insignia to Hyde and St Osyth's, Winchcombe, Colchester, Shrewsbury, Bermondsey and Peterborough, among others.[59] Norton, for its part, had obtained the privilege in 1391, and it was in that year too that the prior of Norton brought off a coup of more permanent value in the elevation of his priory to the status of an abbey, himself winning the title of abbot. Norton's elevation was the first to have been granted to the English Augustinians since the similar promotion of the little house at Creake (Norfolk) in 1231, and it was clearly rated as a singular distinction. Not unreasonably, it has been suggested that this was at least one of the causes of the rebuilding of the abbot's lodgings at Norton in the fifteenth century, then taking the form of a fine new tower house, fashionably embattled in the style of its period.[60]

Another cause, certainly, would have been the growing competition among energetic builders as one superior after another progressively upstaged his rivals. At Canterbury, Prior Thomas Chillenden (1390–1411) amply earned his reputation as 'the greatest Builder of a Prior that ever was in Christes Churche', laying out great sums every year on his schemes.[61] He completed the reconstruction of the nave of the cathedral church, repaired 'at great expense' the 'ancient, ruined and forgotten' water system that had been so remarkable a feature of the twelfth-century monastery, and did much work on the great and privy dormitories, supplying them with new roofs, new windows and new beds. Prior Chillenden's own lodgings inevitably had their share of this expenditure:

Also the prior's bed, with a new study and hall above, and a garderobe practically rebuilt and leaded. Also the passage from the prior's chapel to his chamber newly

119 The prior's lodging and guesthouse at Much Wenlock, probably built for Prior Richard Singer (1486–1521), and constituting the east range of the former infirmary court

120 The upper passage, lit by its remarkable range of windows, of Prior Richard's lodging at Much Wenlock

121 Norton Priory as a Tudor mansion, from an engraving of 1727 made only three years before its demolition; the abbot's tower-house (top left) survived from a fifteenth-century remodelling of the superior's lodgings at Norton, perhaps associated with the elevation of the priory to abbey

122 *Opposite* The nave at Canterbury Cathedral, being one of the many remarkable works of Prior Thomas Chillenden (1390–1411), 'the greatest Builder of a Prior that ever was in Christes Churche'

ceiled and repaired with new windows and a new fireplace. Also a new chamber below built entirely, with a new roof covered with lead. Also another chamber downstairs with a chamber and a decent bath. Also upstairs a new privy chamber with a passage to it, leaded. Also a new place for storage, with a cellar underneath.[62]

Of works like these, the multiplication of new chambers is very much the most significant characteristic. Prior Chillenden must have been familiar with the lodgings of the abbot of Battle, one of his nearer Benedictine neighbours, and there again, both before and after Chillenden's time, the accommodation at the abbot's mansion was expanding. Situated, as was now usual, on the west side of the cloister, the abbot's house at Battle, as reconstructed already in the thirteenth century, began as a first-floor suite of hall, chamber and chapel; in the fourteenth century, private chambers were inserted adjoining the hall; in the fifteenth, a major extension, south of the great chamber, added a new ground-floor hall, private kitchen and further range of lodgings to the complex.[63]

We know that the abbot of Battle lived well in the later Middle Ages. To his household were reserved the cream and the butter from the abbey's dairy at Marley, with the choicest birds and fish: swans and cygnets, dolphins and porpoises, among others.[64] Yet this is not to say that his monks – consumers of cheese and milk, herring, cod and mackerel – were entirely left out of this bonanza. At Durham, in the late fourteenth century, an even richer community of brother Benedictines was assembling the means for a complete remodelling of its domestic accommodation, while leaving the great church it had inherited unchanged. Many of the details of this work survive only in some pious recollections of the early seventeenth century, the so-called *Rites of Durham*. Nevertheless, the great dormitory and cloister at Durham are known to have been rebuilt within the first two decades of the fifteenth century, a new infirmary following in the 1420s.[65] In each campaign, the accents were to be on

comfort and especially on privacy. Thus, of the new dormitory we are told that it was a 'faire large house', re-sited conveniently on the west side of the cloister where there was more space available than on the east. There –

> . . . all the Mounks and the Novices did lye, every Mouncke having a litle chamber of wainscott verie close severall by them selves & ther wyndowes towardes the cloyster, every wyndowe servinge for one Chambre by reasoune the particion betwixt every chamber was close wainscotted one from an other, and in every of there wyndowes a deske to supporte there bookes for there studdie; In the weste syde of the said dorter was the like chambers & in like sort placed with there wyndowes, and desks towardes the fermery [infirmary] & the water, the chambers beinge all well bourded under foute.[66]

In the north cloister alley, every monk had his own study, or 'carrell', all 'fynely wainscotted, and verie close all but the forepart which had carved wourke that gave light in at their carrell doures of wainscott; and in every Carrell was a deske to lye there bookes on'. In the infirmary, the sick had their separate chambers, each with its fireplace. Even the monks' reredorter, or lavatory – 'a faire large house and a most decent place' – had been remodelled to spare the blushes of its users: 'every seate and particion was of wainscott close of either syde verie decent so that one of them could not see one another, when they weare in that place'.[67]

The main omission of the Durham monks from their building programme was as significant as the parts they completed. The old refectory south of the cloister at Durham, dating back to the period of maximum expansion in the twelfth century, was over-large and certainly too cold and draughty for the needs of the late-medieval community. Instead, the monks preferred to dine together in what they called 'the loft', at the west end of the refectory next to their modernized fourteenth-century kitchen from which they drew their food through a hatch. The loft was convenient too for the 'great Cellar, or buttery, where all the drink did stand', and it was not to be until early in the sixteenth century that Prior Thomas Castell improved the seldom used refectory with a new tiled floor and with fine carved half-panelling, over two metres in height, on its long sides to the north and the south. One additional feature of the prior's modernizations was the provision of an open hearth in the centre of the refectory where there had been no such heating before.[68]

For the monks, then, as well as for their abbot, domestic accommodation in the later Middle Ages had taken a turn for the better. St Benedict had told his readers ('if it be possible') to sleep together in one place. 'For bedding,' he had said, 'let this suffice: a mattress, a blanket, a coverlet, and a pillow.'[69] But he had not thought to declare how a great dormitory might, or might not, be divided, and the wainscotted private cubicles of the monks of Durham, comfortably furnished to meet the needs of sleep and study, would everywhere have been a characteristic of English monastic dormitories well before their appearance in the Dissolution inventories in which, quite frequently, they featured. Thus at Ankerwyke (Buckinghamshire), in 1441, the nuns' dormitory had already been partitioned, four of the spaces being reserved for the prioress. And while Bishop Alnwick then told her to 'take downe that perclose [partition] that ye dyde make in the dormytorye', what seems to have worried him at the time was less the divisions already placed between the beds than that 'every nunnes celle be open in toward the dormytory, as your rewle demaundes'.[70] Four years later, in 1445, Bishop Alnwick's commissary, Master John Derby, conducted a visitation of another Benedictine nunnery at Littlemore (Oxfordshire) where he found several of the nuns sharing beds because of the ruinous condition of their dormitory. Littlemore was one of the smaller houses, with very little money for major repairs. Nevertheless, before its suppression by Cardinal Wolsey in 1525, the dormitory had been rebuilt with the prioress's parlour at its northern end, against the wall of the church, and with the individual nuns' cells (separated by a central passage as at Cleeve and Durham) along each side of its length.[71] Bradwell Priory, in Buckinghamshire, suppressed on the same occasion for the endowment of the cardinal's new Oxford college, was surveyed in the late 1520s when an inventory of its goods, demesne lands and principal accommodation was prepared for the use of its lay owners. Bradwell, like Littlemore, was a poor house, and many of its buildings were by then in a state of decay. But noteworthy too were the numerous private lodgings present even at a house of this size: some by the gate, others adjoining the refectory. The community at Bradwell was depleted in its last years, being no more than four or five strong, and this had been one of the reasons advanced by Wolsey for its suppression. In a dormitory thirty feet by twenty-four, obviously built in more generous days, there were only 'ffyve sells in the same that be borded'.[72] Just a few years later, the 'sells in the Dorter of the Cistercian nuns of Catesby (Northamptonshire) were sold off at 6s. 8d. apiece.[73]

What had probably encouraged the partitioning of the dormitories had been the remodelling, sanctioned much earlier, of many monastic infirmaries. Among the works, for example, for which Abbot William of Scarborough (d. 1396) was remembered by his monks was his provision of separate chambers for the sick in the infirmary at Meaux (East Yorkshire); he had also refurnished their dormitory.[74] Infirmaries, like dormitories, had started off as great halls in which heating, although present in some form, was usually remote and ineffective. By the later Middle Ages, other priorities had come to be recognized. Thus the Augustinians of Huntingdon were to be urged by their bishop in 1421/2 to ensure that 'two of the best lodgings in the infirmary, with fireplaces and latrines, be kept completely ready and in fair condition for canons in ill health, to whom, during the time of their infirmity, better, richer and more delicate meats beyond the general commons of the house, shall be supplied out of the common goods of the house, whereby they may be the better restored, and also doctors and medicines, so that with the help of God they may the more quickly recover health'.[75] The very next year, Bishop Fleming of Lincoln was to find himself, at St Frideswide (Oxford), required to order the canons out of their comfortable chambers in the priory's infirmary unless genuinely 'broken down by so great sickness, old age and ill health' as to require such individual attentions.[76]

Although certainly more justifiable on grounds of sound medical practice, the divided infirmary hall of the late-medieval monastery was at least as clear an indicator of the softening regime at many houses as were the partitioned dormitory, the glazed cloister with its individual panelled carrells, and the over-luxurious abbot's lodging. At the great northern Cistercian house of Fountains (West Yorkshire), the thirteenth-century infirmary hall had been a lofty aisled apartment

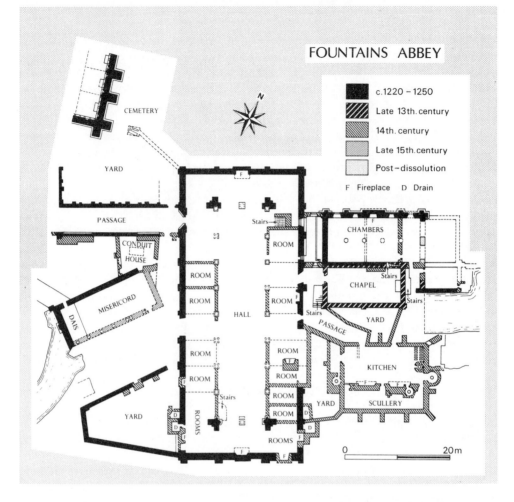

123 The subdivided infirmary hall at Fountains Abbey, with individual fireplaces, a new kitchen and other improvements dating to the later fourteenth and the fifteenth centuries

with fireplaces at each end, dank and draughty at all seasons. Already in the fourteenth century, partitions were being introduced. In the fifteenth century, most of the aisle space on each side of the hall had been divided into small private chambers, many equipped with the individual fireplaces which are still recognizable today as obvious later insertions.[77] Other conversions of this kind have left their mark on the infirmaries of Tintern (Monmouthshire) and Beaulieu (Hampshire), both Cistercian communities like Fountains. At Kirkstall, again in Yorkshire, they were associated with a programme of works which, along with the insertion of floors in the aisles of the infirmary to make two-storey ranges of private chambers, similarly divided the early refectory at the house, now too spacious for its diminished community. The large windows of Kirkstall's refectory were blocked, to be replaced by smaller ones lighting the two floors of the apartment. A chimney was built where the pulpit had been, new pavements were laid, an outer door and stone staircase were added.[78]

124 A view of Beaulieu Abbey from the air, showing the detached infirmary (right) south-east of the cloister, with its own chapel projecting at right-angles, with a misericord attached to its western side and with a dividing wall crossing its centre, placed there in the fifteenth century when the great hall was partitioned in separate chambers

Kirkstall's refectory alterations were an open acknowledgement of a bending of the Rule more blatant than most at this period. Until the fourteenth century, St Benedict's advice to 'abstain entirely from the flesh of four-footed animals' had broadly been accepted by the monks. But even the saint had made an exception of 'the sick who are very weak',[79] and it was this loophole that was to be exploited very commonly in later years to bring entire communities within the range of privileges of the infirm. At the greater monastic houses, of which Fountains again is a good example, infirmaries had been equipped with their separate kitchens and often with another refectory (the *misericord*, or 'indulgence') as well. Through the twelfth century and much of the thirteenth, eating in the misericord had been strictly controlled. Yet before 1300, dispensations to share the meat diet of the infirm were being granted more freely, and it was Benedict XII's general permission of 1336, allowing even the healthy to eat meat in the infirmary provided refectory was still kept, on a rota, by their companions, that finally opened the door to the rest.[80] When Henry V made his attempt in 1421 to bring the English Benedictines back to what he believed to be their original purity of observance, even he had to acknowledge that there were some areas in particular where a return to the Rule was neither practicable any longer nor desirable:

Also, whereas the eating of meat is forbidden to monks except in certain cases, and the infirmity of present day monks and long and established observance has weighed against this rule, it seems very expedient that a gracious modification should be made by apostolic authority, especially in view of the fact that it is expensive and almost insupportable to provide convents, which are a long way from the sea and from waters which could provide an abundance of fish, with other kinds of food than meat; therefore let it be ordained, as the statutes decree, that on all meat days throughout the year half the convent, including the officials who are personally within the gates of the monastery that day, shall dine in the refectory, nor shall they eat meat that day outside, and let them be content in the same refectory with milk foods, fish, and fat of meat like tripe and stuffing.[81]

In effect, Henry V could take his monks no further back than 1336, to the compromise ruling of Benedict XII, and it remained a constant preoccupation of the more concerned reforming bishops after this date to preserve a regime even as moderate as Pope Benedict's. The religious, both monks and nuns, had become increasingly shy of their refectories, so much so that the Benedictines of Humberston (Lincolnshire), by their own confession in 1440, neither ate 'nor have eaten in the frater these twenty years, save only on Good Friday', preferring the comforts of their abbot's hall in its stead.[82] It was at the great house at Peterborough in 1432 that Bishop Gray insisted 'that within the cloister only two places be used for the meals of the brethren, to wit, the frater and the misericord, otherwise called "ly Seyny"; and that henceforward "ly Chymney" [the warming house] be altogether disused'.[83] And it was in direct answer to the complaint that frater was not kept at Wellow (Lincolnshire), an Augustinian community, that Bishop Alnwick, Gray's successor at Lincoln, laid down some explicit rules for future practice at the abbey in the visitation he conducted there personally in 1440:

> Also we enjoin upon you the abbot and convent . . . that, at the seasons of Lent and the Advent of our Lord, and on every Wednesday and Friday out of those seasons, you keep frater and take your food in the same, and have therein some lesson from holy scripture or from some other writing which may edify the hearers during such meals, unless some honest guests or strangers arrive, by reason of whom you, abbot, should be be fittingly excused from frater on such days.[84]

Only the cracks that had recently appeared in the walls of their refectory had prevented the nuns of St Michael's, Stamford, from keeping frater three times a week, on Wednesdays, Fridays and Saturdays. But this claim, made to Bishop Alnwick again in 1440, was in answer to accusations of a practice certainly common in many nunneries well before this date, of eating apart in separate messes, or households.[85] At Stamford, the halls of the prioress and sub-prioress were used for this purpose, and it is not especially surprising that, under a regime of such a kind, the refectory should have been allowed to fall into a state of disrepair. Certainly at St Neots, another common resting-place just off the highway to London, the monks of this much wealthier Benedictine community seem to have managed very well without a refectory, their own being ruined and unusable, through much of the fifteenth century; they dined in the prior's hall instead.[86] Elsewhere, a not uncommon response to the pressure of the times was to be the remodelling of the refectory as a smaller apartment, either by a complete rebuilding on a more restricted site parallel to

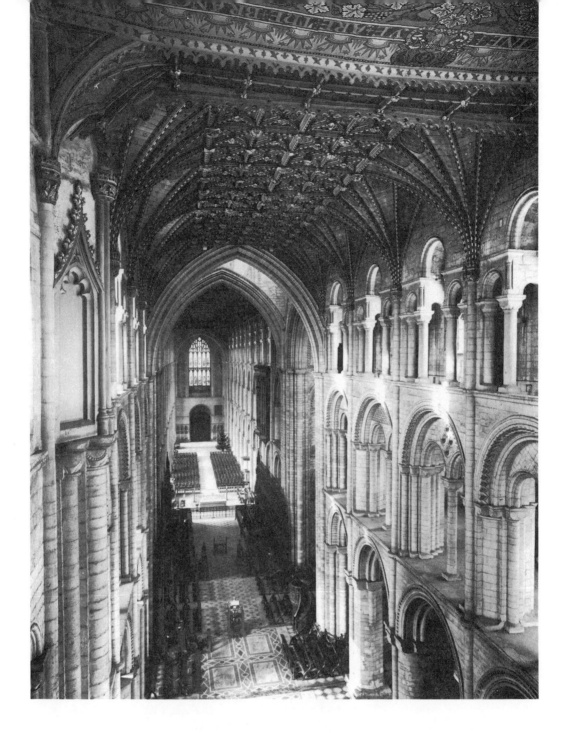

125 Peterborough Abbey: a view westwards down the church of this great house where the monks, by the fifteenth century, had relaxed their Rule, eating in separate households and avoiding the communal frater

the south cloister walk (as at Cleeve and Croxden), or by the shortening of the frater and insertion of a new floor (as at Forde and, very probably, Furness).[87]

Three centuries after the great monastic expansion in the West, what had once been appropriate to the life of religion had become, all too often, a burden. Some of the changes resulted, as we have seen, from a serious retreat in moral purpose. The nun of Stamford who had 'gone away in apostasy, cleaving to a harp-player' was certainly no good example to her sisters,[88] and there were many as irresponsible as herself. But economic pressures were to play their part in the revolution as well. Neither monks nor nuns were as popular in the fifteenth century as they had been back in the twelfth. They collected less from casual benefactions and obtained smaller yields on their estates. An immoral house, as contemporaries well recognized, was quite often a poor or a small house as well. It is not always obvious whether it was the poverty or the immorality that was chiefly to blame, or indeed which preceded the other.

Chapter 7

A Question of Survival

Some of the poorest houses in late-medieval England, and the least well governed, were the alien priories and the priory cells of the original post-Conquest settlement. Semi-conventual cells had always had their problems, and even the rich Benedictines of Durham, with no fewer than nine such dependencies in their charge, found difficulty from the beginning in maintaining a full community at any of them.[1] However, the special burden of the alien houses resided in their status at least as much as in their size. Small, weak and friendless, they were pawns in the war games of kings.

The problems of the Norman monasteries had begun as far back as 1204, when John's loss of Normandy to the French crown had first raised a political barrier between themselves and their English estates, to add to the discomforts of the sea crossing. A few in these circumstances preferred to move out altogether, and there are well-documented exchanges in the late thirteenth century between Bruton and Troarn, Bradenstoke and Saint-Wandrille, giving as their reasons the inconveniences of great distance, the hardships of travel and in particular the perils of the sea.[2] The exchanges were timely, for the renewal of conflict between the kingdoms in 1294 was quickly followed by the prolonged confiscation of alien properties from 1295 to 1303, setting a precedent for repeated exploitation by the crown in future years that would milk the French houses of the bulk of their profits, proceeding through the expulsions of 1378 and 1404 to the dissolution of 1414.[3]

So long as the English wars in France went reasonably well, the alien priories enjoyed some protection from the king. Edward III saw them, as both his father and his grandfather had done, as a useful source of revenue, always good for the occasional imposition about which no Englishman would be found to object. But the mounting xenophobia of the less happy years after 1369 brought uncertainty to all French monks remaining in England, not relieved by the refusal of their Norman superiors throughout the period to contemplate the severing of ties. Among the greater Cluniac houses, the problems of which were somewhat different, Lewes partly sidestepped its difficulties in 1351 by purchasing denizen status. Thetford followed in 1376, Bermondsey in 1381, Lenton, Pontefract and Wenlock in the 1390s.[4] But when in 1414, as the remaining alien houses fell victim to the general suppression, the English Cluniacs implored their abbot for the still greater security of full independence, Abbot Raymond of Cluny dismissed their proposals as '*una magna fatuitas*' (a great folly).[5] It was not until 1480, after repeated attempts to bring it back into the family, that Lewes succeeded in obtaining from the pope its formal release from all allegiance to Cluny and its entry under the protection of St Peter.[6]

The difficulties of the great monastic 'families', among them the Cistercians, were

126 The perils of the sea: a shipwreck scene, with the souls of drowned pilgrims ascending to Heaven as doves, Flemish, late fifteenth century

bad enough. Any suggestion of a foreign allegiance was dangerous. But the worst problems were those of the Norman and other French houses, for it could well be argued (as it was at the time) that they had brought them very largely on themselves. In the early days of the Anglo-Norman settlement, it had rarely paid a French house with possessions in England to undertake the expense of establishing a new community on the profits. Some rationalization of assets had occurred during the thirteenth century, under pressure from the pope among others. On the Bec estates, for example, seven groups were then constituted, each centred on a priory or cell.[7] However, even the relatively wealthy community at Bec, with its unusually extensive English lands, had never felt that it could afford to set up more than four conventual priories on its estates. The other three groups, with Steventon, Wilsford and Ogbourne at the head, were supervised from manorial establishments under the direction of a 'prior', having no more than a single companion at best and frequently residing there on his own. The dangers of such an arrangement were obvious, and it had been these that had led both Innocent III (d. 1216) and Gregory IX (d. 1241) to attempt to establish at least a minimum standard of religious observance on the cells. Nevertheless when, in 1324–5 on the occasion of the second royal confiscation of alien lands, inventories were drawn up at the three Bec 'priories' at Steventon, Wilsford and Ogbourne, the accommodation listed at each of these establishments was obviously in no way monastic. There was a chapel, it is true, at the manor-house at Wilsford. It was equipped, as many manorial chapels must have been, with two suits of vestments and a chasuble, a chalice, some altar cloths and corporals, a missal, a gradual and a manual or ordinal. But chapels featured neither at Steventon nor at Ogbourne, and the monks residing at both these estate-centres were no doubt accustomed to use the neighbouring parish churches for their devotions. In other respects, certainly, the manor-houses were of the familiar hall-and-chamber plan (with annexed kitchen, buttery, brewhouse, bakehouse and dairy) of the contemporary lay estate. In the prior's chamber at Steventon, the king's officials recorded a cash reserve of forty-three shillings, two bed-covers, six sheets and three chests; in the hall, six tables and two pairs of trestles, nine 'worn' (*debiles*) cushions, a bench, three chairs, three forms and a wash-basin. In all three manor-houses, the kitchens were well equipped with a good complement of copper pots and pans, while at Steventon, when the inventory was taken there on 18 October 1324, there was a fine stock of cheeses in the dairy and of pork, ready salted, in the larder. But the only touch of luxury at any of these establishments was the silver plate, of which all three had at least some in their stores. Again Steventon was the best provided in this respect. It had two silver cups, twelve silver spoons and a silver-bound drinking vessel, or mazer; Ogbourne had a small silver cup and four spoons; at Wilsford, there were six silver spoons and two mazers.[8]

Ten days after they had been at Steventon, the king's surveyors, Henry de Pentelawe and John de Brompton, took the inventory of Ivry's much smaller and poorer alien priory at Minster Lovell (Oxfordshire), which was to be one of the houses eventually confiscated by Henry V in the suppressions of 1414. The parish church at Minster Lovell had come to the Benedictines of Ivry (Normandy) in the 1180s by gift of Maud Lovell, a relative by marriage of their founder-patrons, and it was at Minster that Ivry established a centre for the management of its English estates. But although commonly described as a 'priory', the Minster Lovell community never rose above two, nor were its resources at any stage large enough to permit building on a generous scale. In 1324, just as had been the case at the manor-houses of Bec, the accommodation at Minster was limited to a hall, a kitchen and a pantry and buttery. The chamber was not listed, presumably because its contents were not worth recording. The total value of the moveables at the priory was 34s 9d, or about as much as the same officials' valuation of the brewhouse and dairy at Steventon.[9]

Minster Lovell, indeed, was one of those houses which demonstrated very clearly how the evils associated with an inadequate endowment could be aggravated by distance from the mother community. The gross income of the priory, at between eight and twelve pounds, was barely adequate to sustain its two monks once normal expenses had been met. In years of poor harvests or exceptional taxation, a catastrophe would be hard to avoid. During the first royal confiscation of the late 1290s, the imposition by the crown of an annual rent of five pounds immediately crippled the priory's finances. Seized again in 1324, even the king's officials had to concede that there was nothing further to be wrung from the establishment. In 1337, on the occasion of yet another confiscation, the prior had left Minster in the care of a proctor, its income being reported to be 'scarcely sufficient for the sustenance of the prior and his servants'. Certainly, little or nothing was being returned to Ivry by that date, and the connections between the priory and its mother-house in Normandy, though continued still for a few decades yet in the person of the prior himself, were weakening day by day. Whether or not the prior and his companion were permitted to remain there, Minster Lovell came after 1373 into the care of Sir John Lovell 'for as long as the priory shall remain in the king's hand on account of the war with France'. It was his son, William Lord Lovell, who leased the property from Eton College after the former Ivry lands had come to the college in 1441 as part of its foundation endowment.[10]

Sir John Lovell in 1373 had undertaken to 'support all the ordinary and extraordinary charges incumbent on the priory, maintain the houses and buildings of the priory, and leave them in as good a state as he found them in or better'. In the next century, probably at the expense of his son, the parish church was very largely rebuilt. However, it is most unlikely that either Sir John or his successors could have felt much interest in preserving the other buildings which Ivry almost certainly had neglected, and there is nothing now left on their site. All over England the same experience was repeated as the French houses either disposed of their English assets as no longer profitable or, by waiting too long, found themselves the victims of expropriation. The hesitations of the unlucky ones are easy to understand, for the story of confiscation and resumption had been repeated so often by the late fourteenth century that neither then nor after the formal suppression of 1414 was the position of the alien landowner at all clear. In the circumstances, further investment became impossible. In the 1330s and the 1340s, the French houses had continued to put money back into their estates, even making the occasional land purchase; after the mid-century, the story was of neglect and, where possible, of sales.[11] At Allerton Mauleverer (West Yorkshire), the monks of Marmoutier had held the parish church and a small estate, worth just over twenty pounds a year. In 1378, by the estimation of a local jury, their expenses were such that they were making a clear loss, their greatest cost being the maintenance of a prior and two monks to celebrate divine office in the church. This small community had lived in a 'hall with chambers annexed and other offices', described in 1378 as 'dilapidated'.[12]

Of course, wherever responsibilities of this kind could be shed, property previously heavily encumbered by expenses could suddenly become very attractive. Among the custodians of the alien priories in the late fourteenth century were prominent courtiers, many of whom were later successful in converting their custodies to outright purchases.[13] And if much of this land was later made over, in one form or another, to the Church, it was usually because the remaining shreds of conventional prejudice against the disendowment of Christ united in the fifteenth century with a very strong inclination on the part of many noblemen to invest in the security of their souls. Mixed motives at all times were common, the more secure of the religious houses being just as likely as their lay neighbours to look hungrily at the former French lands. When the canons of Michelham (Sussex), in 1379, obtained the custody of Grestain's near-by estate-centre at Wilmington, they must have thought they had brought off a considerable coup. They did it, they claimed, 'to avert the ruin and damage that might have befallen the priory of Wilmington if it had fallen into the hands of laymen'. Nevertheless, had they been successful in retaining the land, they could have doubled the income of their priory.[14] Of more permanence were the purchases, negotiated directly with their former owners, of the alien priories and other estates which together made up the considerable endowments of William of Wykeham's educational establishments at Winchester and New College, Oxford. Among such properties of New College, later to acquire another valuable alien priory at Newington Longeville by gift of Henry VI, were the two Essex houses of Hornchurch (a hospital) and Takeley (a priory), bought from St Bernard Montjoux (Savoy) and St Valery (Picardy) respectively.[15] A third, the alien cell at Harmondsworth (Middlesex), was similarly purchased outright in 1390–91 from the Benedictines of St Catherine-du-Mont (Rouen) for an agreed sum of 8,400 francs, plus extras. It had been the war, the abbot of St Catherine said, that had forced him to dispose of his English estates, rendering them almost worthless to his house. But although this had clearly been his principal motive in the sale, he had other reasons also to be persuaded. Lands in Middlesex were too far distant for efficient management and revenue-collection from Rouen; the sea crossing was difficult and dangerous, the state of the roads insecure; the abbey's representatives in England were unfamiliar with the language and were no doubt gravely homesick in addition.[16]

In due course, all these arguments were to be stood on their heads in a last-ditch defence of the French houses' interests after the suppression of 1414. It was the view, for example, of Abbot Michael of Saint-Evroul (Normandy), expressed in a letter chastising the Carthusians of Henry V's new foundation at Sheen (Surrey) for the part they had played in his loss, that neither the war nor distance were serious impediments to the proper enjoyment of his own abbey's English estates. Without them, his community had been reduced by a half.[17] Ten years later, in 1426, the abbot of Saint-Evroul was still pursuing the same cause at the papal *curia* at Rome, where his audience was not unsympathetic.[18] In general, as was only to be expected, the transition period was characterized by confusion and doubt, creating profitable opportunities for the unscrupulous. St Michael's Mount (Cornwall), formerly a dependent priory of the great Norman house at Mont-St-Michel which it resembled so much in its situation, might at first have been thought to be exempt from suppression under the terms of the act of 1414. But it was a rich prize, one of the best available, and there were soon many claimants to its estates. Initially, the Carthusians of Sheen seem to have been promised it, along with Mont-St-Michel's other valuable priory at Otterton (Devonshire), from which Sidmouth, a large grange, was also managed. However, it was the Bridgettines of Syon (Middlesex), another of Henry V's foundations, who subsequently acquired both the priories and the grange, although they themselves were not to obtain undisputed enjoyment of the estates until King's College (Cambridge), as late as 1468, finally abandoned its own claim to the land.[19]

Whether or not the French houses thought they had much chance of a full recovery of their estates, they continued to behave until towards the end of the fifteenth century as if compensation, at least, would be forthcoming. The effect of this, of course, was to establish a powerful lobby at the English court against any such return of lost lands, while those in possession of former priory buildings experienced every

127 St Michael's Mount (Cornwall) formerly a dependent priory of Mont-St-Michel, in Normandy, but acquired in the fifteenth century by the Bridgettine nuns of Henry V's new foundation at Syon

incentive to demolish them. In these circumstances St Michael's Mount, on its noble rock, was luckier than most of its contemporaries. On the initiative of Edmund Lacy, bishop of Exeter, who visited the Mount on 17 April 1425 when its future was still under discussion, the community (originally three monks) was reconstituted as three chaplains, the senior of whom was styled 'archpriest'. Whatever happened thereafter to the life of the spirit at St Michael's Mount – and under the care of the reform-minded Bridgettines it was probably maintained in some purity – the chaplains undoubtedly kept themselves up to date in the relics they chose to display. They had had a good collection already when they took over the church, including some of the milk and a portion of the girdle of the Virgin Mary, with some stones smuggled home from the Holy Sepulchre in Jerusalem, and with a jaw-bone of the martyred Apollonia of Alexandria, patron saint of all sufferers from toothache. In 1535, the girdle and the jaw-bone were still bravely housed in precious reliquaries of silver-gilt, and they had been joined in the church by evidence of one of the more modern cults, a sword and a pair of spurs of King Henry of Windsor (Henry VI), cruelly done to death – or so at least it suited the Lancastrians and the Tudors to believe – by the Yorkist, Edward IV.[20]

War and distance from home had done much harm to the alien priories. In the late fourteenth century, in common with landowners everywhere, the economy was serving them ill. But another factor too in their unlamented disappearance was a profound change in the climate of belief.

The first signs of a decline in the popularity of the Benedictines were apparent, as we have seen, well before the late fourteenth century. In 1343, Sir Nicholas de Cantilupe's choice of the Carthusians for the new community in his park at Beauvale

128 The chapel at St Michael's Mount, rebuilt in the late fourteenth century and subsequently much altered and restored

was a straw in the wind. With very few exceptions, new foundations in England after this date avoided the traditional orders. St Mary Graces (London), founded in 1350, continued the long-standing royal allegiance to the Cistercian order which had resulted already in Beaulieu (1204), Hailes (1246) and Vale Royal (1274). Like Vale Royal, it was established in fulfilment of a vow drawn from its founder during the perils of a storm at sea.[21] But just as important a consideration in the foundation of St Mary Graces was the death by plague the previous year of Edward III's much loved confessor, Thomas Bradwardine, archbishop of Canterbury elect. St Mary Graces, next to the king's great fortress on Tower Hill, was thus to be a memorial as well as a thank-offering. It shared this role, significantly enough, with another great contemporary foundation, the Charterhouse of the London Carthusians.

In practice, although the Black Death certainly was the initial spur for the London Charterhouse's endowment, it took another two decades (until the early 1370s) for agreement to be reached with the Carthusian General Chapter and for work on the new buildings to begin. Initially, Sir Walter Manny, one of the more enterprising and successful of Edward III's soldiers of fortune, had bought the site for a burial ground during the Black Death, intending to establish there a college of twelve secular priests who would hold in remembrance the fifty thousand citizens believed to have been buried on the spot. Within a decade, Sir Walter had been persuaded by Michael Northburgh, bishop of London (1355–61), to open negotiations with the Carthusians, and it was 'to the most holy monastic life of the Carthusian Order' that Sir Walter professed in 1371 his 'special devotion', placing its members 'above all other religious'.[22] By that time, the old knight's preferences would have been shared by many of his more prominent associates. The London Charterhouse accumulated wealth very quickly, being second only in its endowment, among the English Carthusian houses, to the royal foundation at Sheen (1414). Among its benefactors, pride of place was given to those good and great who had each contributed one cell (or more) to the establishment. One of these, Sir Robert Knollys (d. 1407), had been a companion-at-arms of Sir Walter Manny, He was the 'founder' of the cell lettered 'P'. Cell K was the gift of Mary de Valence, countess of Pembroke; she had been the founder-patron already of the Poor Clares of Denny and of the scholars of Pembroke College (Cambridge).[23] Sir William Walworth, stockfishmonger and twice mayor of London, was a particularly generous supporter of the London Carthusians, contributing cells B, D, G, H and J. Thomas Hatfield, bishop of Durham (1345–81), gave cells R and S. John Buckingham, bishop of Lincoln (1363–98), endowed cell Q.[24]

This cell-by-cell endowment was of course especially attractive to lay benefactors, and the London Charterhouse continued to add new units to its establishment both in the fifteenth and the early sixteenth centuries. However, it was not just as an economical form of personal remembrance that the Carthusians found favour in late-medieval England. Mary de Valence was an important lady, widow of Aymer (d. 1324) and daughter of the Count of St Pol. Yet advanced though her tastes may well have been, her clear preference for the Franciscan nuns, for the poor scholars of Cambridge and for the London Carthusians, was illustrative too of a more general drift in her times. Such inclinations towards the reformist and the educational wings of the Church, increasingly common among potential benefactors after the severe shock of the Black Death, were the cause of dismay among the possessioners. In the later

1360s, when the Benedictine John of Reading wrote his *Chronicle of England*, it was the friars who remained the principal threat to his order. As he saw it, the aftermath of the Black Death, when 'all the wealth of this world' had been left behind, had done the Mendicants particular disservice:

> For these latter found so much superfluous wealth flowing to them from their confessions and the legacies of their penitents, that they would scarcely deign to receive the offerings of the faithful. Without more ado, little heeding their profession and their rule, which consist in mendicant poverty, they gathered from all sides superfluous equipment for their rooms, their tables and their horses, being tempted thereto by the devil; they no longer sought heavenly things, but earthly and carnal pleasures, while asserting in their sermons to the people that Jesus Christ and his disciples had been poor in this life and had begged for their livelihood. And they taught many errors, to say nothing of wickedness.[25]

Certainly, the good fortune of the friars, made more obnoxious by the false piety of their preaching, was the loss of the monks of Westminster, to which community John of Reading belonged. Moreover, as other reforming orders came into fashion, the future promised no better.

No fewer than six out of the nine Carthusian communities in England were founded after the Black Death, all but one of these within two decades of the establishment of the London Charterhouse. They were not – even London and Sheen – exceptionally well endowed. In comparison with other orders, the Carthusians were never very thick on the ground. Nevertheless, their influence was out of all proportion to their numbers. To the chagrin of the black monks and their associates, it was the Carthusians rather than the religious of the older orders who captured the popular imagination. Pondering how to commemorate their long-standing association with Hull, the de la Poles were to consider first the foundation of a collegiate chantry, then of a house of Poor Clares. Their eventual choice in the late 1370s of a community of Carthusians must have been influenced directly by what had happened just a few years before in London. At Coventry, another thriving urban centre, it was John Luscote, the first London prior, who played an important part in the foundation in 1381 of a Charterhouse. Nor were urban locations and burgess patrons the only ones favoured in the expansion. Axholme (Lincolnshire) and Mount Grace (North Yorkshire) enjoyed rural settings such as those originally sought by the order. Both were founded in 1398 on lands provided by the earl of Nottingham (Thomas de Mowbray) and by the duke of Surrey (Thomas de Holand) respectively.[26]

Royal patronage, in one form or another, is recognizable at each of these foundations. Similarly, the next royal initiative in the cause of reform, taken by Henry V in 1415, again returned to the support of the Carthusians. In that year, with the estates of the dissolved alien priories at his disposal, Henry founded two major houses: Sheen (Carthusian) and Syon (Bridgettine). They were both conveniently sited for his palace at Richmond, almost opposite each other on the Thames. To these two houses, within the sound of each other's bells, resorted some of the more austere spirits of the age, much as they had done in the late twelfth century to the earliest Carthusian communities. William of Alnwick and Thomas Fishbourne, the first

129 The fifteenth-century Carthusian priory at Mount Grace from the air, with the church (centre) and great cloister to its north (top). Mount Grace was founded in 1398 during the second phase of Carthusian expansion

confessors and spiritual directors of Syon, had each spent at least a part of his earlier life as a recluse, associated with a traditional Benedictine community. The two first abbesses of Syon, Matilda Newton and Joan North, had been nuns in like fashion of Benedictine houses, the latter at Markyate (Hertfordshire) where she had no doubt heard the message of the St Albans reformers, as well as coming under the influence of Thomas Fishbourne himself during his service as spiritual director of the nuns of Sopwell, in the same county. Appropriately, it was from Mount Grace Priory that the

130 Alan Sorrell's reconstruction of Mount Grace as it might have looked shortly before its suppression, showing the individual cells and gardens of the monks surrounding the great cloister on the left

Carthusians of Sheen obtained the nucleus of their fine library of devotional works. And it was the then prior of Mount Grace, Robert Layton, himself formerly a Benedictine, who stood at the king's side as Henry V's adviser during the abortive proceedings of 1421 when the black monks were urged to reform.[27]

A century later, when Cardinal Wolsey renewed the attack on the Benedictines, the examples of unattainable rigour which their abbots quoted against him were the Carthusians, the Bridgettines and the Friars Observant (the newly arrived fundamentalist wing of the Franciscans). If they were themselves, they claimed, to attempt to impose such stern discipline, their communities would dissolve in apostasy.[28] Yet without it, their prestige unavoidably remained low. As to the relative popularity of the monastic orders by this time, the evidence of contemporary wills is unequivocal. It was the friars who featured most regularly in Londoners' wills, as John of Reading had noticed them beginning to do in the immediate aftermath of the Black Death. But noticeable too was the ascending popularity among the city's testators of the Carthusian communities, especially those of the London Charterhouse and of Sheen.[29] In just the same way, Syon, Sheen, the London

131 Syon House (Middlesex): the eighteenth-century mansion replaced an earlier sixteenth-century conversion of the monastic buildings of the expelled Bridgettine nuns

Charterhouse and Mount Grace were prominent among those very few houses outside their city which the better-off testators of late-medieval Norwich chose to remember in their wills.[30] In Yorkshire, it was Mount Grace again and the Charterhouse at Hull which, together with the friars, remained high in the affections of both gentry and burgesses alike.[31]

On the face of it, monks like the Carthusians who believed in perpetual seclusion, and nuns like the Bridgettines who were both secluded and aristocratic to boot, might each seem an unlikely focus for popular esteem and affection. And certainly their appeal was on a very different level from that of the omnipresent friars of whom it was said, only partly in jest, that 'a fly and a friar will fall in every dish'. Where they scored with their public was in a deeper sympathy than most religious could muster for that mystical spirituality which, in the later Middle Ages, had become one of the principal inspirations of lay piety. There were adherents at Mount Grace of the contemporary Flemish *devotio moderna*, readers of Thomas à Kempis's influential *Imitation of Christ* and sympathizers with those who have since been described as 'Brethren of the Common Life', the followers of Gerhard Groote (d. 1384) of Deventer. At Syon, likewise, there were to be several copies of the *Imitation of Christ* in the fine library built up by the Bridgettine nuns and by the scholars they recruited as confessors, while in Carthusian libraries generally and at Syon again, popular devotional manuals like the *Scale of Perfection* by Walter Hilton were always especially prominent. They were studied alongside that strange hysterical record of an individual's pilgrimage, *The Book of Margery Kempe*, and themselves pointed the way to the complete communion with God of which the English mystics – Richard Rolle and Walter Hilton, Julian of Norwich and the anonymous author of *The Cloud of Unknowing* – wrote with such attractive and compelling eloquence.

Richard Rolle and Walter Hilton both spoke from the depths of their experience as recluses, and it was a similar seclusion that the Carthusians almost alone could offer, through their discipline, to their adherents. Thus at Mount Grace the isolation of the site and the privacy of the monks' individual cells provided the ideal setting for Richard Methley, late in the fifteenth century, both to be exposed to what he recognized as a mystical experience and to attempt later to record it in writing, for 'if naught were said of it haply some might say that it was a thing of naught; and so, following God's will, I will set out as best I can what I have experienced'. Methley had been in the church at Mount Grace when he underwent his visitation, and 'after celebrating Mass was engaged upon thanksgiving in prayer and meditation, when God visited me in power, and I yearned with love so as almost to give up the ghost'. As he would have come to expect from his earlier reading of *The Cloud of Unknowing* and from that French work *The Mirror of Simple Souls* which we know him to have copied in his own hand, Methley lived through a near-total oblivion in the presence of God, finding it as hard as other mystical writers had already done to discover the right words to describe it:

> Then did I forget all pain and fear and deliberate thought of any thing, and even of the Creator. And as men who fear the peril of fire do not cry 'Fire hath come upon my house; come ye and help me', since in their strait and agony they can scarce speak a single word, but cry 'Fire, Fire, Fire!' or, if their fear be greater they cry 'Ah! Ah! Ah!', wishing to impart their peril in this single cry, so I, in my poor way. For first I oft commended my soul to God, saying: 'Into thy hands', either in words or (as I think rather) in spirit. But as the pain of love grew more powerful I could scarce have any thought at all, forming within my spirit these words: 'Love! Love! Love!' And at last, ceasing from this, I deemed that I would wholly yield up my soul, singing, rather than crying, in spirit through joy: 'Ah! Ah! Ah!'[32]

It so happened that God had visited Methley in the church at Mount Grace, and not in his cell or in the fields. However, the church itself (never of much importance as a centre of religious life at Mount Grace) played little part in the experience, and a more usual condition of encounters of this kind was that they should be allowed to develop in seclusion. Such necessarily personal dialogues with the Holy Ghost were of course antithetical to the whole purpose and meaning of religious communities as St Benedict and his followers had designed them. In their time, the monks of Hailes had received Margery Kempe kindly, taking even her scolding for their 'many great oaths and horrible' in good part (above, p. 83). But they can hardly have been persuaded that her individual brand of emotional excess could long serve as a model for their own community.[33] Margery, in the company of the mystics with whom in spirit she was one, might have been harmless enough. Elsewhere, her passionate pursuit of her individual love affair with God was enough to put the monks, as a group, on the defensive.

They had more than Margery, as it happened, to trouble them. Margery had not questioned the authenticity of the Holy Blood of Hailes, but there were those who did just this in her time, and the assault on pilgrimages and on relics for which the Lollards became known was already not the most dangerous of their heresies. Late-medieval dissent, both within the Church and outside it, had taken two paths

132 Remains of the church (left) at Mount Grace Priory, where Richard Methley had his encounter with God; the small size of the building was characteristic of the Carthusians, for whom devotions in the privacy of the cell took a larger part in their routine than communal worship in the choir

potentially threatening to the monks. Since the time of St Francis in the early thirteenth century, poverty and the apostolic life had been preached energetically by the Mendicants. It was only a short step, soon taken, to an outright attack on all property in the Church as a direct contradiction of Christ's teaching. Simultaneously, an even greater threat to monasticism (because more difficult to answer) arose in the growing emphasis on the value of the personal dialogue with God, as practised among others by the Carthusians. Uthred of Boldon (d. 1397), sub-prior of Durham and three times prior of Durham's rest-house at Finchale, had learnt the skills of academic debate as a scholar at Oxford, becoming a worthy opponent there of the friars. But his position was essentially a defensive one, and the craft he developed was apologetics. Against those who attacked the excessive wealth of the higher clergy and their too frequent participation in government, Uthred of Boldon was able to deploy Aristotelian arguments in favour of rule by a natural élite. The clergy, being both more spiritual and more literate than the greater part of their contemporaries, were better equipped to hold property and to govern – in the language of the controversy of Uthred's day, better fitted to exercise 'dominion'. As for the personal encounter with God and the value of direct experience of the Holy Spirit, Uthred was careful not to be too dismissive. There was no one way of life that alone could be seen as the guaranteed path to perfection. The contemplative life – the path of the Carthusians – had its merits. But it was the 'mixed life', part contemplative and part active, of his own community at Durham that Uthred urged especially on his readers.[34]

Uthred's arguments were too academic to appeal to a very wide audience. In any event, the movement against the possessioners had become by this time an instinctive reaction against wealth even amongst those who, like John Wyclif himself, were fully equipped to engage in the debate on Uthred's level. Wyclif answered Uthred moderately enough, but his feelings were not always so contained.

He was to describe the religious orders – the monks, the canons and the friars together – as 'a flock of the fiend's children', while one of his most damaging assertions was that they had taken to themselves 'the fourth part [of all] that should be in their brethren's hands', being the 'most greedy purchasers in earth'.[35]

When Wyclif wrote about dominion and grace, he was picturing a return to an idealized theocratic monarchy, such as Charlemagne might perhaps have maintained. Grace would be judged in the next world, not in this one; and always provided that the Church acknowledged its dependence on the State, it might keep its lands, exercising dominion over them as before.[36] However, if Wyclif thought nothing of popular sovereignty and would have rejected common ownership of the land, his followers were quite pardonably misled by the fire of his debate to read more into his arguments than he intended. As Wyclif wrote and taught at Oxford in the 1360s and 1370s, and as the papacy lost its leadership in the Great Schism, the attack on the possessioners gathered strength. It was no longer Wyclif's views alone that were being condemned at Archbishop Courtenay's London synod of 1382, a year after the Peasants' Revolt, for many of the 'erroneous conclusions' listed at the time were popular, not scholarly, in their origin. Certainly, they were uniformly hostile to the monks. Among the beliefs condemned in 1382 were the conclusions that 'if anyone enters any private religious order, he hereby becomes more unable and unsuitable for the observance of God's mandates'; that 'the saints who instituted any private religious orders, whether of possessioners or of mendicants, committed sin in so doing'; and that 'the religious men who live in private religious orders are not of the Christian religion'. More dangerous still were the 'erroneous conclusions' that touched directly on issues of property – 'that temporal lords may, at their will, take away the temporal goods of ecclesiastics who are habitually delinquent, and that the people may, at their will, correct delinquent lords'; further 'that tithes are pure alms, and that parishioners may withhold them on account of the sins of their curates, and at their will give the tithes to others'.[37]

Henry Knighton, a canon of Leicester, believed Lollard opinions to have 'prevailed to such an extent that half the population or more were won over to their sect, some from their hearts, others from shame or fear'; they had become so bold 'that in public places they shamelessly barked like dogs with unwearying voices'.[38] But Leicester itself, with other Midland cities, was a stronghold of Lollardy, and it is doubtful whether the Lollards made many converts in more rural areas, while even those they had won were lost to the cause as it was driven into impossible extremes. The first major disendowment proposals, presented as a Commons petition in 1410, although couched in especially attractive terms as they estimated the wealth of the monks, never stood a chance of success.[39] Far from advancing the disendowment campaign, Lollard sponsorship, by awakening new fears in the conservative community, contributed materially to its suppression.[40] Nevertheless, many of the criticisms that had been made of the Church were too near the mark to be dismissed. If anything Wyclif had underestimated the proportion of the nation's wealth held under the 'dead hand' (*mortmain*) of the Church. Increasingly there were those, the plunderers of the alien priories among them, who wanted a share of these riches for themselves.

The spoliation of the monastic Church, beginning long before the Dissolution, was made the easier by economic adversity, by shaken self-confidence and by the merely lukewarm support of its friends. Already, while John XXII was pope (1316–34), the current economic difficulties of the Cistercians had been explained to him as a consequence not of their own bad management of their estates but of other misfortunes out of their control – of the greed of their neighbours, of perpetual wars and natural calamities, of taxes from which they ought to have been (and were no longer) exempt.[41] None of these problems went away in the fourteenth century. For many, too, the fifteenth century had nothing more promising to bring.

Among the possessioners, the true crisis developed about a half century after the reverses of the Black Death. Skilled administrators – Thomas Chillenden (d. 1411) at Christ Church (Canterbury), Thomas de là Mare (d. 1396) and John of Whethamstede (d. 1465) at St Albans – were successful in averting the worst troubles. Nor was there to be any time, as we have seen, when the greater houses stopped extending and improving their buildings. But the clearest symptom of economic distress, the abandonment of demesne farming in favour of leasing, was to be recognizable at all major houses before 1400. Some communities took longer than others to adjust to their new situation. Durham, Battle and Westminster were all slow to change. Yet at Durham, the point of decision in favour of general leasing of the demesne seems to have been reached no later than the second decade of the fifteenth century;[42] at Battle, although the monks were exceptionally efficient farmers, keeping a number of their estates long in hand, demesne farming on a very large scale had ceased much earlier, in the 1380s;[43] at Westminster, a sluggish and conservative estate management system had nevertheless begun moving in the direction of widespread leasing from the first signs of a collapse of cereal prices in the mid-1370s.[44]

In general, while there are many purely local explanations for the abandonment of demesne farming by individual houses, including the coastal inundations that touched Battle,[45] what finally persuaded most communities to lease their demesnes was the clear failure of agricultural prices to keep up with costs, in particular to match escalating wages. Manorial discipline had been one of the casualties of the Black Death and subsequent plagues. Labour, now permanently in short supply, could fix its own price. When the monks and their fellow landowners attempted to regulate wages, the response, not infrequently, was violence on the land; in 1381, there was rebellion.

The reaction of the monks to violence of this kind, as indeed to the violence of war, matched that of other similarly threatened landowners of the period. Making common cause with their better-off neighbours, they protected their buildings with high precinct walls, pierced only by formidable gatehouses. They dug moats at their manors and sometimes round their own houses as well. They demonstrated their allegiances, and invoked their friends, by magnificent heraldic displays. Obviously, the degree of threat varied with the situation and wealth of each house. Many monastic communities were never defended, except in the most nominal way. But for the Premonstratensians of Alnwick, in the Northumbrian Marches, the danger of a Scottish attack, even under the shadow of the great Percy fortress they neighboured, was clearly so continuous that some investment in self-defence became essential. Before the end of the fourteenth century, the entire abbey precinct at Alnwick had been surrounded by a high boundary wall, to form a large semicircular enclosure protected on the south by the River Alne. To the north-west, against the main road from Alnwick to Eglingham, a formidably battlemented and machicolated late-medieval gatehouse is now the only standing building at the abbey. Dating, like the former precinct wall, to the late fourteenth century, this gatehouse carries the heraldry of the Percy patrons of Alnwick and of their Lucy associates. It was in 1376, we know, that the abbot of Alnwick had given a great feast at his house for Henry de Percy, 'our noble advocate', just the year before Lord Percy contrived his elevation to the ancient but long extinct earldom of Northumberland. Percy came accompanied by thirteen knights and by a great host of other relatives and friends, over a thousand in number, for whom the cloister itself was temporarily put in service as a dining hall.[46]

Alnwick's nearest neighbours in religion, the Carmelite friars of Hulne, just a couple of miles up the road towards Eglingham, were as reluctant as the canons to place their faith only in God. Prominent at Hulne again was a strong precinct wall, still surviving to its full length round the site; and here the defences were completed before the end of the fifteenth century by a great residential tower house, very much in the regional tradition.[47] Contemporaneously, it was with tower houses like Hulne's that the local aristocracy defended its estates against the Scots, while in Scotland too the raids of the English were met with identical precautions. The extraordinarily lavish fifteenth-century rebuilding of the great church at Melrose, north of the border in Roxburghshire, followed a history of destruction by the English royal armies, including two serious pillagings in 1322 and 1385, during the second of which the church and other buildings were burnt down.[48] In Dumfriesshire, to the west, the Cistercians of Sweetheart were to surround themselves with a stone precinct wall, almost four metres in height, on three sides of their site, while a water-filled ditch closed off the fourth to the south.[49] Inchcolm Abbey, on its island site on the Firth of Forth, rightly judged itself to be especially exposed to the English. A fourteenth-century choir book, surviving from Inchcolm, contains the prayer – 'Save this choir, which sings thy praise, from the invasions of the English.' The prayer dates to about 1340, and it followed a raid of 1335 when the English had broken into the monastery. They were back again in 1385, and it was not until the comprehensive fortification of the site by Abbot Walter Bower in the 1420s and 1430s that the canons could remain there throughout the year, even in the summer when the raids were most threatening.[50]

Inevitably coastal sites were always especially at risk, at least as much in the South as in the North. Michelham, in Sussex, was to become one of the more complete examples of a defended priory site, with encircling moat and strong fifteenth-century gatehouse tower, fortified in this way against the French. And indeed piratical raids on the south coast of England during the Hundred Years War became so frequent, whether in reality or merely in threat, that it would have been an improvident community which, by the late fourteenth century, had done nothing to forestall and deflect them. Thus the fortifications of the Cistercians of Quarr, on the painfully vulnerable Isle of Wight, licensed in 1365, could only just have been completed in 1377 when they passed their first test in averting the French during an otherwise disastrous landing that year.[51] Simultaneously, down in the South-West, the neighbouring Devonshire communities of Buckland and Tavistock were both to be fortified against the Breton pirates who were making the sea and its environs so unsafe; while still in 1535, at St Michael's Mount (Cornwall), 'habiliments of war', including bows and breastplates, hand-guns and cannons, bills and 'three old poleaxes of iron', figured prominently in the inventory of that date.[52]

It was probably one of the earliest invasion threats of the Hundred Years War that persuaded the monks of Battle (Sussex) to apply to the king in the summer of 1338 for a licence to fortify their abbey. Certainly, a powerful fleet of French marauders was cruising the south coast at the time, nor was this threat to be lifted decisively until the English naval victory at Sluys in 1340 put an end for the moment to such activities. In the meantime, Abbot Alan of Ketling would have begun on the great gatehouse which still stands to its full height as the principal entry to Battle's precincts. Equipped with polygonal turrets at the angles and rising clear above the line of the adjoining ranges, the gatehouse is a magnificent structure very exactly illustrating the double purpose – to protect and to overawe – that such entrances were intended to fulfil.[53]

By then Bury (Suffolk) already had its twelfth-century gate-tower, south of the abbey church, which, like the gate at Battle, dominated the street it confronted. In the fourteenth century, not content with this, the monks of Bury built themselves another gatehouse, more magnificent than the last, as the main entrance to the northern part of a defended precinct, newly fortified against a return of the rioting which had done such damage to the church and its treasures in 1327. Unlike the twelfth-century gate, the functions of which were wholly peaceable, no monastic gatehouse of the mid-fourteenth century would be considered complete without some trappings of war. At Bury, the single gate-opening is defended by a portcullis. Hidden behind the statuary, now removed, of the once ornate façade – a composition intended both to instruct and to edify the passer-by – are the arrow-slits of quite another purpose.[54]

Separate lodgings, over the gate, characterized both Bury and Battle. And it was this residential use of the gatehouse tower, already familiar at comparable military buildings of the time, that was to be important again at Thornton, in Lincolnshire, one of the wealthier Augustinian houses. The rebuilding of Thornton had been continuing steadily since the late thirteenth century (above, pp. 111–12). Towards the end of the next century it was almost complete, and it was in the 1380s, perhaps hurried by the memory of the Peasants' Revolt, that the entire monastic assemblage at Thornton was rounded off with an exceptionally handsome gatehouse, among the more splendid survivals of its class. Incorporated in the Thornton gatehouse, in exactly the same manner as they would be again at many contemporary castle entrance-towers, were impressive halls at first- and second-floor level, each with adjoining bedchambers equipped with fireplaces of their own and individual garderobes.[55] Although later made more prominent and aggressive than it had originally been by the addition of an elaborate sixteenth-century barbican, the Thornton gatehouse nevertheless exemplifies that community of interest, in property and government, that had developed in England by the later Middle Ages between the aristocracy and the princes of the Church. It was a prestige building, bold and commanding, having little obviously to do with those pastoral

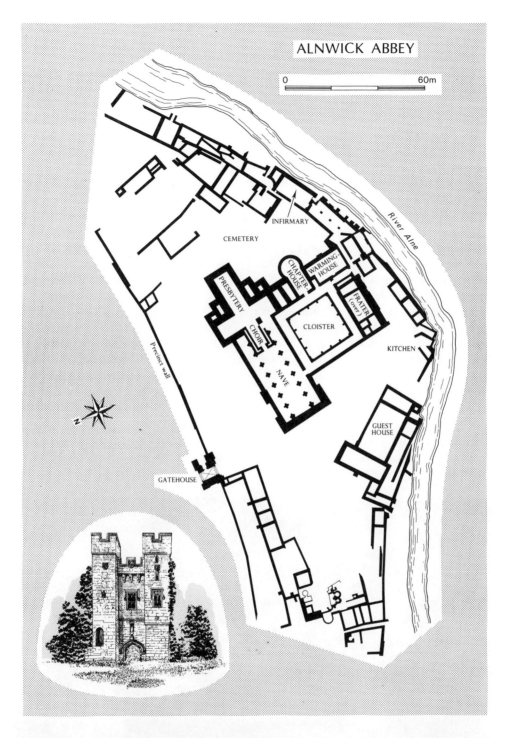

ALNWICK ABBEY

0   60m

INFIRMARY

CEMETERY

River AIne

CHAPTER-HOUSE

WARMING-HOUSE

PRESBYTERY

FRATER (over)

CHOIR

CLOISTER

Precinct wall

NAVE

KITCHEN

GUEST HOUSE

GATEHOUSE

N

133 Alnwick Abbey (Northumberland): a Premonstratensian house fortified in the late fourteenth century with a strong precinct wall (left) and great gatehouse (bottom left) facing the main road. Alnwick was under Percy patronage in its later years, and its gatehouse – the east front of which is reproduced here from a drawing of 1858 – was lavishly decorated with Percy and Lucy heraldry (after W. H. St John Hope, *Arch. J.*, 44 (1887))

responsibilities that had brought the Augustinians to Lincolnshire in the first place.

To many, in any event, those responsibilities had altered in emphasis. Much of the property that came to the Church in the later Middle Ages – more than a quarter of all grants to the possessioner orders during the reign of Edward III – was assigned to a particular purpose.[56] Monastic communities had always recognized an obligation to commemorate their founders. But the emphasis, so characteristic of the fourteenth and fifteenth centuries, on a commemorative function alone, was something new. It brought both profit and pain to the monks.

In point of fact, the elaborate burial arrangements of the higher clergy and the local aristocracy dominate the later history of many houses. Indeed, Maxstoke (Warwickshire), an Augustinian priory of unusually late foundation, owed its very existence to the desire of William de Clinton, newly created earl of Huntingdon, to commemorate the line he still hoped to establish in perpetuity. Coinciding in date with his own elevation to the earldom on 10 March 1337, William de Clinton promoted the collegiate chantry he had founded just a few years before at the parish church at Maxstoke (near which he was also to build a fine castle) into an independent Augustinian community of the statutory prior and twelve canons. He endowed the priory with, among other things, three parish churches, the appropriation of which he was busy negotiating in the 1340s, not long before his death in 1354 brought all these projects and his line to an end.[57] In the event, William de Clinton's priory, although never a rich one, survived through in fair shape until the Dissolution. It thus held in long remembrance its founder's wishes, as did that

134 Hulne Priory from the air: this Carmelite house, exposed in Northumberland to Scottish cattle-raiders and other marauders, was defended in the later Middle Ages with a strong precinct wall, to which a substantial tower-house (left centre) was added before the end of the fifteenth century (*British Crown copyright reserved*)

135 Hulne as it is today, with its former defensive tower rising behind the 'Gothick' summer-house built in the late eighteenth century for the then duke of Northumberland on part of the west claustral range

other characteristic product of Edwardian piety, the re-founded Premonstratensian abbey at Leiston (Suffolk), which was to prosper under the patronage of Robert de Ufford (d. 1369), first earl of Suffolk, to which dignity he had been raised in 1337 at the same time as William de Clinton received his earldom of Huntingdon. Leiston, originally set on an exposed coastal site, had suffered badly in the floods of the earlier part of the century, and it was largely as a result of the generosity of the ageing earl that the community was able to move, in the mid-1360s, to a new site away from the sea.[58] Within a generation, all but the church of the canons' fine new buildings, lately reconstructed 'in a safer place at grievous cost', had been 'totally destroyed by fire with their corn and goods of no small value'. An appeal against further taxes, favourably received by the king in the autumn of 1380, reported the canons of Leiston to be 'so burdened with debt that they may not content their creditors, pay the said tenths and support other charges, and have not the means honourably to maintain themselves'.[59]

Leiston, like Maxstoke, rose above its difficulties, and if chantry foundations could occasionally go wrong – as was to be the case with Bishop Hotham's recent endowment of Welbeck (Nottinghamshire) in the 1340s and quite possibly with Richard le Scrope's proposals for Easby (North Yorkshire) just before the end of the same century as well[60] – the balance of advantage more often came to favour the

136 Melrose Abbey, in Roxburghshire, as rebuilt in the fifteenth century following a succession of disastrous English raids

137 Sweetheart Abbey (Dumfriesshire), one of the Scottish abbeys fortified against the English in the later Middle Ages

138 Inchcolm Abbey, in the Firth of Forth, first systematically fortified against the English in the 1420s and 1430s (*British Crown copyright reserved*)

religious. It is true that the nuns of Lacock (Wiltshire), by an agreement dated 3 May 1352, bound themselves to sing a memorial mass, with penitential psalms, every 3 August in perpetuity for the soul of the deceased John Goudlyne; they were to record their undertaking in Lacock's book of obits and would remember John Goudlyne always among their benefactors. Yet in return they were to receive fair payment 'for carrying on their own arduous business', while six of the nuns who were present at John's obsequies were to be rewarded on that day with a gallon of wine which they might exchange, if they preferred, for a six-pence pittance.[61]

On a larger scale, one of the more important of the later acquisitions of Owston Abbey, in Leicestershire, was the Coleville manor in Muston and Normanton which came to the canons as the endowment of a chantry, set up in the late 1360s by Robert Coleville, lord of Bytham, and his wife. In the 1380s, the stipends of the two chaplains maintaining the chantry cost Owston no more than ten pounds, while the rents receivable from the lands of the endowment totalled over thirty pounds in all.[62] When similar sums are done on the obit accounts of the wealthy Benedictines of Glastonbury, it is immediately clear that the monks themselves were absorbing a good part of the proceeds. Thus the revenues accruing to the keeper of the anniversary of Abbot John de Cancia in 1539, the year of Glastonbury's suppression, were recorded then as £26 5s 7½d, of which only a proportion was assigned to the expenses of the obit, the balance being shared out among the monks: 16s 10d to the abbot, 12s 7½d to the prior, and 8s 5d to each monk. From the proceeds of the anniversary of Walter Monyton that same year, the cash doles of the monks of Glastonbury, already among the most generous in the land, benefited by 5s a head.[63]

An inevitable consequence of benefactions like these was that the monastic churches of late-medieval England, like the parish churches and cathedrals of their day, came to be filled with funerary monuments and with chantry chapels of great (and increasing) splendour. The memorial works of Henry VII on his own behalf at Westminster Abbey are well known; they remain among the greater glories of the church. But the king was lavish too in the commemoration of others of his line, including Prince Arthur, his eldest son, who died on 2 April 1502. Before the year was out, Henry had met the cost of a memorial window in the north transept of Malvern Priory (Worcestershire), completing a re-glazing scheme which has left Malvern still with one of the finest assemblages of such glass in the country. In the meantime, he had paid generously towards Arthur's funeral at Worcester and had probably taken the first steps already in the commissioning of the fine monument placed next to the high altar in the cathedral. Prince Arthur's chapel at Worcester was not begun before 1504. However, the prince had been laid there, 'at the South End of the High Altar of that Cathedrall Church', soon after his death, amidst great ceremonial and to such displays of grief that 'he had a hard Heart that wept not'. Certainly, the English gift for public display, on which in these times we still congratulate ourselves, was very much in evidence at Prince Arthur's obsequies in 1502. The prince had died at Ludlow Castle, and it was from Ludlow that the corpse was brought, on a specially prepared funerary carriage, by slow stages south to Worcester. The first stage, completed on St Mark's Day (25 April), followed the highway due east to Bewdley: 'It was the foulest cold windye and rainey Daye, and the worst Waye that I have seene: Yea, and in some Places they were faine to take Oxen to draw the Charre, so ill was the Waye.' From Bewdley, officials rode ahead to prepare the reception at Worcester, 'and suffered no Man nor other to enter the Gate of that Cittie untill the Tyme the Corpes was come'. And then 'every Thinge was ordered as followeth' –

Fresh Scocheons were sett on the Charre, and draught Horses were mended, and vi^{xx} [120] new Torches delivered to the vi^{xx} Torch Bearers at the Towne's End. That Daye

139 The great encircling moat, comparatively rare at monastic houses of any size, at Michelham Priory (Sussex), defended in this way against the French whose piratical raids, during the fourteenth century, terrorized the south coast of England (*British Crown copyright reserved*)

140 Michelham's handsome fifteenth-century gatehouse tower, defending the bridge over the moat

was faire, and then the Gentlemen rode Two and Two together, and all the other as were before ordered. The Order of Fryers censed the Corpse at the Towne's End, and then proceeded to the Gate of that Cittie: At which Gate were the Bayliffs, and the honest Men of that Cittie on Foote. Alonge in a Rowe on everye Side were the Vicar Generall or Chauncelor of the Bishopps of that See, with a good Number of secular Canons in graye Amys [amices], with rich Copes: And other Curats, secular Priests, Clerks, and Children, with Surplisses in great Number, and I suppose all the Torches of the Towne.

At the cathedral gate, four bishops (of Lincoln, Salisbury, Chester, and Worcester) censed the corpse which was then removed from its carriage and received by the prior and convent of Worcester in full pontificals, attended by the abbots of Gloucester and of Evesham, of Chester, Shrewsbury, Tewkesbury, Hailes and Bordesley, all richly robed as before. Carried through the cathedral in procession, the prince's bier was laid under a canopy ('herse') which was 'the goodlyest and best wrought and garnished that ever I sawe'.

There were xviii Lights [candles], Two great Standards, a Banner of the King's Armes, a Banner of the Kinge of Spaine's Armes, a Banner of the Queen's Armes, a Banner of the Queene of Spaine's Armes, a Banner of the Prince's Armes, a Banner

141 The fourteenth-century barn at Buckland Abbey (Devonshire): one of its defensive arrow-slits may be seen between the second and the third buttresses from the right

142 Battle Abbey's handsome mid-fourteenth-century residential gatehouse, seen from within the abbey precinct

143 The original twelfth-century entrance tower at Bury St Edmunds, datable to 1120–48, which also served as a belfry

144 Bury's answer to the riots of 1327: a strong gatehouse completed before 1346 and equipped with a portcullis and with arrow-slits

of the Princesse's Armes, Two of Wales, One of Kadwallader, a Bannerell of Normandye, a Banerell of Guien, a Banerell of Cornwall, a Banerell of Chester, a Banerell of Poyctowe, and 100 Pencills [pennons] of divers Badges; also the rich Cloth of Majestie, well frindged and double rayled, covered with black Cloth, was layed under Foote, which after was the Fees of the Officers of Armes.

The ceremonial pomp of the event, bringing together in deliberate and familiar association images of Church and State, continued through to the end. It was the earls of Shrewsbury and of Kent who carried Prince Arthur's embroidered coat of arms in the final procession; other leading members of the aristocracy and of the prince's household bore his shield, his sword ('the Point forward'), and his crested helm. Four knights led Lord Garrard, the young son and heir of the earl of Kildare, 'armed with the Prince's owne Harneys on a Courser [charger] richly trapped with a Trapper of Velvet embrothered with Needleworke of the Prince's Armes, with a Pollaxe in his Hande, the Head downwards, into the Midst of the Queere [choir], where the Abbot of Tewksbury, Gospeller of that Masse, received the Offring of that Horse'. After further rich offerings, an address, a 'great generall Dole of Groates to every poore Man and Woman', and 'divers and many Anthemes', Prince Arthur's body was laid in the grave 'with Weeping and sore Lamentation'. Then –

His Officer of Armes, sore weeping, tooke of his Coate of Armes, and cast it along over the Chest right lamentably. Then Sir William Ovedall Comptroller of his Houshold, sore weeping and crying, tooke the Staffe of his Office by both Endes, and over his owne Head brake it, and cast it into the Grave. In likewise did Sir Ric. Croft

145 The imposing outer face of the great gatehouse at Thornton (Lincolnshire), built in the 1380s, perhaps in response to recent troubles in the Peasants' Revolt (1381); part of the brick-built sixteenth-century barbican is visible on the left

Steward of his Houshold, and cast his Staffe broken into the Grave. In likewise did the Gentlemen Ushers their Roddes. This was a piteous Sight to those who beheld it. All Things thus finished, there was ordeyned a great Dinner . . .[64]

Whether mourning or feasting together, the monks and the aristocracy, by the Late Middle Ages, had established a fair working relationship. It is true that patrons were accustomed, as always, to make a variety of demands upon the monastic houses. The right of burial within the church was only one of many privileges to which the founder and his kin became entitled, while legitimate claims on the hospitality of a house could sometimes be pushed to intolerable lengths. An aristocratic widow, taking refuge in a nunnery, might bring jealousies and dissensions with her, refusing obedience to the prioress as did Isabel Lady Clinton at Wroxall (Warwickshire) in the 1320s, or obtaining for herself some particular favour as in the private room granted to Dame Margaret Darcy at Heynings (Lincolnshire) in 1393 'on account of the nobility of her race'.[65] Eleanor Lady Audley was a boarder at Langley (Leicestershire), to which she brought useful additional income. Yet, as the prioress was to complain in 1440, her noble guest 'has a great abundance of dogs, insomuch that whenever she comes to church there follow her twelve dogs, who make a great uproar in church, hindering them in their psalmody, and the nuns hereby are made terrified'.[66]

Such behaviour at Langley must have been enough to cause even the gentlest of sisters to sigh. Nor would community discipline have been made any easier for the nuns of Elstow (Bedfordshire) at about that time by the presence within their walls of

146 Thornton Abbey's gatehouse from within the precinct, showing the fine windows lighting the first- and second-floor halls

147 A nobleman receives extreme unction, with priests, monks and family in attendance. French, late fifteenth century

married corrodians, as a result of whose 'performance of conjugal rites between the same, encouragement of fleshly desire may easily be offered, at any rate to women in religion'.[67] But to see hospitality, or even the taking in of lodgers and corrodians, as invariably oppressive, is to make light of a role which the religious themselves were accustomed to take very seriously. St Benedict had told his followers, 'Let all guests that come be received like Christ, for he will say: "I was a stranger and ye took me in." And let fitting honour be shown to all, but especially to churchmen and pilgrims.' He had warned them, 'In the reception of poor men and pilgrims special attention should be shown, because in them is Christ more truly welcomed; for the fear which the rich inspire is enough of itself to secure them honour.'[68] In precisely that spirit, one of the last acts of the Cistercians of Cleeve (Somerset), shortly to be driven from their house, was to frame an inscription above their new gate: 'Gate be open, shut to no honest person' (*porta patens esto / nulli claudaris honesto*).[69] Hospitality, as they saw it, was a duty, no whit the worse for being something of a pleasurable distraction in addition.

Indeed, groan though the monks might over the cost of hospitality, there is much to suggest that, at any rate at the larger houses, the responsibility had been gladly assumed. Basingwerk (Flintshire), in common with the other Welsh houses of the Cistercian order, had never been especially rich. Yet in the fifteenth century it was to build itself new guest quarters so attractive to visitors that they flocked there in great

148 Leiston Abbey (Suffolk), a Premonstratensian house of no more than modest means which was nevertheless rebuilt in lavish style in the 1360s, on a new site away from the sea, with the assistance of its magnate benefactor, Robert de Ufford, earl of Suffolk (d. 1369)

149 The east end of the church at Leiston, showing something of the former high decorative quality of the stonework

numbers, no doubt being drawn by the additional incentive of a choice of French or Spanish wines with their meals.[70] At Durham of course, being one of the greater monasteries, the provision was especially lavish. There the monks kept a 'famouse house of hospitallitie called the geste haule', priding themselves on a standard of entertainment that 'both for the goodnes of ther diete, the sweete & daintie furneture of there Lodgings, & generally all things necessarie for traveillers' was not inferior to any place in England. The guest hall at Durham was 'a goodly brave place much like unto the body of a church with verey fair pillers supporting yt on ether syde and in the mydest of the haule a most large Raunge for the fyer'. Next to it, 'the chambers & lodginges . . . weare most swetly keept, and so richly furnyshed that they weare not unpleasant to ly in, especially one chamber called the Kyngs chamber deservinge that name, in that the king him selfe myght verie well have lyne in yt for the princelynes therof'. As for the food, it 'came from the great kitching of the prior, the bread & beare from his pantrie and seller, yf they weare of honor they weare served as honorably as the prior him selfe, otherwise according to there severall callinges'.[71]

Both those who sat down with the prior of Durham and those who attended him at table were 'gentlemen and yeomen of the best in the countrie', his house deserving no less. The association was of great mutual significance. As a manipulator of patronage, none would be more adroit than John Wessington, prior of Durham (1416–46), much of whose time was to be spent in adjusting the claims of patrons of his house so as to procure what advantage he could for the priory.[72] He practised an ancient skill. Earlier, it had been said at Leicester of William of Clown (d. 1378), a 'most pious abbot of devout memory . . . a lover of peace and quiet', that 'in hunting of the hare he was reckoned the most notable and renowned among all the lords of the realm, so that the King himself [Edward III] and his son Prince Edward [the Black Prince] and divers lords of the realm had an annual engagement to hunt at his entertainment. Nevertheless he would often say in private that the only reason why he took delight in such paltry sports was to show politeness to the lords of the realm, to get on easy terms with them and win their good will in matters of business.'[73] Abbot William's contemporary, Thomas de la Mare, abbot of St Albans (1349–96), had similar ascetic

150 Donor figure of Henry VII in the north transept window at Malvern Priory church

151 Prince Arthur's Chantry Chapel next to the high altar at Worcester Cathedral, begun in 1504 and subsequently protected against damage at the Reformation by its associations with the Tudor dynasty

152 Interior of Prince Arthur's
     Chantry at Worcester, with the
     prince's plain tomb-chest
     (bottom left) under a handsome
     lierne-vault and surrounded by
     high-quality stone-carving

impulses which he likewise suppressed in the interests of the community he headed. In private, he wore a hair shirt, rose early, ate seldom and drank little. But he loved beautiful things, was a generous host and collected many valuable gifts from his guests. Among those who came was Joan, princess of Wales and mother of Richard II, who later gave a gold collar to the saint, a silver cup to Abbot Thomas and a cask of wine annually to the community for many years. Richard II offered another gold collar at St Alban's shrine; Mary, countess of Pembroke, gave a silver-gilt reliquary of St Vincent; Robert of Walsham, confessor to the Black Prince, donated four hundred marks towards building works at the abbey; the duke of Gloucester, Thomas of Woodstock, gave six cloths of gold and an enamelled gold collar set with sapphires.[74]

153 The gatehouse at Cleeve (Somerset), as remodelled by Abbot Dovell shortly before the suppression of his house

This partnership between the wealthy had much to recommend it, yet there was a darker side to the relationship as well. By Thomas de la Mare's day, it had been some time already since the superiors of the great possessioner houses had occupied, as of right, positions of influence at the king's court. Without a natural entrée of their own to the highest circles, the monks had turned increasingly to their local magnates for support, and they had had to pay heavily for it in concessions. On the high altar at Durham, an 'excellent fine booke verye richly covered with gold and silver' listed St Cuthbert's benefactors, showing how highly the custodians of the saint's great lands 'esteemed their founders and benefactors, and the dayly and quotidian remembrance they had of them in the time of masse and divine service'.[75] But this 'most divine and charitable affection to the soules of theire benefactors as well dead as livinge' was far from being the only charge to be laid on St Cuthbert's estate. During the fifteenth century in particular, while factional disputes were least controlled, the greater monasteries everywhere recruited lay stewards from among the aristocracy of the region. Of course, they changed sides and switched their advocates when it suited

154 Basingwerk (Flintshire): this small Cistercian community was one of several in Wales which, during the last century of monasticism in the principality, earned a good reputation for the consistently high quality of its hospitality (*British Crown copyright reserved*)

155 Late-medieval heraldic tiles from Malvern Priory, in Worcestershire, commemorating the community's aristocratic patrons

them, but what they could not do at any time was to manage without advocates at all.[76]

Inevitably, the price the religious houses paid for the support of their lay friends would be measured in terms of land. When, late in the fourteenth century, the monks had first leased their demesnes, they had quite often found peasant cultivators to take on their estates, whether cooperatively or alone as individuals. A hundred years later, the situation had changed completely. Land units had grown larger; leases had lengthened; the gentry had taken control. Practice varied between houses, and there were even some, like the Premonstratensians of Croxton (Leicestershire), who strongly resisted the intrusion of the gentry as leaseholders.[77] However, for most communities the convenience of long-term leasing was too obvious to contest, the need for powerful local advocacy too acute. In the East Midlands, the earls of Huntingdon were hereditary stewards of more than one house; prominent local gentry – Babingtons and Pooles, Wigstons and Purefoys, Greys, Giffords, Ratcliffes and many others – were stewards, bailiffs, rent-collectors and lessees.[78] All these men had a claim on the monastic houses, at which very many of them enjoyed special privileges and from which a fair number in addition drew fees. They were interested – a good deal too interested – in monastic lands. One of the most revealing documents of the Dissolution years is a report of the complaints of Edward Calthrope, 'founder' and patron by recent inheritance of the little Trinitarian friary at Ingham (Norfolk), who believed himself cheated of his rights. The prior and his brethren at Ingham, anticipating suppression of their community, had sold their entire estate to a near neighbour, William Woodhouse, contrary to the assurances given some time before to the aspiring heir, Edward Calthrope, 'that in case they did either sell or alienate the same or any part thereof, that the same Edward should have it before any other man, forasmuch as it was founded by his ancestor, and the said Edward also next heir to the foundation'. By this action, Calthrope stood to lose for ever his foundation 'and also his bargain of the prior and convent'. It was the view of Calthrope's kinsman, Richard Wharton, writing to Thomas Cromwell on his behalf, that 'forasmuch as the said Edward is the founder, and also had a special promise of the prior and convent, to buy the same in case they did sell it, after my poor mind it were most reasonable that he should have the bargain and preferment before any other'.[79] Late in 1535, when Wharton wrote, many would have been of like mind with himself. There were sharks enough already in the sea.

Chapter 8

Indian Summer and Collapse

It is abundantly clear that the revived interest of aristocracy and gentry in the monastic lands coincided with a general return to profitability. Still, in the late fifteenth century, leases were long and rents were low. Yet the population of England, after its sharp descent and long stagnation, had begun to rise again. Demand for land was picking up and its price improving; the market for farm produce, as for all commodities, was enlarging year by year.

The monastic houses which had kept control of their lands were especially well placed to profit by price movements of this kind. Small communities, always more likely than the greater corporations to practise direct farming on their own account, enjoyed a new lease of life. They had come dangerously near collapse in the difficult years, and some indeed had perished. But like any contemporary landowner, they could not fail to benefit from the ascent of prices and depression of wages which agriculture experienced as population grew and demand caught up with supply. The pace of change, inevitably, was slow. There was nothing yet to equal the dramatic inflation of later Tudor times, out of which property-holders everywhere made their fortunes. In many houses, returning prosperity may have passed largely unnoticed, to be dissipated by the sort of management that allowed the Cistercians of Whalley (Lancashire) to lay out fully two-thirds of their large annual income on the purchase of foodstuffs and drink.[1] Nevertheless, resources were still found – by the monks of Whalley among others – for a renewal of building on an appreciable scale. And this was work on which houses of no more than moderate means were as likely to be active as the traditionally wealthy possessioners.

One contemporary writer, a Venetian, was to describe the 'enormously rich Benedictine, Carthusian, and Cistercian monasteries', loaded with church plate and other treasures, as 'more like baronial palaces than religious houses'. In England in the 1490s, by his account, there was not a house even of mendicant friars that was without its silver 'crucifixes, candlesticks, censers, patens, and cups . . . besides many other ornaments worthy of a cathedral church in the same metal'.[2] Popular piety had served the Mendicants this well, as indeed it had favoured the Carthusians. Less fashionable orders, whether the Benedictines or the once prosperous Cistercians, had long ceased to collect bequests or other donations on such a scale as to make each of their houses a treasure-chest. Yet one of the benefits of a long existence had already been the accumulation of interests and properties so diverse in character and considerable in range that it would have been an unlucky community which, by the early sixteenth century, would see no improvement in any part of its revenues.

Indeed, active building abbots reappear at just this time to engage in campaigns where a primary emphasis was almost always to be placed on display. Church towers,

156 The great fifteenth-century central tower, known as 'Bell Harry', at Christ Church (Canterbury)

for example, were a common addition to buildings already of some splendour. Gatehouses were rebuilt; guest and other lodgings were improved; the superior's quarters, in very many communities, either were given a face-lift or were entirely remodelled in the likeness, and with the comforts, of a manor-house. Partly as a result of earlier pressures to economize, the life-style of an abbot had become increasingly secularized. Some superiors, at first forced to move out of their communities to save money in hospitality and other charges, found themselves better suited by the freedom of their manor-houses and increasingly reluctant to return. It was to be said, for example, of the abbot of Bury in 1535 that he 'lay much forth in his granges', where 'he delighted much in playing at dice and cards, and therein spent much money, and in building for his pleasure'.[3] At Glastonbury, the abbey in 1539 was 'great, goodly, and so princely as we have not seen the like'. Yet the abbot still had his 'four fair manor places . . . the furthermost but three miles distant'.[4] If any of these 'goodly mansions' had been even half as comfortable as that same abbot's fine manor-house at Ashbury (Berkshire), a useful staging-post on his way up to London, he might indeed have found reason to linger there.[5]

The abbots of Bury and of Glastonbury were Benedictines, but it had never been the custom of every order to encourage its superiors to stay away. Accordingly, the modernization of the superior's lodgings at the monastic house itself became a characteristic indicator of returning prosperity as fortune at last favoured the landowner. The Benedictines, of course, were as prone to such refurbishments as any others. Milton (Dorset) and Muchelney (Somerset) were both black-monk houses of

157 The abbot of Glastonbury's
    manor-house at Ashbury
    (Berkshire), rebuilt in the late
    fifteenth century as a
    comfortable staging-post on the
    road from Somerset to London

158 Abbot William Middleton's hall
    at Milton Abbey (Dorset), with
    its carved oak screen (restored
    but largely original), dated
    1498

159 The former abbot's lodgings at Muchelney (Somerset), rebuilt on a newly luxurious scale in the early sixteenth century

160 The great gatehouse, elaborately ornamented with flushwork panelling in the East Anglian manner, of St Osyth's Priory (Essex), built in the late fifteenth century

161 View of the great hall (centre) and adjoining entrance tower of Abbot Charde's palatial lodgings at Forde (Dorset), rebuilt shortly before the Dissolution

more than average wealth. Each, at the very end of the fifteenth century or early in the sixteenth, was equipped with fine new lodgings for the abbot, thoroughly secular in flavour.[6] Such lordly halls and well-heated, panelled chambers were repeated everywhere at houses of comparable status. Among the better-endowed Augustinian communities were the abbeys of Notley (Buckinghamshire) and St Osyth (Essex), both of which were to take advantage of improving times to rebuild and extend their abbots' quarters. At St Osyth, too, Abbot Vintoner's new lodgings had succeeded by only a few years the total transformation of his abbey's approaches as the gatehouse

162 Detail of windows in the north alley of Abbot Charde's new cloister at Forde; the Dissolution stopped building before the other cloister alleys could be completed

164 The west tower at Shap (Westmorland), built by
Richard Redman in *c.* 1500 as an especially handsome addition to this otherwise modest Premonstratensian house

163 Robert King's new tower at his lodgings at Thame, built in the last decade of his community's
existence

was grandly rebuilt.[7] Meanwhile the Cistercians, always among the richer of the
reformed orders, had resumed again those building programmes for which once they
had been especially well known. Thomas Charde, last abbot of Forde (Dorset), was to
build himself a great hall at least as fine as that of the Benedictine William Middleton
(of Milton) or the Augustinian John Vintoner (of St Osyth). He had begun the
reconstruction of the cloister at Forde, completing the surviving north alley, when the
community he directed was dissolved.[8] At Thame (Oxfordshire), in exactly these
years, Abbot Robert King extended his lodgings with a handsome new tower,
expensively panelled within.[9] John Paslew at Whalley (Lancashire), another last
abbot, was responsible for the commissioning of a separate mansion, east of the great
cloister, which would later make up – as the others did too – the core of a post-
Dissolution establishment.[10]

Among these building abbots, so often the last of their line, many would have
taken their example from such great figures of the late-medieval Church as Richard
Redman of Shap (Westmorland), the leading English Premonstratensian of his day,
and Marmaduke Huby of Fountains (West Yorkshire), the Cistercian. Bishop Redman
died in 1505, Abbot Huby in 1526. Both had made their mark as gifted administrators
and busy reformers; characteristically, they had also been energetic in building. It
was not that Shap itself was ever a wealthy community. But Richard Redman,
simultaneously abbot of Shap and bishop of St Asaph (1471), Exeter (1495) and Ely

(1501) in succession, remained loyal to the house that had brought him originally to prominence. It was towards the end of Redman's long abbacy that the monastic church at Shap acquired the great west tower which is now the abbey's most prominent memorial.[11] There is more than merely local significance in such a work. Amongst the many prohibitions that the former reforming orders had come, by the late fifteenth century, to ignore, was the twelfth-century rejection of towers. Certainly, in late-medieval England, where noble towers were springing up at most parish churches and at almost every other religious institution in the land, self-denial in this respect would have become especially difficult for the monks. Marmaduke Huby has been described with good reason as 'by far the most distinguished Cistercian abbot of his age'.[12] Before his election to the abbacy of Fountains in 1495, he had taken his part in the purging of the Welsh houses, and he knew very well the dangers to his order of a corrupt leadership and of a discipline that was overly relaxed. Yet it was Huby who rebuilt the abbot's lodgings at Fountains in sumptuous style, with fine bay windows, side-wall fireplaces, and private latrines. And it was to

165 Abbot Marmaduke Huby's great tower at Fountains Abbey: one of the many building works of this remarkable man who has been described as 'by far the most distinguished Cistercian abbot of his age'

166 The church at Bolton Priory from the air, showing Prior Richard Mone's incomplete sixteenth-
century west tower (left), with the present parish church still occupying the body of the nave
(centre), and the roofless fourteenth-century transepts and presbytery (right) (*British Crown copyright reserved*)

Huby again that Fountains owed the handsome north tower which was to be the most
spectacular of all his many works.[13]

Marmaduke Huby's tower at Fountains was a lavish composition, rich in heraldry
including his own, and further decorated with pious inscriptions dedicating this
magnificence to God. Many came to Fountains in Huby's day, among them very
probably the abbot of Furness (Lancashire) who began his own west tower at just
about this time.[14] However, more directly competitive both in the quality of its
decoration and in its intended scale was the magnificent west tower of the
Augustinians of Bolton, among Huby's nearest neighbours in religion. The tower at
Bolton Priory was begun in 1520 by Richard Mone, last prior of the community. It
still carries the inscription – 'In the year of our Lord MVCXX R[ichard Mone] began
this foundation, on whose soul God have mercy, Amen.' But it never got beyond the
head of the great west window, at which point the life of the community ran out.

Accordingly, the church at Bolton, which continued in use as the parish church after the suppression of 1540, preserves uniquely two west fronts: the fine early-thirteenth-century façade of the original building and existing church, with its intended replacement, Prior Mone's incomplete west front, largely hiding the work which he had expected in due course to demolish.[15] Indeed, there are few more poignant memorials to English monasticism than this great skeleton of a church in which the parish still worships, occupying no more than the nave. In the perfect setting of unspoilt Wharfedale, it is a spot of great beauty and of that particularly agreeable brand of melancholy that accompanies reflections on the past.

Certainly, even before the suppression of their communities made philosophizing of this kind the familiar coin of successive generations of antiquaries, the monks themselves had revived an old interest in the lessons of their own long history. Marmaduke Huby was among those superiors who habitually showed an intelligent concern for the past, and it is in the attitudes of men of Huby's quality and influence that it becomes possible to discern some hint of a self-generated renewal.[16] Fifteenth-century monks had many reasons, most of them intensely practical, for raking through the ashes of the past. Disendowment proposals, despite the collapse of Lollardy, were still in the air. More than ever, monasticism needed its propagandists, both in general and more specifically in the courts. Defence of threatened property, restoration of failing morale, the instruction and enlightenment of influential visitors – all these gave purpose to monastic chroniclers who, like Thomas Burton of Meaux (Yorkshire) early in the century, 'collected together many ancient documents and long forgotten parchments', including 'some which had been exposed to the rain, and others put aside for the fire'.[17] But something else was also present in the writings of Thomas Burton, as it would be in those of his successors. Genuine intellectual curiosity had been awakened. In a man like Richard Kidderminster, abbot of Winchcombe (1488–1527), the antiquarian and the humanist were very close together. And he was far from alone in these new leanings.[18] In the cathedral register at Winchester, four documents dating to 1470 were written in what is clearly a humanistic script. They are precious evidence of the existence of a small coterie of humanists amongst the Benedictines of Winchester, about which almost every other detail is now hidden.[19]

The humanism of William Selling (d. 1494), monk and eventually prior of Christ Church, Canterbury, would have been acquired in Italy itself, where he studied some years and to which he is known to have returned several times.[20] Yet by the early sixteenth century, the Renaissance had reached and was infusing the North. In the 1520s and 1530s young monks of an intellectual turn of mind might be followers of Erasmus, lovers of the new learning: we know of such, for example, at the great black-monk houses at Evesham (Worcestershire) and Glastonbury (Somerset).[21] Meanwhile in building projects of the period, the characteristic flavour of the Renaissance had arrived. Muchelney and Notley, St Osyth, Forde and Thame all make use of Renaissance decorative devices – mermen and mermaids, sphinxes, putti and arabesques – or display Renaissance symmetry in their planning. Certainly, in the new tower at Thame (Oxfordshire) Abbot King's private parlour was thoroughly Italianate in taste. Arabesques and roundels, urns, mermaids, scrolls and putti

THE ABBEYS AND PRIORIES OF MEDIEVAL ENGLAND

decorated the frieze. On the east wall of the chamber, a display of heraldry commemorated Robert King and his friends. They were not, in the context of these threatening years, a particularly savoury collection. The last abbot of Thame was himself clearly the associate of precisely that group which, in serving as Henry VIII's commissioners for the Suppression, was likely to profit most from the scattering of the community he led. King in his turn would become first bishop of the new diocese of Oxford; his relative by marriage, John Lord Williams of Thame, came immediately into possession of the former abbey, dissolved in 1539. Other shields in the panels frame the arms of Lee and Clarke, Barentyne, Wenman (the later owners of Thame), Norreys and Fermor, with the mitre and arms of Bishop Longland of Lincoln and the escutcheon – in bolder relief than the others – of the abbot's other patron, Henry VIII.[22] These men were in touch with the latest thinking, among the dominant figures of their day. Not one would exhibit the smallest interest in preserving a life of religion at Thame.

In practice, then, the new learning threatened suppression at least as much as it promised renewal. When Erasmus took his cool look at the monastic life, he dissolved more of its protective myths than he intended. In one of his most widely read works, the *Enchiridion* (1504), he had written –

167 The fine surviving fireplace, already Renaissance in flavour, in the sixteenth-century abbot's lodgings at Muchelney

168 Abbot King's parlour in his new tower at Thame, with its up-to-date Renaissance plasterwork in a style still rare in Europe north of the Alps

The monastic life should not be equated with the virtuous life: it is just one type of life that may be either advantageous or not according to the individual's dispositions of mind and body. I would no more persuade you to it than I would dissuade you from it.[23]

The *Enchiridion* was not generally available in an English translation until 1533. However, in the meantime Erasmus himself had made several visits to England, counting many in positions of power and intellectual leadership as friends. Among these, Henry VIII and John Longland, the patrons of Abbot King of Thame, were of course prominent. But the circle included Foxe and Warham, Fisher, Gardiner, Colet and More; Wolsey, most dangerously, was a sympathizer. Not all these men would travel the whole way with Henry. Yet none could have remained uninfluenced by the Erasmian view of the monasteries as a backward-looking anachronism: out of date, out of sympathy and ripe to fall.[24] Dean Colet it had been who, in a celebrated sermon to Convocation in 1511, had urged the assembled clergy to rehearse 'the laws that command them [the monks, canons, and religious men] to go the strait way that leadeth unto heaven, leaving the broad way of the world; that commandeth them not to turmoil themselves in business, neither secular nor other; that command that they sue not in princes' courts for earthly things. For it is in the Council of Chalcedon that monks ought only to give themselves to prayer and fasting, and to the chastening of their flesh, and observing of their rules.'[25] But the call to reform – which had been heard and ignored before – was in the event less threatening than the pragmatic solution of Cardinal Wolsey: to sever the limbs worst infected. Almost thirty religious houses, of different orders and condition, came under the cardinal's knife. With few exceptions, it was an Erasmian assessment of their negative worth that let the breakers in.

Wolsey's suppressions were intended to finance great collegiate foundations of his own. St Frideswide's (Oxford), a comparatively wealthy Augustinian community, lost its site to Cardinal College, while the revenues of some twenty other suppressed religious houses were brought together in the college's endowment.[26] But although it is true that Cardinal Wolsey's suppressions, because of their scale and their timing in the 1520s, were to prove especially influential, they were not without precedent even then. During the economic recession of the previous century, several of the smaller Augustinian houses had followed the alien priories into oblivion. Some had merged with, or been absorbed by, neighbours – the diminutive priory of Chetwode (Buckinghamshire), too poor to sustain itself or the parish churches for which it was responsible, had been swallowed by Notley, a brother in religion in the same county; eight years later, in 1468, Wormegay (Norfolk) was absorbed by Pentney, larger and luckier than its neighbour; in 1476, another Norfolk community, at Great Massingham, merged with the wealthier West Acre Priory 'in consideration of the nearness of the places and since there is no other place of religion to which it can be so conveniently and suitably united'.[27] However, efforts like these to keep the canons' endowment within their own Augustinian family had become rarer over the years. Selborne (Hampshire) was one of the smaller houses of the order. Like others of its kind, it had never fully recovered from the misfortunes visited upon it by the Black Death. In 1484, ruinous and with only one aged canon (calling himself the 'prior') in residence, Selborne was granted to Magdalen College, Oxford. Its patron, Bishop Waynflete of Winchester, was also the founder of the college.[28]

Other patrons before Wolsey had similarly seen the advantages to themselves of such a move. As always, it was the smaller Augustinian houses and the poorest nunneries that were at risk. In 1497, the Benedictine nunnery of St Mary and St Radegund (Cambridge), 'which is of the foundation and patronage of the bishop', was closed by John Alcock, bishop of Ely (1486–1500). Alcock's stated purpose was to

169 Remains of the church at Creake Abbey (Norfolk), a poverty-stricken Augustinian community suppressed in 1506 after an epidemic had carried off its remaining canons. Creake became a part of the founding endowment of Margaret Beaufort's Christ's College, Cambridge

found a college in its stead, later to become known as Jesus College although at first called the College of St Mary the Virgin, St John the Evangelist and St Radegund the Virgin by Cambridge. Characteristically, while the college was to maintain a master, six fellows and 'a certain number of scholars to be instructed in grammar', a large part of its purpose was memorial. In effect, the bishop's foundation was to become a chantry, 'to pray and celebrate divine service daily for the king, his queen Elizabeth, his mother Margaret, his son Arthur prince of Wales, and his second son the duke of York, his other children, the bishop of Ely, and for the soul of the king's father Edmund earl of Richmond'.[29]

At St Radegund's, poverty had been brought on the house 'by reason of the dissolute conduct and incontinence of the prioress and nuns, on account of their vicinity to the University of Cambridge'. A more unfortunate case, certainly less deserving of an early suppression, was the little Augustinian abbey at Creake, in Norfolk, which became part of the endowment, after 1506, of Margaret Beaufort's Christ's College, Cambridge. Creake, despite its elevation from priory to abbey in 1231, had never been rich. Yet there is no doubt that it would have survived until the general suppression of the lesser houses in 1536 had it not been for two major catastrophes. In 1483, or thereabouts, a disastrous fire burnt out the abbey church, destroying at the same time a number of the conventual buildings; the church was never fully rebuilt. Then, in 1506, an epidemic carried off the entire remaining community at Creake, with the result that, religious life having come to an end at the abbey, the crown might reclaim it as patron. Margaret, countess of Richmond and Derby, Henry VII's mother, had come under the influence of the Erasmian John Fisher, bishop of Rochester (1504–35). It was on his advice that she turned away from her initial project to extend the ancient royal abbey at Westminster, exchanging it instead for the more contemporary purpose of furthering the new learning at the universities. Creake, which came to the Lady Margaret on 14 July 1507 by gift of her son, was one element only in the many useful and pious works of this devout lady of whom, as Fisher said, 'All England for her death had cause of weeping.' They included the two Lady Margaret divinity professorships established in 1502 at Oxford and Cambridge, the latter held by Fisher and Erasmus in succession, with Christ's College itself in 1505, and with the posthumous St John's College (Cambridge), founded in 1509–11 on the site of the former Augustinian hospital ('now in a most impoverished and dilapidated condition') of St John the Evangelist in that city.[30]

At this time still, the ruin and decay of individual religious houses was almost always the reason originally advanced for their suppression. Yet it is clear that poor economic circumstances, anyway known to have been ameliorating just then, were rarely the only – or even the most important – cause of such closures. Cardinal Wolsey's suppressions of 1524–5 and 1527–8, although claimed to be of houses where 'neither God was served, nor religion kept', included several communities whose relative prosperity suggests at least the potential for self-generated reform and renewal, whatever the state in which Wolsey himself may have encountered them. Daventry (Northamptonshire), a former Cluniac house, was very far from bankruptcy in 1525 when suppressed for the cardinal's educational purposes. And the same could be said of the Benedictines of Wallingford (Berkshire), dismissed in

1528, as of the Austin canons of Lesne and Tonbridge, both in Kent, sent packing three years earlier. Bayham Abbey, in Sussex, was the only Premonstratensian house to fall in Wolsey's suppressions, and although not rich, it was far from being the poorest of its order. Its buildings, as is still obvious, were exceptionally handsome, and in the church the nave, at least, had been reconstructed as recently as the fifteenth century. In 1525, when Wolsey's agents stopped worship at Bayham, there was a riot among the canons' supporters in the neighbourhood. Briefly, a new abbot was elected and the former canons reinstated until Wolsey and his men regained control.[31]

In the final event, the full-scale assault on the religious houses of England came from two directions, and this was what made it so dangerous. Thus one of the grounds for the suppression of a community could be the evil ways of its members; another, its irreducible poverty. Since slack discipline and poverty so often coincided, the case for closure was easy to present and very difficult, even for a convinced churchman, to answer.

Few so much as tried. Robert Sherburne, bishop of Chichester (1508–36), was exceptionally quick off the mark in his premature expulsion ('for their evil ways') of the prior and canons of the little Augustinian community at Shulbred (Sussex). A decade before the first Act of Suppression of 1536, he had deposed the prior and dismissed the canons, going even further as he 'pulled down a chapel made with pillars of marble, he pulled down the frater, much of the church, he converted to his own use tiles upon the houses and the lead under the pipes, all the pavement of the frater, three chalices with all the household fitments, leaving bare walls'.[32] What actually happened at Shulbred is not entirely clear. Yet the defences of monasticism were crumbling day by day, incapable of resisting the growing public pressures for a more purposeful redistribution of what was now seen as the Church's wasted endowment.

In 1521, Luther had joined the attack on the monasteries in his abrasive and influential *De votis monasticis*. In the cause of Christian liberty, he declared monasticism a sham: a selfish pursuit of individual salvation at the cost of the whole community of believers.[33] As Erasmus said, 'I laid a hen's egg; Luther hatched a bird of quite a different species.' But Luther himself could not have gone far without the support of the many who had come to think as he did. Before the English suppressions of 1536–40, there had been a wholesale dissolution in Switzerland as early as 1524; entire orders had been suppressed in Scandinavia, others in northern Germany.[34] In attacking first the lesser houses, Henry VIII and his advisers struck where monasticism as a whole was at its weakest. It was not difficult to persuade an already pliant Parliament that 'it is and shall be much more to the pleasure of Almighty God and for the honour of this his realm that the possessions of such spiritual religious houses, now being spent, spoiled, and wasted for increase and maintenance of sin, should be used and converted to better uses'. Such praiseworthy ambitions were never realized. But even a cynic could not have disputed the grounds on which the earliest suppressions were proposed. The act of 1536 begins with a preamble which, for all its polemical tone, was essentially just in its conclusions:

Forasmuch as manifest sin, vicious, carnal and abominable living, is daily used and committed amongst the little and small abbeys, priories, and other religious houses of monks, canons, and nuns, where the congregation of such religious persons is under the number of twelve persons, whereby the governors of such religious houses and their convents, spoil, destroy, consume, and utterly waste as well their churches, monasteries, priories, principal houses, farms, granges, lands, tenements, and hereditaments, as the ornaments of their churches and their goods and chattels to the high displeasure of Almighty God, slander of good religion, and to the great infamy of the King's Highness and the realm if redress should not be had thereof, And albeit that many continual visitations hath been heretofore had by the space of two hundred years and more, for an honest and charitable reformation of such unthrifty, carnal, and abominable living, yet little or none amendment is hitherto had, but their vicious living shamelessly increaseth and augmenteth . . . so that without such small houses be utterly suppressed and the religious persons therein committed to great and honourable monasteries of religion in this realm, where they may be compelled to live religiously for reformation of their lives, there can else be no reformation in this behalf: In consideration whereof the King's most royal Majesty, being supreme head in earth under God of the Church of England . . . [having laid these circumstances before Parliament, received the petition that it be enacted that] . . . his Majesty shall have and enjoy to him and to his heirs for ever all and singular such monasteries, priories, and other religious houses of monks, canons, and nuns, of what kinds or diversities of habits, rules, or orders soever they be called or named, which have not in lands, tenements, rents, tithes, portions, and other hereditaments above the clear yearly value of two hundred pounds.[35]

The dispossessed heads of houses, out of the king's 'most excellent charity', were to be provided with pensions; the remainder, if unwilling to be placed in the surviving larger houses, were to 'have their capacities, if they will, to live honestly and virtuously abroad, and some convenient charity disposed to them towards their living'.[36]

The passing of the lesser houses was not unlamented. It led directly into the Pilgrimage of Grace. Nevertheless, it is not hard to see that honourable men could have found it in their hearts to accept, and even to welcome, such a purge. Many exceptions were allowed to the suppressions of 1536; there were plans abroad for a more equitable redistribution of former monastic wealth; few believed that the king would go further. In the circumstances, it was easy to be persuaded, as Henry himself held, that 'there be none houses suppressed, where God was well served, but where most vice, mischief and abomination of living was used'.[37]

In the monasteries themselves, opinion was fatally divided. With many others, the monks of Peterborough, assembled in their great chapter-house on 27 July 1534, had acknowledged the king as head of the Church and had denied the authority of the pope:

Know all men to whom this present writing shall come, that We, the Abbot and

170 The stubs of walls at the formerly great Cluniac priory of St Pancras, Lewes, demolished professionally by Giovanni Portinari and his crew during the winter of 1537–8, working on behalf of Thomas
Cromwell

> Convent of Burgh S. Peter, of the diocese of Lincoln, with one mouth and voice,
> and with unanimous consent and assent, by this our writing given under our
> common seal in our Chapter House . . . will always display entire, inviolate,
> sincere, and perpetual, fidelity, regard and obedience towards our Lord King
> Henry the eighth, and towards Queen Anne his wife . . . Also that we always hold
> it confirmed and established, and always will hold, that the aforesaid Henry our
> King is the head of the church of England. . . . And also that the bishop of Rome,
> who in his bulls takes the name of Pope, and claims for himself the pre-eminence of
> the chief pontiff, has no other greater jurisdiction assigned to him by God in this
> realm of England than any other foreign bishop.[38]

Later, under pressure of events, they and their kind would be forced to go much
further. The Benedictines of Worcester, when Bishop Latimer conducted a reforming
visitation at their cathedral priory in 1537, were still (in his judgement) guilty of
'ignorance and negligence . . . idolatry and many kinds of superstitions and other
enormities'. To remedy these, Latimer characteristically proposed the purchase of
English-language bibles, to be kept in church and cloister, with daily lectures,
readings and sermons.[39] Yet just a year later, the abbot of Hailes (Gloucestershire)
would already be thanking God, as he packed away his famous relic, the Holy Blood,
that 'he lived in this time of light and knowledge of His true honour, which he has
come to through reading the Scripture in English'. Similarly hoping to save her
house, Katharine Bulkeley, abbess of Godstow (Oxfordshire), assured Thomas
Cromwell that 'ther is nother Pope nor Purgatorie, Image nor Pilgrimage, ne prayinge
to dede Saintes, usid or regarded amongeste hus', while the Cistercians of Biddlesden
(Buckinghamshire) guaranteed their pensions by departing in the opinion that 'the
manner and trade of living which we and others of our pretensed religion have
practised and used many days, doth most principally consist in dumb ceremonies and
in certain constitutions of Roman and other forinsical potentates'.[40]

Of course, what was said quite freely in 1538 had been exceptional two years earlier. Nevertheless, the number of religious prepared of their own accord to abandon their way of life in 1536 is already testimony enough to the degree of demoralisation in their communities. It was the Augustinians, with saleable skills as priests, who were the readiest to go; Carthusians, more confident of their personal route to salvation, preferred to stay; nuns had little choice but to remain where they were, if they could.[41] Confidence in the value of a religious life had sagged so alarmingly that even the more eloquent of the monks' defenders were inclined to stress other qualities as of greater importance in presenting the case for their preservation. Robert Aske, leader of the northern rising called the Pilgrimage of Grace, lost his life in the cause he had espoused. Yet when he came, shortly before his execution, to record his thoughts on why the lesser monasteries of his region should have been preserved, the 'divine service of almighty God' was scarcely more important in his list of their purposes than the charitable succour of the poor. He could see –

> . . . none hospitality now in those places kept . . . Also divers and many of the said abbeys were in the mountains and desert places, where the people be rude of conditions and not well taught the law of God, and when the said abbeys stood, the said people had not only worldly refreshing in their bodies but also spiritual refuge both by ghostly living of them and also by spiritual information and preaching . . . for none was in these parts denied, neither horsemeat nor mansmeat, so that the people were greatly refreshed by the said abbeys, where they now have no such succour . . . Also the abbeys were one of the beauties of this realm to all men and strangers passing through the same; also all gentlemen were much

171 Earthworks on the site of Kirkstead Abbey, dissolved in 1537 and one of the more effectively demolished of the Lincolnshire houses

succoured in their needs with money; their young sons there succoured, and in the nunneries their daughters brought up in virtue; and also their evidences and money left to the uses of infants in abbeys' hands, always sure there; and such abbeys as were near the danger of sea banks were great maintainers of sea walls and dykes, maintainers and builders of bridges and highways, and other such things for the commonwealth.[42]

If utility alone had been the measure of worth, then some houses at least might have been spared, as indeed the king's commissioners occasionally urged. Catesby (Northamptonshire) and Polesworth (Warwickshire), houses of 'virtuous and religious' women, were among those strongly recommended for preservation at the time: Catesby on the argument that it stood 'in such a quarter much to the relief of the king's people, and his grace's poor subjects there likewise much relieved', Polesworth because 'the town and nunnery standeth in a hard soil and barren ground, and to our estimations, if the nunnery be suppressed, the town will shortly after fall to ruin and decay'.[43] And Polesworth, whether for this reason or another, survived the first round of suppressions in 1536, to be dissolved only in 1539. Yet sooner or later neither utility nor virtue would suffice. Luther had hatched his bird. There was no defence of monasticism in England that, at that hour, could stand up against such criticism.

Ultimately, the effect of the civil disturbances in Lincolnshire and in the North, through the autumn and winter of 1536–7, was to hasten a further programme of closure of the greater monasteries only just becoming the policy of the king. Henry VIII's attitude to the greater houses was still very uncertain. Farcical though they turned out to be, Henry's re-foundations at Bisham (Berkshire) and Stixwould (Lincolnshire) were sufficient to establish that, for the king at least, reform rather than suppression continued possible.[44] Rich communities had many friends. In practice, it remained politically out of the question even to contemplate dissolution until the abbot of Furness, under pressure for his role in the Pilgrimage of Grace, himself showed the path to surrender.

The community at Furness, although less active than some in the support of the rebels, had spoken out openly against the king, doubting Henry's supremacy in the Church. When Robert Radcliffe, lately created earl of Sussex and a close confidant of the king, entered Lancashire early in 1537 to settle the unquiet county, his progress was marked by executions. The abbot of Furness was unnerved. On Radcliffe's suggestion, he surrendered his house as a voluntary 'discharge of conscience'; his community followed him in the same.[45] From this time onwards, one community after another was to be persuaded to accept what was invariably described as an entirely 'voluntary' liquidation. Accordingly when, after many of the remaining houses had already fallen, a second act for the dissolution of the monasteries was drafted in 1539 to legalize the transfer of their properties to the crown, this voluntary element had become dominant. The monastic superiors, it was claimed, had granted their houses and lands to the king 'of their own free and voluntary minds, good wills and assents, without constraint, coaction, or compulsion of any manner of person or persons'.[46] It was as if every community were as willing to depart as the Gilbertines of Fordham

(Cambridgeshire) who, as early as 1535, had told Dr Legh that they desired nothing so much as to be set 'at liberty out of this bondage, which they are not able longer to endure, as they say, but should fall into desperation or else run away'; or indeed as those nuns of Denny, in the same county, who – a day or two before, and with equal lack of success – had 'most instantly desired with weeping eyes to go forth', importunately crying, to Dr Legh again, that they lived there 'against their conscience'.[47]

We cannot, of course, know the full circumstances of each and every surrender. But acts of defiance were certainly few, and the more common case, as John Husee predicted before the end of 1537, was that 'most will go down by consent of their abbots and priors'. Husee was the steward of Arthur Plantagenet, Viscount Lisle (d. 1542), at that time deputy of Calais, and it was his earnest hope, as he wrote to his master on 11 December 1537, that 'something will fall to your lordship'.[48] During the following months, as 'the abbeys go down as fast as they may', Lisle and his friends were all in the market for whatever abbeys God and the king might send them. One of the earliest of the greater houses to go had been the Cluniac priory at Lewes (Sussex), surrendered to the king on 11 November 1537 and marked out by Thomas Cromwell as his own. Much of it had already been destroyed before the end of March 1538, 'plucked down' professionally by Giovanni Portinari and by the crew of demolition men he had imported for the purpose from London.[49] Meanwhile, others were proving themselves as quick to ensure that the 'nests' should go, 'for fear the Birds should build therein again'.[50] Dr London's notorious destruction of the shrine of Our Lady at Caversham (Oxfordshire), which he defaced 'thorowly in exchuying of any

172 Remains of the crossing and south transept of the abbey church at Roche, the suppression of which (in 1538) was later described in such detail by Michael Sherbrook

173 The nave at Worcester: a great cathedral priory which, after the suppression proceedings of 1540, preserved both buildings and endowment largely intact as a cathedral of Henry VIII's reformed Church

176 The spacious interior of Malvern's church, greatly improved during the important building works of the fifteenth century when new windows were inserted and a tower built over the crossing

suppressed houses' as well of men as of wemen, they be in manner all gon that night I have taken ther surendre and streightway in new apparell'.[56] His colleague, Dr Layton, found the same to be the case at the king's recent re-foundation at Bisham (Berkshire) to which monks had been im orted from Chertsey. Bisham, when Richard Layton took its surrender late in June 1538, was in a poor condition. The crops in the fields were good, but there was 'not one bushel of wheat, malt or other grain' in the granary, the cattle were few and poor, there were no hangings on the walls, and the abbot had sold off the church plate and vestments, being 'so good a husband[man] that doubtless within one year, I judge verily, he would have sold the house, lands, and all, for white wine, sugar, borage leaves, and sack, whereof he sips nightly in his chamber till midnight'. The monks, under such leadership, were 'of small learning, and much less discretion'. On 22 June, as Layton wrote, they were already 'much desirous to be gone'. The previous day, while Layton himself had held an auction of old vestments in the chapter-house, 'they the monks cried a new mart in the cloister; every man bringing his cowl cast upon his neck to be sold, and sold them indeed'.[57]

Much the most complete description of these events survives, albeit at second hand, in Michael Sherbrook's polemical treatise, *The Fall of Religious Houses*, on which he probably began no earlier than the late 1560s. When he wrote, Sherbrook had recently been instituted rector of Wickersley, his own birthplace. Born in 1535, he was still very young when the neighbouring Roche Abbey was suppressed. Nevertheless he could claim, plausibly enough, to remember the time when bells still hung in the tower at Roche, and his closest relations were themselves present, he tells us, during the destruction that followed the surrender. It was to them that he turned in later years for an account of what actually happened. Roche's fall was a spectacle, Sherbrook commented, that –

175 The former priory church at Malvern (Worcestershire), purchased by the townspeople immediately after the departure of the monks and converted to the use of the parish

whole week here to set everything in due order.' Dr London took advantage of his stay to make a preliminary list of the images and relics at Reading Abbey, condemned with all other such 'superstitions' in the Ten Articles of 1536. Much of Reading's great collection dated back to the twelfth century, and it was as authentic as any such accumulation could have been (above, p. 79). But Dr London, characteristically, treated it with scant respect. He noted 'two pieces of the holy cross', with some of the more obviously important relics including 'a bone of saint Edward the Martyr's arm', 'saint James' hand', 'saint Philip's stole' and 'a bone of Mary Magdalene, with other more'. However, he soon lost heart, ending his list – 'There be a multitude of small bones, laces, stones, and arms, which would occupy four sheets of paper to make particularly an inventory of every part thereof. They be all at your lordships [Thomas Cromwell's] commandment.'[53]

The abbot of Reading had shown Dr London his relics 'with good will', and a fair part of the success of the commissioners in securing voluntary surrenders over the almost three years that it took the remaining great houses to fall, resulted from the promises they could make. In the first suppressions of 1536–7, the monks had departed with diminutive 'capacities'; they had been allowed their beds ('given to them by the Lord the King's Commissioners, of the Lord the King's alms') but little else.[54] By 1538, when there was plainly nowhere else for them to go, the terms had become more generous. As Dr London told Cromwell of the Reading Franciscans, '[I have] clearly despatched all the friars out of the doors in their secular apparel, and have given to every one of them money in their purses, and have clearly paid their debts.'[55] It was to be his experience as a much-travelled commissioner that at all the

176 The spacious interior of Malvern's church, greatly improved during the important building works of the fifteenth century when new windows were inserted and a tower built over the crossing

suppressed houses' as well of wemen, they be in manner all gon that night I have taken ther surendre and streightway in new apparell'.[56] His colleague, Dr Layton, found the same to be the case at the king's recent re-foundation at Bisham (Berkshire) to which monks had been im orted from Chertsey. Bisham, when Richard Layton took its surrender late in June 1538, was in a poor condition. The crops in the fields were good, but there was 'not one bushel of wheat, malt or other grain' in the granary, the cattle were few and poor, there were no hangings on the walls, and the abbot had sold off the church plate and vestments, being 'so good a husband[man] that doubtless within one year, I judge verily, he would have sold the house, lands, and all, for white wine, sugar, borage leaves, and sack, whereof he sips nightly in his chamber till midnight'. The monks, under such leadership, were 'of small learning, and much less discretion'. On 22 June, as Layton wrote, they were already 'much desirous to be gone'. The previous day, while Layton himself had held an auction of old vestments in the chapter-house, 'they the monks cried a new mart in the cloister; every man bringing his cowl cast upon his neck to be sold, and sold them indeed'.[57]

Much the most complete description of these events survives, albeit at second hand, in Michael Sherbrook's polemical treatise, *The Fall of Religious Houses*, on which he probably began no earlier than the late 1560s. When he wrote, Sherbrook had recently been instituted rector of Wickersley, his own birthplace. Born in 1535, he was still very young when the neighbouring Roche Abbey was suppressed. Nevertheless he could claim, plausibly enough, to remember the time when bells still hung in the tower at Roche, and his closest relations were themselves present, he tells us, during the destruction that followed the surrender. It was to them that he turned in later years for an account of what actually happened. Roche's fall was a spectacle, Sherbrook commented, that –

177 *Left* Muchelney from the air, showing the parish church (left) immediately north of the excavated foundations of its vastly greater neighbouring abbey (*British Crown copyright reserved*)

178 *Right* The former abbey church at Tewkesbury, preserved at the Dissolution to serve the parish, despite its exaggerated scale (*British Crown copyright reserved*)

. . . would have made an Heart of Flint to have melted and weeped to have seen the breaking up of the House, and their sorrowfull departing; and the sudden spoil that fell the same day of their departure from the House. And every Person had every thing good cheap; except the poor Monks, Fryers, and Nuns that had no Money to bestow of any thing: as it appeared by the Suppression of an abbey, hard by me, called the Roche Abbey; a House of White Monks; a very fair builded House all of Freestone . . . At the Breaking up whereof an Uncle of mine was present, being well acquainted with certain of the Monks there; and when they were put forth of the House, one of the Monks, his Friend, told him that every one of the Covent had given to him his Cell, wherein he lied: wherein was not any thing of Price, but his Bed and Apparell, which was but simple and of small Price. Which Monk willed my Uncle to buy something of him; who said, I see nothing that is worth Money to my use: No said he; give me ii^d for my Cell Door, which was never made with v^s. No said my Uncle, I know not what to do with it (for he was a Young Man unmarried, and then neither stood need of Houses nor Doors). But such Persons as afterward bought their Corn or Hay or such like, found all the doors either open or the Locks and Shackles plucked away, or the Door itself taken away, went in and took what they found, filched it away.

Some took the Service Books that Lied in the Church and laid them upon their Waine Coppes [waggon floors] to peice the same; some took Windowes of the Hay laith [barn] and hid them in their Hay; and likewise they did of many other Things: For some pulled forth the Iron Hooks out of the walls that bought none, when the yeoman and Gentlemen of the Country had bought the Timber of the Church: For the Church was the first thing that was put to the spoil; and then the Abbat's Lodgine, Dortor, and Frater, with the Cloister and all the Buildings thereabout, within the Abbey Walls: for nothing was spared but the Ox-houses and swinecoates and such other Houses of Office, that stood without the Walls . . . It

179 The present parish church at Binham (Norfolk), formerly the nave of the much larger church of the Benedictine priory on the site

would have pitied any Heart to see what tearing up of the Lead there was, and plucking up of Boards, and throwing down of the Sparres; and when the Lead was torn off and cast down into the Church, and the Tombs in the Church all broken ... and all things of Price, either spoiled, carped [plucked] away or defaced to the uttermost.

The persons that cast the Lead into foders, pluck'd up all the Seats in the Choir, wherein the Monks sat when they said service; which were like to the Seats in Minsters, and burned them, and melted the Lead therewithall: although there was wood plenty within a flight shot of them ...

For the better Proof of this my Saying, I demanded of my Father, thirty years after the Suppression, which had bought part of the Timber of the Church, and all the Timber in the Steeple, with the Bell Frame, with other his Parteners therein (in the which steeple hung viii, yea ix Bells; whereof the least but one, could not be bought at this Day for xx^{li}, which Bells I did see hang there myself, more than a year after the Suppression) whether he thought well of the Religious Persons and of the Religion then used? And he told me Yea: For said He, I did see no Cause to the contrary: Well, said I, then how came it to pass you was so ready to distroy and spoil the thing that you thought well of? What should I do, said He; might I not as well as others have some Profit of the Spoil of the Abbey? For I did see all would away; and therefore I did as others did.[58]

Sherbrook's description of the destruction of Roche is circumstantial enough to carry conviction. It is fully supported, moreover, in the archaeological record of such sites.[59] Yet the fate of individual members of the religious communities was only exceptionally to be as dismal as Sherbrook suggested much later. At Roche itself, the monks had not departed empty-handed. They had been given twenty shillings each towards their new clothing, with half the agreed year's pension in advance; the abbot had left with his books, with plate and household stuff, with a chalice, a

180 Lanercost Priory (Cumberland) from the air; the nave at Lanercost is still in use as the parish church, although the former transepts, crossing and presbytery are in ruins (*British Crown copyright reserved*)

181 The east end of the abbey
church at Pershore
(Worcestershire): an unusual
post-Dissolution conversion in
which the transepts, crossing,
and presbytery were preserved
for the use of the parish, while
the Lady Chapel and nave were
demolished

182 The present parish church at
Beaulieu (Hampshire), formerly
the refectory of this great
Cistercian house, seen through
the chapter-house entrance

183 Thomas Wriothesley's sixteenth-century gatehouse at Titchfield (Hampshire), cutting through the former nave of the Premonstratensian abbey suppressed in 1537

184 Mottisfont (Hampshire): a country house re-fashioned from the crossing (left) and nave (centre) of the former priory church, first by Lord Sandys in *c.* 1540 and then by Sir Richard Mill two centuries later

vestment, and £30 in cash.[60] Even after the quite extensive cloister sales which were conducted on the premises at the suppression, the payment of 'rewardes' to the departing superior, to his community, and to their servants not infrequently left the royal commissioners temporarily but substantially out of pocket. At Dale (Derbyshire), a Premonstratensian house surrendered in October 1538, none of the canons had gone away with less than a pound and most had had twice that sum; the abbot had been paid off with £6 13s 4d; John of the Henhouse had been granted eight shillings. Having collected what they could from the sale of grain and cattle, as well as from the disposal of church and other furnishings including the iron railings and 'tymber worke ther' of the founder's tomb, the commissioners had nothing in hand, 'for they have payd more then have recevyd by the summe of vijl. xvijs. vyd'.[61] Dieulacres (Staffordshire) was a richer house, and the commissioners finished, after their various disbursements, almost twice as deeply in debt. Here both the 'rewardes' on departure and the agreed future pensions totalled more than those at Dale. The abbot of Dieulacres was to collect a pension – as it turned out, for many years – of £60 annually, as against the £26 13s 4d assigned to the late abbot of Dale. Pensions of between £6 and forty shillings were common to both monks and canons, many of whom are known to have been drawing them still well into the 1550s.[62]

185 The rich Augustinian priory of St Osyth (Essex), suppressed in 1539 and later converted (after 1558) into the country house of Lord Darcy, who built the great tower (top right) (*British Crown copyright reserved*)

186 Sir Richard Grenville's economical conversion, undertaken in the late 1570s, of the former Cistercian church at Buckland (Devonshire), re-using its central tower and crossing as the pivot of his Elizabethan country house

187 Forde Abbey (Somerset), where Abbot Charde's work of the immediately pre-Dissolution period (centre) was subsequently developed into a substantial mid-seventeenth-century mansion by Sir Edmund Prideaux, a wealthy lawyer and Parliamentarian who became attorney-general to Oliver Cromwell (*British Crown copyright reserved*)

The subsequent fortunes of the ex-religious have been much debated, and it is no doubt true that some, in future years, would share the sad experience of the Lincolnshire pensioners, 'in especyall of the porest sorte havyng the smallest pencyons', who were complaining to the Edwardian commissioners by the mid-century that 'they have bene so delayed and dryven frome tyme to tyme and place to place for the payment of the saide pencyons, besydes the exaction of rewardes to the receyvor and his servauntes, as dyverse of them have spente the whole value of ther pencion or [before] they coulde gette it, and other some halfe or parte theroff to the utter decay of ther lyving'.[63] Yet for most, the system had worked well enough at the start, and there is good reason to believe that, among the more compliant, severe deprivation was rare.[64] Especially fortunate were the former monastic cathedrals – 'dens of loitering lubbers' – where much of the old-style organization survived in fact, if not in name. Among the deans and chapters of the six new cathedrals of the Henrician Reformation, each of them created out of a former monastic community, a similar continuity was maintained.[65] But the 'cushioned ease' of the former abbot of Tavistock, living just up the hill from the ruins of the house he had once ruled,[66] was not exceptional, nor was it impossible, in the comparatively relaxed circumstances of Henry VIII's later years, to keep at least the shadow of a religious life in being. One of the purchasers of surplus church goods at Beeleigh (Essex) in 1536 was 'my lorde Abbotte' who secured for himself, for 3s 4d, 'j vestment of yellowe sylke in Jh'us Chapell'.[67] We do not know, of course, what purpose the abbot may have had for this vestment. However, it is certain that when, on the surrender of the Nunnaminster (Winchester) in 1539, the last abbess, Dame Elizabeth Shelley, retained for her own use a 'little chalice of silver and parcel gilt', she saw it still as an object of persisting religious significance. Mistress Shelley and her former sisters in religion, some eight of them in all, continued to live as neighbours in the same parish in Winchester, where they may have practised a life in common. Donating the chalice to Winchester College, in the chapel of which she was later buried, Dame Elizabeth made it a condition of her gift that the 'nunnery of St Mary's in Winchester shall have it again in case it be restored and come up again in her time'.[68]

Nothing of the kind ever happened. The Nunnaminster, although its site is known, has left little of significance above ground. Luckier were those establishments in which, for one reason or another, the interest of a layman became engaged. Church fittings, obviously, had their uses. Both at Roche and at Tavistock, the local churchwardens were to make substantial purchases of vestments and other furnishings when the goods of the two abbeys were put up for sale.[69] And it was no doubt a purchase of this kind that brought the fine choir stalls, only lately fitted at Easby (North Yorkshire), to their present position in the parish church of neighbouring Richmond.[70] In a swift move of unusual initiative and daring, the men of Malvern (Worcestershire) bought the priory church, extensively rebuilt in the previous century, for the use thereafter of their parish, thus ensuring a survival that even Latimer had wanted, 'natt in monkrye, God forbyd!' but for preaching.[71]

The church at Great Malvern replaced an existing parish church, then allowed to decay and disappear. It reversed the usual pattern, where the parish church – as at Muchelney (Somerset) or Kenilworth (Warwickshire) – more commonly survived the destruction of its great neighbour.[72] Understandably, if a conventual church were already in use by lay parishioners, its preservation – in whole or in part – was secured. Thus it was as parish churches of exceptional magnificence that Boxgrove (Sussex), Christchurch (Dorset) and Tewkesbury (Gloucestershire) came through the holocaust relatively intact, complete with their fine founders' tombs. Where, for one reason or another, the preservation of the entire monastic church proved impracticable, the east (or conventual) end of the building – including presbytery, transepts and crossing – might be sold off with the former domestic ranges of the house. Only the nave, as at Binham (Norfolk), Bolton (West Yorkshire) or Lanercost (Cumberland), walled off from the rest, would be kept for the parishioners, as it had been traditionally in the past. Certainly unusual was the solution reached at Pershore (Worcestershire), where it was the presbytery that was retained, complete with crossing and both transepts, the north of which subsequently collapsed. And odder still was the case of Beaulieu (Hampshire), shorn of its great church but provided soon afterwards with facilities for worship in the former monastic refectory.

One of the churches preserved in this way for parochial purposes was the incomplete building at Milton (Dorset), at which the nave, after the fire of 1309, had never been fully reconstructed. Milton had been bought, the year after its surrender, by Sir John Tregonwell, one of the king's commissioners in the county, and it was he who re-modelled Abbot Middleton's fine lodgings (above, pp. 210–13) as the nucleus for a new mansion of his own.[73] Others in his position, whether because there was an adequate parish church already in being or because their plans left no room for such provision, were clearly better suited if religion on the site were cut short. Within a few days of the fall of Titchfield (Hampshire), the royal commissioners were writing to Thomas Wriothesley, its new owner, to outline their plan for a major conversion. 'All the church,' they said, 'must [come] down with the steeple, only that portion which is north from the steeple and knit with the dorter to stand, for your dining parlour and chapel beneath, and for lodging above of two storeys if you list, leaded and battled above with fair crests and prospects east, west, and south upon your garden, orchard and court.' They promised Wriothesley a mansion fit for the king, his unpredictable master, to visit 'and for any baron to keep his hospitality in'; they proposed a sale of church fittings (altars, images and alabaster carvings), urging 'Mistress Wriothesley, nor you neither, be not meticulous nor scrupulous to make sale of such holy things'; and they concluded with the reassurance – 'As for plucking down of the church [it] is but a small matter, minding (as we doubt not but you will) to build a chapel.'[74]

Titchfield, with its pompously embattled gatehouse tower, driven through the body of the former nave, is probably the most insensitively arrogant of such church conversions. But there were to be precisely contemporary re-fashionings of this kind at Netley and at Mottisfont, only a few miles away, carried out respectively for William Paulet and William Lord Sandys. At Netley where, in contrast to Titchfield, the cloister had been south of the church, Paulet created his courtyard mansion by replacing the former refectory by a central southern gatehouse, making a new hall and a kitchen out of the nave (above, Fig. 42). Shorn of its presbytery and north transept, the nave at Mottisfont still does duty as the frame of Lord Sandys' original post-Dissolution mansion and of its eighteenth-century re-fashioning.

Wriothesley, Paulet and Sandys were all prominent at court; they belonged to a group which, confident in its modernity, could contemplate such sacrilege with few qualms. Others, of course, were less certain. Among the many stories later collected by Sir Henry Spelman to illustrate the 'strange misfortunes and grievous accidents' that had befallen the luckless owners of former monastic sites, was one concerning Binham Priory, in Norfolk. Binham had been granted to the Paston family, and it was Edward Paston who, inheriting the ruins, decided to build a mansion in their place. However, as soon as the work of clearance began, 'a piece of wall fell upon a workman, and slew him: perplexed with this accident in the beginning of this business, he [Edward Paston] gave it wholly over, and would by no means, all his life after, be persuaded to re-attempt it, but built his mansion-house, a very fair one, at Appleton'.[75] Later, as was only to be expected, some of the inhibitions would die away, and it is to the energetic conversions of Lord Darcy at St Osyth's (Essex) after 1558, of Sir Richard Grenville at Buckland (Devonshire) in the 1570s, and of Sir Edmund Prideaux at Forde (Dorset) as late as the 1650s, that we owe what survives of these interesting and important buildings. There is nothing, moreover, in the workmanlike conversion of the little priory cell at Calwich (Staffordshire), where a Lancashire man 'hath made a parlour of the chancel, a hall of the church, and a kitchen of the steeple', to suggest that lay owners, even of the less sophisticated sort, were long held back by their misgivings.[76] In the meantime, though, a sense of desolation had developed. Shakespeare writes of those 'bare ruin'd choirs where late the sweet birds sang'; Donne of the winds which 'in our ruin'd Abbeyes rore'. In humbler but no less poignant vein, Francis Trigge would report in 1589: 'Many do lament the pulling downe of abbayes. They say it was never merie world since.'[77]

That merriment, too, had been cut short too abruptly, with heedless and casual brutality. Perhaps the saddest single memorial of the suppression of the religious houses is a note that has survived in a bible from Evesham (Worcestershire), one of the last of the great abbeys to be surrendered. The bible, appropriately enough, is a first edition of the English-language translation known as the Matthew Bible (1537), approved by the reformers for use at the monasteries. It was the possession of John Alcester, last sacristan of Evesham, who used it for miscellaneous notes and jottings, including liturgical memoranda appropriate to his office, proverbs, music and historical memorials of the abbey. Alcester had been present when the commissioners required the final surrender of his community. They did it, he noted, on 30 January 1540 'at Evensong tyme, the convent beyng in theyre quere at thys verse *Deposuit potentes*, and wold not suffir them to make an end'.[78]

Abbreviations

Agric. H. R.	*Agricultural History Review*
Ant. J.	*Antiquaries Journal*
Arch.	Archaeology, archaeological
Arch. J.	*Archaeological Journal*
Archit.	Architecture, architectural
BAR	British Archaeological Reports
B.I.H.R.	*Bulletin of the Institute of Historical Research*
Bodleian	Bodleian Library, Oxford
Cal. C. R.	*Calendar of the close rolls preserved in the Public Record Office*
Cal. P. R.	*Calendar of the patent rolls preserved in the Public Record Office*
Cambridge	University of Cambridge: Committee for Aerial Photography
E.H.R.	*English Historical Review*
Ec. H. R.	*Economic History Review*
Hist.	History, historical
Inst.	Institute
J.	*Journal*
J.B.A.A.	*Journal of the British Archaeological Association*
J. Eccl. H.	*Journal of Ecclesiastical History*
J. Hist. Geog.	*Journal of Historical Geography*
J. Med. H.	*Journal of Medieval History*
Lincoln Visitations	A. Hamilton Thompson (ed.), *Visitations of Religious Houses in the Diocese of Lincoln*, 3 vols, Lincoln Record Society 7, 14 and 21, 1914–29
Med. Arch.	*Medieval Archaeology*
Medieval Religious Houses	David Knowles and R. Neville Hadcock, *Medieval Religious Houses. England and Wales*, Longmans, 1953
Monastic Order	David Knowles, *The Monastic Order in England*, Cambridge University Press, 1963 (2nd edn)
Monastic Sites from the Air	David Knowles and J. K. S. St Joseph, *Monastic Sites from the Air*, Cambridge University Press, 1952
NMR	National Monuments Record
pers. comm.	personal communication

Proc.	*Proceedings*
PSA	Property Services Agency: Photographic Library
RCHM	Royal Commission on Historical Monuments
Religious Orders	David Knowles, *The Religious Orders in England,* 3 vols, Cambridge University Press, 1956 (2nd edn)
Soc.	Society
Trans.	*Transactions*
Trans. Inst. Brit. Geog.	*Transactions of the Institute of British Geographers*
T.R.H.S.	*Transactions of the Royal Historical Society*
VCH	*Victoria History of the Counties of England*

Guides to individual religious houses, published by Her Majesty's Stationery Office on behalf of the Department of the Environment, by the National Trust, and by other bodies, are cited below by author (where given), title and date, thus:

J. G. Coad, *Hailes Abbey,* 1970

Mottisfont Abbey, 1973

Notes and References

Chapter 1   An Alien Settlement

1   Quoted by Antonia Gransden, 'Cultural transition at Worcester in the Anglo-Norman period', in *Medieval Art and Architecture at Worcester Cathedral* (ed. Glenys Popper), 1978, p. 10.
2   R. W. Southern (ed.), *The Life of St Anselm, Archbishop of Canterbury, by Eadmer*, 1962, p. 51.
3   Henry Thomas Riley (ed.), *Gesta Abbatum Monasterii Sancti Albani a Thoma Walsingham*, Rolls Series, 1867, i: 62.
4   David C. Douglas and George W. Greenaway (eds.), *English Historical Documents 1042–1189*, 1953, pp. 606–7.
5   Donald Matthew, *The Norman Monasteries and their English Possessions*, 1962, pp. 30–32.
6   Marjorie Morgan, *The English Lands of the Abbey of Bec*, 1968 (revised edn), p. 11.
7   Ibid., pp. 10–11.
8   Donald Matthew, op. cit., pp. 55–6.
9   John Le Patourel, *The Norman Empire*, 1976, pp. 317–18.
10 For the date of foundation, see Rose Graham, 'Four alien priories in Monmouthshire', *J.B.A.A.*, 35 (1929), p. 103.
11 Donald Matthew, op. cit., pp. 56–7.
12 Rose Graham, op. cit., pp. 120–21.
13 Emma Mason, 'English tithe income of Norman religious houses', *B.I.H.R.*, 48 (1975), pp. 91–4. For a useful general survey of the whole foundation process at alien priories like Wootton Wawen, see Donald Matthew, op. cit., pp. 44–65.
14 Eleanor Searle, *Lordship and Community. Battle Abbey and its Banlieu 1066–1538*, 1974, p. 22.
15 Ibid., p. 21.
16 For a re-dating of the Conqueror's appeal to Abbot Hugh, see Frank Barlow's 'William I's relations with Cluny', *J. Eccl. H.*, 32 (1981), pp. 131–41; and see also the same author's *The English Church 1066–1154*, 1979, pp. 184–5. A useful general account of 'The coming of the Cluniacs' was published by Brian Golding in the *Proceedings of the Battle Conference on Anglo-Norman Studies III* (ed. R. Allen Brown), 1981, pp. 65–77.
17 D. C. Douglas and G. W. Greenaway (eds.), op. cit., pp. 605–6. The charter, which is undated, must belong on internal evidence to the years 1078–82.
18 A. W. Clapham, *English Romanesque Architecture after the Conquest*, 1934, pp. 71–3.
19 For an account of the monastic colonisation of Scotland, see G. W. S. Barrow, 'Scottish rulers and the religious orders 1070–1153', *T.R.H.S.*, 3 (1953), pp. 77–100.
20 Helen Clover and Margaret Gibson (eds.), *The Letters of Lanfranc, Archbishop of Canterbury*, 1979, pp. 30–33.
21 Ibid., pp. 88–9.
22 Ibid., pp. 34–5.
23 D. C. Douglas and G. W. Greenaway (eds.), op. cit., pp. 631–5.
24 *Monastic Order*, pp. 114–15.
25 Ibid., pp. 113–14.
26 D. C. Douglas and G. W. Greenaway (eds.), op. cit., pp. 634–5.
27 W. T. Mellows (ed.), *The Chronicle of Hugh Candidus, a Monk of Peterborough*, 1949, pp. 84–5, quoted in translation by Edmund King, *Peterborough Abbey 1086–1310*, 1973, p. 13.
28 R. W. Southern, 'Aspects of the European tradition of historical writing: 4. The sense of the past', *T.R.H.S.*, 23 (1973), p. 246.
29 Antonia Gransden, *Historical Writing in England c. 550 to c. 1307*, 1974, pp. 279–80.
30 R. B. Dobson, *Durham Priory 1400–1450*, 1973, p. 11 and passim.
31 R. W. Southern, op. cit. (1973), pp. 249–50.

32 L. F. Salzman, *Building in England down to 1540*, 1967 (2nd edn), p. 364.
33 Quoted by B. Dodwell, 'The foundation of Norwich Cathedral', *T.R.H.S.*, 7 (1957), p. 9.
34 L. F. Salzman, op. cit., pp. 361–2, 364.
35 D. C. Douglas and G. W. Greenaway (eds.), op. cit., p. 624. For a recent account of his works at Worcester, see R. D. H. Gem, 'Bishop Wulfstan II and the Romanesque cathedral church of Worcester', in *Medieval Art and Architecture at Worcester Cathedral* (ed. Glenys Popper), 1978, pp. 15–37.
36 Alfred Clapham, *St Augustine's Abbey*, 1955, p. 17.
37 L. F. Salzman, op. cit., p. 364.
38 Rose Graham, *The History of the Alien Priory of Wenlock*, 1965, pp. 7–8.
39 David Baker, 'Excavations at Elstow Abbey, Bedfordshire, 1966–68. Second interim report', *Bedfordshire Arch. J.*, 4 (1969), p. 30.

Chapter 2   The Reforming Summer

1   The changing role of Cluny is usefully discussed in the epilogue to H. E. J. Cowdrey's *The Cluniacs and the Gregorian Reform*, 1970, pp. 253–65.
2   Quoted by Rose Graham and A. W. Clapham, 'The Order of Grandmont and its houses in England', *Archaeologia*, 75 (1924–5), p. 162.
3   Quoted by J. C. Dickinson, *The Origins of the Austin Canons and their Introduction into England*, 1950, p. 152.
4   *Monastic Order*, p. 206; Rose Graham, 'Excavations on the site of Sempringham Priory', *J.B.A.A.*, 5 (1940), p. 76.
5   The verdict is William of Newburgh's, quoted by Giles Constable, 'Ailred of Rievaulx and the nun of Watton: an episode in the early history of the Gilbertine Order', *Studies in Church History, Subsidia*, 1978, p. 221.
6   Ibid., p. 222 (the story is told by Gerald of Wales).
7   Susan Wood, *English Monasteries and their Patrons in the Thirteenth Century*, 1955, pp..26–7.
8   Charles Peers, *Kirkham Priory*, 1946, p. 1.
9   Emma Mason, 'English tithe income of Norman religious houses', *B.I.H.R.*, 48 (1975), pp. 91–4, and the same author's 'Timeo barones et donas ferentes', *Studies in Church History*, 15 (1978), pp. 69–70.
10 H. Mayr-Harting, 'Functions of a twelfth-century recluse', *History*, 60 (1975), pp. 345, 349.
11 D. C. Douglas and G. W. Greenaway (eds.), *English Historical Documents 1042–1189*, 1953, pp. 694–7.
12 Richard Mortimer, 'Religious and secular motives for some English monastic foundations', *Studies in Church History*, 15 (1978), pp. 78–9.
13 A. G. Dyson, 'The monastic patronage of Bishop Alexander of Lincoln', *J. Eccl. H.*, 26 (1975), pp. 1–24.
14 J. C. Dickinson, 'English regular canons and the Continent in the twelfth century', *T.R.H.S.*, 1 (1951), pp. 74–6; for the full foundation narrative, see Dugdale's *Monasticon Anglicanum* (eds. J. Caley, H. Ellis and B. Bandinel), 1846, vi: i: 344–8.
15 D. C. Douglas and G. W. Greenaway (eds.), op. cit., p. 694.
16 Elizabeth M. Hallam, 'Henry II as a founder of monasteries', *J. Eccl. H.*, 28 (1977), pp. 122–5.
17 Elizabeth M. Hallam, 'Henry II, Richard I and the order of Grandmont', *J. Med. H.*, 1 (1975), pp. 165–86.
18 Elizabeth M. Hallam, op. cit. (1977), pp. 117–18; *Monastic Order*, pp. 200, 204; Thomas S. R. Boase, 'Fontevrault and the Plantagenets', *J.B.A.A.*, 34 (1971), especially pp. 4–7.
19 J. C. Dickinson, op. cit. (1950), p. 99.
20 Quoted by R. W. Southern in an account, unusually sympathetic, of Augustinian origins (*Western Society and the Church in the Middle Ages*, 1970, pp. 241–50).
21 For a fuller discussion, see my own *The Parish Churches of Medieval England*, 1981, especially pp. 6–7.
22 Giles Constable, *Monastic Tithes from their Origins to the Twelfth Century*, 1964, p. 138.

23   B. R. Kemp, 'Monastic possession of parish churches in England in the twelfth century', *J. Eccl. H.*, 31 (1980), p. 143.

24   Ibid., p. 138.

25   Giles Constable, op. cit., p. 110, where this passage appears in full; it is reproduced by kind permission of Professor Constable, complete with his additions.

26   For a useful summary discussion of the debate on this matter, see Marjorie Chibnall, 'Monks and pastoral work: a problem in Anglo-Norman history', *J. Eccl. H.*, 18 (1967), pp. 165–72.

27   Susan Wood, *op. cit.*, 1955, p. 25.

28   Ibid., passim, but see especially pp. 101–21.

29   W. A. Pantin, 'Notley Abbey', *Oxoniensia*, 6 (1941), pp. 23–4.

30   Richard Mortimer (ed.), *Leiston Abbey Cartulary and Butley Priory Charters*, Suffolk Charters 1, 1979, p. 22.

31   R. H. Hilton, *The Economic Development of some Leicestershire Estates in the 14th and 15th Centuries.* 1947, pp. 109–11.

32   A. N. Webb (ed.), *An Edition of the Cartulary of Burscough Priory*, Chetham Society 18, 1970, pp. 12–14.

33   Dorothy M. Owen, *Church and Society in Medieval Lincolnshire*, 1971, p. 51.

34   J. C. Dickinson, op. cit. (1950), pp. 116–18, 126.

35   Ibid., p. 118.

36   See figure 3 in David M. Robinson's *The Geography of Augustinian Settlement in Medieval England and Wales*, BAR British Series 80 (i), 1980, p. 24.

37   J. C. Dickinson, op. cit. (1950), p. 128.

38   W. E. Wightman, 'Henry I and the foundation of Nostell Priory', *Yorkshire Arch. J.*, 41 (1963), pp. 57–8.

39   For Westminster, see Barbara Harvey, *Westminster Abbey and its Estates in the Middle Ages*, 1977, p. 42.

40   E. O. Blake (ed.), *The Cartulary of the Priory of St Denys near Southampton*, Southampton Records Series 24, 1981, pp. xxv, xxvii–xxviii.

41   *Monastic Order*, pp. 227–8.

42   D. C. Douglas and G. W. Greenaway (eds.), op. cit., p. 692.

43   Bennett D. Hill, *English Cistercian Monasteries and their Patrons in the Twelfth Century*, 1968, pp. 30–36.

44   Ibid., pp. 34–5.

45   For parallel analyses of the Fountains foundation story, differing only in emphasis, see Denis Bethell, 'The foundation of Fountains Abbey and the state of St Mary's York in 1132', *J. Eccl. H.*, 17 (1966), pp. 11–27, and L. G. D. Baker, 'The foundation of Fountains Abbey', *Northern History*, 4 (1969), pp. 29–43.

46   Denis Bethell, op. cit., p. 12; R. Gilyard-Beer, *Fountains Abbey*, 1970, p. 5.

47   R. Gilyard-Beer, op. cit., pp. 6–7.

48   D. C. Douglas and G. W. Greenaway (eds.), op. cit., p. 697.

49   R. Gilyard-Beer, op. cit., pp. 22–3; Charles Peers, *Rievaulx Abbey*, 1967, p. 8.

50   *Monastic Order*, p. 259.

51   Ibid., pp. 754–5 (Additional Note D: 'The origin of the lay brothers'); and see also Giles Constable, '"Famuli" and "conversi" at Cluny. A note on Statute 24 of Peter the Venerable', *Revue Bénédictine*, 83 (1973), pp. 326–50.

52   Christopher J. Holdsworth, 'The blessings of work: the Cistercian view', *Studies in Church History*, 10 (1973), pp. 59–76.

53   For Cistercian estate policy, especially in the north of England, see my own *The Monastic Grange in Medieval England*, 1969, passim.

54   R. Gilyard-Beer, op. cit., pp. 23–4.

55   C. A. Ralegh Radford, *Cymmer Abbey*, 1946.

56   J. S. Richardson and Marguerite Wood, *Melrose Abbey*, 1949, p. 18.

57   J. S. Richardson, *Sweetheart Abbey*, 1951, p. 14.

58   Owen Ashmore, *A Guide to Whalley Abbey*, 1968.

59   T. Jones Pierce, 'Strata Florida Abbey', *Ceredigion*, 1 (1950), p. 26.

60 A. Hamilton Thompson, *Roche Abbey*, 1954.

61 Rose Graham and A. W. Clapham, op. cit., pp. 170–71; D. Knowles, 'The revolt of the lay brothers of Sempringham', *E.H.R.*, 50 (1935), pp. 465–87.

62 For the riots in the 1190s at Strata Florida, see T. Jones Pierce, op. cit., p. 21.

63 Colin Morris, 'Equestris ordo: chivalry as a vocation in the twelfth century', *Studies in Church History*, 15 (1978), p. 92.

64 Ibid., p. 88.

Chapter 3   A Spirit of Compromise

1 *Monastic Order*, p. 252.

2 Ibid., pp. 297–8.

3 Bennett D. Hill, *English Cistercian Monasteries and their Patrons in the Twelfth Century*, 1968, pp. 64–6.

4 C. A. F. Meekings and R. F. Hunnisett, 'The early years of Netley Abbey', *J. Eccl. H.*, 30 (1979), pp. 1–37.

5 Sally Thompson, 'The problem of the Cistercian nuns in the twelfth and early thirteenth centuries', *Studies in Church History, Subsidia*, 1978, pp. 227–52.

6 *Monastic Order*, pp. 668–77.

7 Mary Suydam, 'Origins of the Savigniac Order. Savigny's role within twelfth-century monastic reform', *Revue Bénédictine*, 86 (1976), pp. 94–108.

8 Bennett D. Hill, op. cit., pp. 112–13.

9 Mary Bayliss, 'Dieulacres Abbey', *North Staffordshire J. Field Studies*, 2 (1962), p. 79.

10 J. M. Wagstaff, 'The economy of Dieulacres Abbey, 1214–1539', ibid., 10 (1970), pp. 83–101.

11 Glanmor Williams, *The Welsh Church from Conquest to Reformation*, 1962, pp. 164–5, 348; for Aberconway in particular, see Rhŷs W. Hays, *The History of the Abbey of Aberconway 1186–1537*, 1963, pp. 116–19.

12 Peter Fergusson, 'The south transept elevation of Byland Abbey', *J.B.A.A.*, 38 (1975), pp. 155–76.

13 P. K. Baillie Reynolds, *Croxden Abbey*, 1946. At Pontigny in the mid-1180s and at Clairvaux itself even earlier, the building of similarly elaborate east ends must have provided further justification, if such were needed, for this plan (M.-A. Dimier, 'Origine des déambulatoires à chapelles rayonnantes non saillantes', *Bulletin Monumental*, 110 (1957), pp. 23–33).

14 Charles Peers, *Rievaulx Abbey*, 1967.

15 Sally Thompson, op. cit., pp. 231–2.

16 A. G. Dyson, 'The monastic patronage of Bishop Alexander of Lincoln', *J. Eccl. H.*, 26 (1975), p. 19; Janet E. Burton, *The Yorkshire Nunneries in the Twelfth and Thirteenth Centuries*, Borthwick Papers 56, 1979, p. 4.

17 Sally Thompson, op. cit., pp. 236–8; Brenda M. Bolton, 'Mulieres sanctae', *Studies in Church History*, 10 (1973), pp. 78–9.

18 David M. Robinson, *The Geography of Augustinian Settlement in Medieval England and Wales*, BAR British Series 80 (i), 1980, pp. 24–7.

19 J. C. Dickinson, *The Origins of the Austin Canons and their Introduction into England*, 1950, pp. 143–8.

20 Ibid., pp. 135–6.

21 *Medieval Religious Houses*, pp. 145, 151, 155. Leprosy was no longer endemic by the fourteenth century, many leper hospitals either closing or becoming, as here, an almshouse.

22 Ibid., pp. 173–5.

23 Richard Mortimer (ed.), *Leiston Abbey Cartulary and Butley Priory Charters*, Suffolk Charters 1, 1979, pp. 1–3.

24 H. M. Colvin, *The White Canons in England*, 1951, p. 31.

25 Ibid., pp. 33–5.

26   Ibid., p. 37; S. E. Rigold, *Bayham Abbey*, 1974, pp. 5–6.

27   H. M. Colvin, op. cit., p. 30.

28   *Monastic Sites from the Air*, pp. 170–73.

29   Charles Peers, *Byland Abbey*, 1952, p. 3.

30   L. A. S. Butler, *Neath Abbey*, 1976, p. 6.

31   H. M. Colvin, op. cit., p. 29.

32   H. Mayr-Harting, 'Functions of a twelfth-century recluse', *History*, 60 (1975), p. 349.

33   *Monastic Order*, p. 360.

34   J. C. Dickinson, op. cit., p. 153; David M. Robinson, op. cit., pp. 50, 239.

35   Bryan Waites, 'The monastic settlement of North East Yorkshire', *Yorkshire Arch. J.*, 40 (1959–62), pp. 478–95.

36   *Religious Orders II*, p. 256.

37   H. M. Colvin (ed.), *The History of the King's Works, Volume I. The Middle Ages*, 1963, i: 87–90.

38   Quoted by W. L. Warren, *Henry II*, 1973, pp. 212–13.

39   Ibid., p. 214; *Monastic Order*, pp. 381–3.

40   *Monastic Order*, pp. 383–4.

41   Ibid., pp. 385–6.

42   Christopher Harper-Bill, 'Monastic apostasy in late-medieval England', *J. Eccl. H.*, 32 (1981), p. 10.

43   *Religious Orders II*, p. 129.

44   *Religious Orders III*, p. 159.

45   H. E. Butler (ed.), *The Chronicle of Jocelin of Brakelond*, 1949, pp. 39–41.

46   H. M. Colvin, op. cit. (1951), p. 164.

Chapter 4   Affluence, Investment and Growth

1   H. E. Butler (ed.), *The Chronicle of Jocelin of Brakelond*, 1949, p. 1.

2   A. R. Bridbury, 'The farming out of manors', *Ec. H. R.*, 31 (1978), pp. 503–20.

3   Barbara Harvey, *Westminster Abbey and its Estates in the Middle Ages*, 1977, pp. 83–4.

4   H. E. Butler (ed.), op. cit., pp. 58–9.

5   P. D. A. Harvey, 'The English inflation of 1180–1220', *Past & Present*, 61 (1973), pp. 3–30.

6   Eleanor Searle, *Lordship and Community. Battle Abbey and its Banlieu 1066–1538*, 1974, pp. 104–5.

7   Ibid., pp. 151–2.

8   Barbara Harvey, op. cit., p. 64.

9   Edmund King, *Peterborough Abbey 1086–1310. A Study in the Land Market*, 1973, pp. 144–5.

10   Barbara Harvey, op. cit., pp. 65–6.

11   H. Mayr-Harting (ed.), *The Acta of the Bishops of Chichester 1075–1207*, Canterbury and York Society 60, 1964, pp. 62–70.

12   For two recent comments on the alleged 'crisis' and its implications, see D. A. Carpenter, 'Was there a crisis of the knightly class in the thirteenth century? The Oxfordshire evidence', *E.H.R.*, 95 (1980), pp. 721–52, and R. H. Britnell, 'Minor landlords in England and medieval agrarian capitalism', *Past & Present*, 89 (1980), pp. 3–22.

13   Barbara Harvey, op. cit., p. 65.

14   Eleanor Searle, op. cit., pp. 154–8; Edmund King, 'Large and small landowners in thirteenth-century England. The case of Peterborough Abbey', *Past & Present*, 47 (1970), p. 48.

15   David Postles, 'Problems in the administration of small manors: three Oxfordshire glebe-demesnes, 1278–1345', *Midland History*, 4 (1977), p. 2.

16   C. A. F. Meekings and R. F. Hunnisett, 'The early years of Netley Abbey', *J. Eccl. H.*, 30 (1979), p. 20.

17   J. Ambrose Raftis, *The Estates of Ramsey Abbey*, 1957, pp. 109–12.

18   H. E. Hallam, *Settlement and Society. A Study of the Early Agrarian History of South Lincolnshire*, 1965, p. 218; and see also the same author's 'Goll Grange. A grange of Spalding Priory', *Reports and Papers Lincolnshire Archit. and Arch. Soc.*, 5 (1953–4), pp. 1–18.

19   Quoted by H. C. Darby, *The Medieval Fenland*, 1974 (2nd edn), p. 52.

20   Edmund King, op. cit., 1973, p. 74.

21   Ibid., pp. 74–81.

22   H. C. Darby, R. E. Glasscock, J. Sheail and G. R. Versey, 'The changing geographical distribution of wealth in England: 1086–1334–1525', *J. Hist. Geog.*, 5 (1979), pp. 247–62.

23   Kenneth H. Rogers (ed.), *Lacock Abbey Charters*, Wiltshire Record Society 34, 1978, p. 46.

24   Antonia Gransden, 'The growth of the Glastonbury traditions and legends in the twelfth century', *J. Eccl. H.*, 27 (1976), pp. 337–58; for a note on recent excavations at Glastonbury, thought to have identified the site of the monks' twelfth-century diggings, see *Med. Arch.*, 9 (1965), p. 182.

25   For Gervase of Canterbury's description of the fire and the subsequent rebuilding of the choir, see L. F. Salzman, *Building in England down to 1540*, 1967 (2nd edn), pp. 369–75.

26   Mavis Mate, 'Coping with inflation: a fourteenth-century example', *J. Med. Hist.*, 4 (1978), pp. 102–3; for the heavy expenses incurred earlier at the translation of the relics, see the same author's 'The indebtedness of Canterbury Cathedral Priory 1215–95', *Ec. H. R.*, 26 (1973), p. 184.

27   J. Wickham Legg and W. H. St John Hope, *Inventories of Christchurch Canterbury*, 1902, pp. 34–9, 41, 137.

28   Charlotte Augusta Sneyd (ed.), *A Relation, or rather a True Account, of the Island of England*, Camden Society 37, 1847, pp. 30–31.

29   *Mottisfont Abbey*, 1973, p. 4.

30   T. Jones Pierce, 'Strata Florida Abbey', *Ceredigion*, 1 (1950), p. 31.

31   John Brownbill (ed.), *The Ledger-Book of Vale Royal Abbey*, Lancashire and Cheshire Record Society 68, 1914, p. 9.

32   Denis Bethell, 'The making of a twelfth-century relic collection', *Studies in Church History*, 8 (1972), p. 65.

33   Ibid., p. 66.

34   Ibid., pp. 67–8.

35   J. Wickham Legg and W. H. St John Hope, op. cit., p. 38.

36   J. S. Richardson and Marguerite Wood, *Melrose Abbey*, 1949, p. 22.

37   Colin Morris, 'A critique of popular religion: Guibert of Nogent on *The Relics of the Saints*', *Studies in Church History*, 8 (1972), pp. 55–60.

38   Harry Rothwell (ed.), *English Historical Documents 1189–1327*, 1975, pp. 669–70.

39   L. F. Salzman, op. cit., p. 381.

40   H. E. Butler, op. cit., pp. 116–17.

41   Barbara Harvey, op. cit., pp. 43–4.

42   Ibid., p. 44.

43   H. M. Colvin (ed.), *The History of the King's Works, Volume I, The Middle Ages*, 1963, i: 130–57.

44   J. G. Coad, *Hailes Abbey*, 1970, p. 6.

45   W. Butler-Bowdon, *The Book of Margery Kempe 1436*, 1936, p. 163.

46   R. N. Hadcock, *Tynemouth Priory and Castle*, 1952, pp. 3–5, 10–12.

47   Alfred Clapham, *Whitby Abbey*, 1952, pp. 3–5, 14–15.

48   Peter Draper, 'Bishop Northwold and the cult of Saint Etheldreda', in *Medieval Art and Architecture at Ely Cathedral* (eds. Nicola Coldstream and Peter Draper), 1979, pp. 8–27.

49   H. E. Butler, op. cit., p. 96.

50   L. F. Salzman, op. cit., p. 381.

51   Ibid., pp. 378–9.

52   Charles Peers, *Rievaulx Abbey*, 1967, pp. 8–10.

53   John Blair, Philip Lankester, and Jeffrey West, 'A Transitional cloister arcade at Haughmond Abbey, Shropshire', *Med. Arch.*, 24 (1980), pp. 210–13, 240–41.

54   *Lacock Abbey*, 1977, pp. 25–6.

55   Nikolaus Pevsner, *North-East Norfolk and Norwich*, 1962, pp. 89–90.

56   L. F. Salzman, op. cit., p. 368.

57   Ibid., pp. 377–8, 390–91.

58   S. E. Rigold, *Lilleshall Abbey*, 1969, p. 10.

59   C. A. Ralegh Radford, *St Dogmael's Abbey*, 1962, p. 17.

60   J. Beverley Smith and B. H. St J. O'Neil, *Talley Abbey*, 1967, pp. 11–15.

61   C. A. Ralegh Radford, *Cymmer Abbey*, 1946.

62   L. F. Salzman, op. cit., pp. 376–7.

63   *VCH Hertfordshire*, 1908, ii: 484–5.

Chapter 5   Times of Plenty, Times of Sorrow

1   For one of the more comprehensive accounts of these difficulties, see John R. H. Moorman, *Church Life in England in the Thirteenth Century*, 1945, pp. 302–13.
2   Rose Graham, 'The conflict between Robert Winchelsey, archbishop of Canterbury, and the abbot and monks of St Augustine's, Canterbury', *J. Eccl. H.*, 1 (1950), p. 47.
3   Mavis Mate, 'The indebtedness of Canterbury Cathedral Priory 1215–95', *Ec. H. R.*, 26 (1973), p. 192.
4   W. G. D. Fletcher, 'Visitations of Wenlock Priory in the thirteenth century', *Trans Shropshire Arch. Soc.*, 9 (1909), pp. 141–6.
5   Derek Baker, 'Heresy and learning in early Cistercianism', *Studies in Church History*, 9 (1972), pp. 93–107.
6   H. E. Butler (ed.), *The Chronicle of Jocelin of Brakelond*, 1949, p. 29.
7   For the small estates, see R. H. Britnell, 'Minor landlords in England and medieval agrarian capitalism', *Past & Present*, 89 (1980), pp. 3–4. And see also David Postles, 'The manorial accounts of Oseney Abbey, 1274–1348', *Archives*, 14 (1979), pp. 75–80.
8   R. A. L. Smith, *Canterbury Cathedral Priory. A Study in Monastic Administration*, 1943, passim; E. Stone, 'Profit-and-loss accountancy at Norwich Cathedral Priory', *T.R.H.S.*, 12 (1962), pp. 25–48; Ian Kershaw, *Bolton Priory. The Economy of a Northern Monastery 1286–1325*, 1973, pp. 45–7; Barbara Harvey, *Westminster Abbey and its Estates in the Middle Ages*, 1977, p. 149.
9   *Lincoln Visitations II*, p. 174.
10 Eileen Power, *Medieval English Nunneries c. 1275 to 1535*, 1922, p. 219.
11 *Med. Arch.*, 23 (1979), pp. 250–51.
12 David Baker, 'Excavations at Elstow Abbey, Bedfordshire, 1968–1970', *Bedfordshire Arch. J.*, 6 (1971), pp. 55–64.
13 For these totals, see *Religious Orders II*, pp. 256, 260–61.
14 Kenneth H. Rogers (ed.), *Lacock Abbey Charters*, Wiltshire Record Society 34, 1978, p. 20.
15 Ibid., loc. cit.
16 Eileen Power, op. cit., p. 213.
17 Ibid., p. 212.
18 Janet E. Burton, *The Yorkshire Nunneries in the Twelfth and Thirteenth Centuries*, Borthwick Papers 56, 1979, p. 33.
19 W. A. Pantin, *The English Church in the Fourteenth Century*, 1955, pp. 126–7; K. L. Wood-Legh, *Studies in Church Life in England under Edward III*, 1934, pp. 8–9.
20 Marjorie Morgan, *The English Lands of the Abbey of Bec*, 1968 (revised edn), pp. 31–2.
21 Ibid., p. 29.
22 C. A. Ralegh Radford, *Ewenny Priory*, 1952, p. 25.
23 F. J. E. Raby and P. K. Baillie Reynolds, *Thetford Priory*, 1979, pp. 5–7.
24 G. H. Cook (ed.), *Letters to Cromwell and Others on the Suppression of the Monasteries*, 1965, pp. 89–90.
25 Elizabeth S. Eames, *Catalogue of Lead-Glazed Earthenware Tiles in the Department of Medieval and Later Antiquities, British Museum*, 1980, i: 202–3.
26 James G. Mann, 'Butley Priory, Suffolk', *Country Life*, 25 March 1933, pp. 308–14; J. N. L. Myres and W. D. Caröe, 'Butley Priory, Suffolk', *Arch. J.*, 110 (1933), pp. 177–281; Nikolaus Pevsner, *Suffolk*, 1961, pp. 137–40.
27 Charles Peers, *Kirkham Priory*, 1946.
28 D. W. Maclagan, *Tewkesbury Abbey* (undated).
29 L. A. S. Butler, *Neath Abbey*, 1976, pp. 8, 17.
30 R. Gilyard-Beer, *Guisborough Priory*, 1955.
31 Ibid., p. 5.
32 O. E. Craster, *Tintern Abbey*, 1956, pp. 8–10.
33 S. E. Rigold, *Bayham Abbey*, 1974, pp. 7–8.
34 Ibid., pp. 24–7.
35 Alfred Clapham and P. K. Baillie Reynolds, *Thornton Abbey*, 1956.
36 Ibid., p. 8.

37 Barbara Harvey, op. cit., p. 51; R. M. Haines, 'The appropriation of Longdon Church to Westminster Abbey', *Trans Worcestershire Arch. Soc.*, 38 (1961), pp. 39–52.

38 A. H. Davis (ed.), *William Thorne's Chronicle of Saint Augustine's Abbey, Canterbury*, 1934, pp. 439–40.

39 F. R. Chapman (ed.), *Sacrist Rolls of Ely*, 1907, ii:50–51.

40 Ibid., i:11.

41 L. F. Salzman, *Building in England down to 1540*, 1967 (2nd edn), p. 390.

42 Ibid., p. 394.

43 Laurence Keen, 'The fourteenth-century tile pavements in Prior Crauden's chapel and in the south transept', in *Medieval Art and Architecture at Ely Cathedral* (eds. Nicola Coldstream and Peter Draper), 1979, pp. 52–3; for a discussion of the schools of masons working at Ely on the choir, Lady Chapel, and octagon, see Nicola Coldstream's 'Ely Cathedral: the fourteenth-century work' (ibid., pp. 28–46).

44 Elizabeth S. Eames, op. cit., pp. 34–6; for the cheaper imitations, see the same author's 'Medieval pseudo-mosaic tiles', *J.B.A.A.*, 38 (1975), pp. 81–9.

45 Granville T. Rudd and Bernard B. West, 'Excavations at Warden Abbey in 1960 and 1961', *Bedfordshire Arch. J.*, 2 (1964), pp. 58–72, also Evelyn Baker, pers. comm.; Patrick Greene, 'Norton Priory, Cheshire', *Current Archaeology*, 70 (1980), pp. 343–9.

46 C. A. Ralegh Radford, *Strata Florida Abbey*, 1949, p. 6.

47 Elizabeth S. Eames, *Medieval Tiles. A Handbook*, 1968, pp. 9, 14.

48 Nicola Coldstream, 'English decorated shrine bases', *J.B.A.A.*, 129 (1976), pp. 31–4.

49 *VCH Sussex*, 1937, ix:103.

50 Nicola Coldstream, op. cit. (1976), pp. 18–19; David Hinton, 'Bicester Priory', *Oxoniensia*, 33 (1968), pp. 25–6, 39.

51 R. M. Haines (ed.), *A Calendar of the Register of Wolstan de Bransford, Bishop of Worcester 1339–49*, Worcestershire Historical Society 4, 1966, pp. ix–x.

52 Harry Rothwell (ed.), *English Historical Documents 1189–1327*, 1975, p. 773.

53 Ibid., pp. 686–7, 771.

54 Henry Richard Luard (ed.), *Annales Monastici*, Rolls Series, 1869, iv:537.

55 James Lee-Warner, 'Petition of the prior and canons of Walsingham, Norfolk, to Elizabeth, Lady of Clare. Circa A.D. 1345', *Arch. J.*, 26 (1869), pp. 166–73.

56 Harry Rothwell (ed.), op. cit., pp. 685–6.

57 E. O. Blake (ed.), *The Cartulary of the Priory of St Denys near Southampton*, Southampton Records Series 24, 1981, pp. xxxviii–xxxix.

58 Ibid., p. 1.

59 H. P. R. Finberg, *Tavistock Abbey. A Study in the Social and Economic History of Devon*, 1969 (2nd edn), pp. 260–61.

60 H. P. R. Finberg, *West-Country Historical Studies*, 1969, pp. 169–81.

61 M. L. Parry, *Climatic Change, Agriculture, and Settlement*, 1978, passim (but see especially pp. 65–6, 97–100, 103–5, 124–5).

62 Ian Kershaw, *Bolton Priory. The Economy of a Northern Monastery 1286–1325*, 1973, pp. 13–14, 113–17.

63 Ibid., p. 121.

64 Ibid., p. 17.

65 *Monastic Sites from the Air*, pp. 46–7, 256–7; for descriptions and plans, see also the papers by W. H. St John Hope. 'On the Premonstratensian abbey of St Mary at Alnwick, Northumberland', *Arch. J.*, 44 (1887), pp. 337–46, and 'On the Whitefriars or Carmelites of Hulne, Northumberland', ibid., 47 (1890), pp. 105–29.

66 Eileen Power, op. cit., p. 427.

67 *Medieval Religious Houses*, p. 228.

68 Rosalind M. T. Hill, *The Labourer in the Vineyard. The Visitations of Archbishop Melton in the Archdeaconry of Richmond*, Borthwick Papers 35, 1968, pp. 18–19.

69 Ian Kershaw, 'The great famine and agrarian crisis in England 1315–1322', *Past & Present*, 59 (1973), pp. 3–50.

70 R. M. Haines (ed.), *Calendar of the Register of Adam de Orleton, Bishop of Worcester 1327–1333*,

Worcestershire Historical Society 10, 1979, pp. 66–7.

71   Ibid., p. 143.

72   For the still continuing debate about soil exhaustion, see especially R. H. Britnell, 'Agricultural technology and the margin of cultivation in the fourteenth century', *Ec. H. R.*, 30 (1977), pp. 53–66, and W. Harwood Long, 'The low yields of corn in medieval England', ibid., 32 (1979), pp. 459–69.

73   N. M. Trenholme, *The English Monastic Borough*, 1927, pp. 31–44.

74   Rosamond Faith, 'The class struggle in fourteenth-century England', in *People's History and Socialist Theory* (ed. R. Samuel), History Workshop Series, 1981, p. 52.

75   N. M. Trenholme, op. cit., pp. 57–65.

76   Mavis Mate, 'Coping with inflation: a fourteenth-century example', *J. Med. H.*, 4 (1978), p. 103.

77   A. R. Bridbury, 'Before the Black Death', *Ec. H. R.*, 30 (1977), pp. 407–9; and see also N. J. Mayhew, 'Numismatic evidence and falling prices in the fourteenth century', ibid., 27 (1974), pp. 1–15.

78   Rose Graham, 'Excavations on the site of Sempringham Priory', *J.B.A.A.*, 5 (1940), pp. 86–90.

79   C. T. Flower and M. C. B. Dawes (eds.), *Registrum Simonis de Gandavo, Diocesis Saresbiriensis A.D. 1297–1315*, Canterbury and York Society 40, 1934, pp. 272–3.

80   For a good description of the church at Milton, including a comment on the results of exploratory excavations there on the nave, see *RCHM Dorset*, 1970, iii:183–9.

81   *Religious Orders II*, pp. 10–11.

82   William Dugdale, *Monasticon Anglicanum* (eds. J. Caley, H. Ellis, and B. Bandinel), 1846, iv:226–8; and see also Eileen Power, op. cit., p. 180.

83   J. C. Dickinson, 'Early suppressions of English houses of Austin canons', in *Medieval Studies presented to Rose Graham* (eds. Veronica Ruffer and A. J. Taylor), 1950, pp. 65–6.

84   D. G. Watts, 'A model for the early fourteenth century', *Ec. H. R.*, 20 (1967), p. 547.

85   Frances M. Page, *The Estates of Crowland Abbey, A Study in Manorial Organization*, 1934, pp. 120–21.

86   For these views, see A. R. Bridbury, 'The Black Death', *Ec. H. R.*, 26 (1973), pp. 577–92.

87   For a useful recent full-length study of the impact of plague on late-medieval England, based on Norwich diocese testamentary records, see Robert S. Gottfried's *Epidemic Disease in Fifteenth-Century England. The Medical Response and the Demographic Consequences*, 1978.

88   John Hatcher, *Plague, Population and the English Economy 1348–1530*, 1977, pp. 17–18.

89   Eleanor Searle, *Lordship and Community. Battle Abbey and its Banlieu, 1066–1538*, 1974, pp. 261–2.

90   Eileen Power, op. cit., pp. 181–2.

91   Carson Ritchie, 'The Black Death at St Edmund's Abbey', *Proc. Suffolk Institute of Archaeology*, 27 (1955–7), pp. 47–50.

92   J. Ambrose Raftis, *Warboys. Two Hundred Years in the Life of an English Mediaeval Village*, 1974, pp. 216–24; Barbara Harvey, op. cit., pp. 244–6; Frances M. Page, op. cit., p. 125.

Chapter 6   Bending the Rule

1   William Abel Pantin (ed.), *Documents Illustrating the Activities of the General and Provincial Chapters of the English Black Monks 1215–1540*, Camden Third Series 54, 1937, iii:123–4.

2   Justin McCann, *The Rule of St Benedict*, 1972, pp. 110–11, 160–61.

3   Ibid., pp. 70–71.

4   Ibid., pp. 84–5; R. W. Southern (ed.), *The Life of St Anselm, Archbishop of Canterbury, by Eadmer*, 1962, p. 40.

5   *Religious Orders I*, pp. 88–91; Janet E. Burton, *The Yorkshire Nunneries in the Twelfth and Thirteenth Centuries*, Borthwick Papers 56, 1979, p. 31.

6   Justin McCann, op. cit., pp. 154–5.

7   C. H. Talbot (ed.), *Letters from the English Abbots to the Chapter at Cîteaux 1442–1521*, Camden Fourth Series 4, 1967, p. 15.

8   Christopher Harper-Bill, 'Monastic apostasy in late-medieval England', *J. Eccl. H.*, 32 (1981), p. 16.

9   Ibid., p. 8.

10 For a useful discussion of these privileges and dispensations, see *Religious Orders II*, pp. 170–74.

11 *Lincoln Visitations III*, pp. 221, 225.

12 Ibid., p. 224.

13 A. R. Myers (ed.), *English Historical Documents 1327–1485*, 1969, p. 840.

14 *Lincoln Visitations I*, pp. 22–3.

15 Justin McCann, op. cit., pp. 110–11.

16 Eileen Power, *Medieval English Nunneries c. 1275 to 1535*, 1922, pp. 291, 293–4. As Miss Power remarks, in a characteristic footnote, 'it is a pity that the word [*accidie, accidia*] has fallen out of use. The disease has not.' (p. 293).

17 R. B. Dobson, *Durham Priory 1400–1450*, 1973, in particular pp. 65–72.

18 G. H. Cook, *Letters to Cromwell and Others on the Suppression of the Monasteries*, 1965, p. 109.

19 Christopher Harper-Bill, 'Cistercian visitation in the Late Middle Ages: the case of Hailes Abbey', *B.I.H.R.*, 53 (1980), pp. 111–12.

20 Joyce Youings, *The Dissolution of the Monasteries*, 1971, p. 153.

21 For an early example of regulations concerning blood-letting, see David Knowles (ed.), *The Monastic Constitutions of Lanfranc*, 1951, pp. 93–5.

22 R. M. Haines (ed.), *Calendar of the Register of Adam de Orleton, Bishop of Worcester 1327–1333*, Worcester Historical Society 10, 1979, p. 164.

23 R. A. L. Smith, *Canterbury Cathedral Priory. A Study in Monastic Administration*, 1943, p. 46.

24 Joseph Henry Dahmus (ed.), *The Metropolitan Visitations of William Courteney, Archbishop of Canterbury 1381–1396*, 1950, pp. 46–7, 159–60.

25 *Religious Orders I*, p. 284; *Religious Orders II*, pp. 42, 47, 246; Henry Thomas Riley (ed.), *Gesta Abbatum Monasterii Sancti Albani*, Rolls Series, 1867, ii: 399–400.

26 Harry Rothwell (ed.), *English Historical Documents 1189–1327*, 1975, pp. 751–5.

27 J. S. Brewer (ed.), *Giraldi Cambrensis Opera. Speculum Ecclesiae*, Rolls Series, 1873, iv: 40.

28 Harry Rothwell (ed.), op. cit., pp. 756–7.

29 R. M. Haines (ed.), op. cit., p. 163.

30 Eileen Power, op. cit., p. 304.

31 *Lincoln Visitations II*, pp. 3–4, 176.

32 Ibid., pp. 166, 168.

33 *Lincoln Visitations III*, p. 314.

34 Ibid., p. 310.

35 Mary Bateson, 'Archbishop Warham's visitation of monasteries, 1511', *E.H.R.*, 6 (1891), pp. 28–30.

36 The point is well made in *Religious Orders I*, p. 289.

37 Ian Keil, 'The chamberer of Glastonbury Abbey in the fourteenth century', *Proc. Somersetshire Arch. and Natural Hist. Soc.*, 107 (1963), pp. 79–92, and the same author's 'Impropriation and benefice in the later Middle Ages', *Wiltshire Arch. and Natural Hist. Magazine*, 58 (1961–3), pp. 351–61.

38 Eileen Power, op. cit., p. 339.

39 A. R. Myers (ed.), op. cit., p. 810.

40 *Lincoln Visitations II*, p. 84.

41 G. H. Rooke, 'Dom William Ingram and his Account-Book, 1504–1533', *J. Eccl. H.*, 7 (1956), pp. 30–44.

42 Harry Rothwell (ed.), op. cit., p. 671 (the 64th canon of the Fourth Lateran Council).

43 Mackenzie E. C. Walcott, 'Inventories of (I.) St Mary's Hospital, or Maison Dieu, Dover; (II.) The Benedictine priory of St Martin New-work, Dover, for monks; (III.) The Benedictine priory of SS. Mary and Sexburga, in the Island of Shepey, for nuns', *Archaeologia Cantiana*, 7 (1868), p. 296.

44 W. G. Clark-Maxwell, 'The outfit for the profession of an Austin canoness at Lacock, Wilts. in the year 1395, and other memoranda', *Arch. J.*, 69 (1912), pp. 117–18. For dowries and other fees, see Eileen Power, op. cit., pp. 16–24.

45 For a good collection of sale records, see Mackenzie E. C. Walcott, 'Inventories and valuations of religious houses at the time of the Dissolution, from the Public Record Office', *Archaeologia*, 43 (1871), pp. 201–49.

46 Philip Rahtz and Susan Hirst, *Bordesley Abbey, Redditch, Hereford-Worcestershire. First report on excavations 1969–1973*, BAR British Series 23, 1976, p. 22.

47   David A. Walsh, 'A rebuilt cloister at Bordesley Abbey', *J.B.A.A.*, 132 (1979), pp. 42–9.
48   J. G. Coad, *Hailes Abbey*, 1970, pp. 17–18.
49   L. F. Salzman, *Building in England down to 1540*, 1967 (2nd edn), pp. 448–50.
50   Derek Baker, 'Old wine in new bottles: attitudes to reform in fifteenth-century England', *Studies in Church History*, 14 (1977), p. 206.
51   Philip Rahtz and Susan Hirst, op. cit., p. 20; *Religious Orders II*, pp. 125–7.
52   *Monastic Sites from the Air*, pp. 100–101.
53   R. Gilyard-Beer, *Cleeve Abbey*, 1960.
54   F. J. E. Raby and P. K. Baillie Reynolds, *Castle Acre Priory*, 1952; P. A. Faulkner, 'A model of Castle Acre Priory', *Med. Arch.*, 6–7 (1962–3), pp. 300–303.
55   A. R. Myers (ed.), op. cit., pp. 787–8.
56   D. H. S. Cranage, 'The monastery of St Milburge at Much Wenlock, Shropshire', *Archaeologia*, 72 (1922), pp. 122–8; Rose Graham, *The History of the Alien Priory of Wenlock*, 1965.
57   *Religious Orders III*, p. 82.
58   For a useful discussion of one of these, see 'Wenlok's Household' in the introduction to Barbara Harvey's *Documents Illustrating the Rule of Walter de Wenlok, Abbot of Westminster, 1283–1307*, Camden Fourth Series 2, 1965, pp. 6–10.
59   Alfred H. Sweet, 'The apostolic see and the heads of English religious houses', *Speculum*, 28 (1953), p. 479.
60   J. Patrick Greene, 'The elevation of Norton Priory, Cheshire, to the status of mitred abbey', *Trans Hist. Soc. Lancashire and Cheshire*, 128 (1978), pp. 97–112.
61   R. A. L. Smith, op. cit., p. 194.
62   L. F. Salzman, op. cit., p. 397.
63   Harold Brakspear, 'The abbot's house at Battle', *Archaeologia*, 83 (1933), pp. 143–4.
64   Eleanor Searle and Barbara Ross (eds.), *The Cellarers' Rolls of Battle Abbey 1275–1513*, Sussex Record Society 65, 1967, p. 19.
65   R. B. Dobson, op. cit., pp. 78, 293–4.
66   J. T. Fowler (ed.), *Rites of Durham, being a Description or Brief Declaration of all the Ancient Monuments, Rites, & Customs belonging or being within the Monastical Church of Durham before the Suppression*, Surtees Society 107, 1903 (for 1902), p. 85.
67   Ibid., pp. 51, 83, 86.
68   Ibid., pp. 68, 86–7; Eric Gee, 'Discoveries in the frater at Durham', *Arch. J.*, 123 (1966), pp. 69–78.
69   Justin McCann, op. cit., pp. 70–71, 126–7.
70   *Lincoln Visitations II*, p. 9.
71   W. A. Pantin, 'Minchery Farm, Littlemore', *Oxoniensia*, 35 (1970), pp. 19–26.
72   Dennis C. Mynard, 'Excavations at Bradwell Priory', *Milton Keynes J. Arch. and Hist.*, 3 (1974), pp. 32–5.
73   Mackenzie E. C. Walcott, op. cit. (1871), p. 241.
74   Edward A. Bond (ed.), *Chronica Monasterii de Melsa*, Rolls Series, 1868, iii: 224.
75   *Lincoln Visitations I*, p. 75.
76   Ibid., p. 97.
77   R. Gilyard-Beer, *Fountains Abbey*, 1970, pp. 61–2.
78   David E. Owen, C. Vincent Bellamy and C. M. Mitchell, *Kirkstall Abbey Excavations 1955–1959*, Thoresby Society 48, 1961, pp. 5, 113–15.
79   Justin McCann, op. cit., pp. 96–7.
80   *Religious Orders I*, p. 282.
81   A. R. Myers (ed.), op. cit., p. 788.
82   *Lincoln Visitations II*, pp. 141–2, 144.
83   *Lincoln Visitations I*, p. 102.
84   *Lincoln Visitations III*, p. 393.
85   Ibid., p. 349; Eileen Power, op. cit., pp. 316–18.
86   C. F. Tebbutt, 'St Neots Priory', *Proc. Cambridge Antiquarian Soc.*, 59 (1966), pp. 73–4.
87   R. Gilyard-Beer, *Cleeve Abbey*, 1960, pp. 33–5; P. K. Baillie Reynolds, *Croxden Abbey*, 1946; *RCHM Dorset*, 1952, i: 240, 242–3; J. C. Dickinson, *Furness Abbey*, 1965, p. 12.
88   *Lincoln Visitations III*, p. 348.

Chapter 7   A Question of Survival

1   For a comprehensive discussion of Durham's problems at its cells, see R. B. Dobson, *Durham Priory 1400–1450*, 1973, pp. 297–341.
2   Donald Matthew, *The Norman Monasteries and their English Possessions*, 1962, pp. 99–103; Vera C. M. London (ed.), *The Cartulary of Bradenstoke Priory*, Wiltshire Record Society 35, 1979, p. 150.
3   Donald Matthew, op. cit., p. 81ff; Marjorie Morgan, 'The suppression of the alien priories', *History*, 26 (1941–2), pp. 204–12.
4   *Religious Orders II*, p. 168.
5   Rose Graham, 'The English province of the order of Cluny in the fifteenth century', *T.R.H.S.*, 7 (1924), p. 108.
6   A. R. Myers (ed.), *English Historical Documents 1327–1485*, 1969, p. 811.
7   Marjorie Morgan, *The English Lands of the Abbey of Bec*, 1968 (revised edn), pp. 20–21.
8   Marjorie Morgan, 'Inventories of three small alien priories', *J.B.A.A.*, 3 (1939), pp. 141–9.
9   A. J. Taylor, 'The alien priory of Minster Lovell', *Oxoniensia*, 2 (1937), pp. 103–17. For a surviving building of this type, compare Cogges (Oxfordshire), a former cell of Fécamp, recently the subject of research by John Blair and J. M. Steane (*Med. Arch.*, 25 (1981), pp. 190–92).
10 A. J. Taylor, op. cit., pp. 110–14.
11 Donald Matthew, op. cit., pp. 103–5.
12 *VCH Yorkshire*, 1913, iii: 387.
13 K. B. McFarlane, *Lancastrian Kings and Lollard Knights*, 1972, pp. 190–92.
14 W. Budgen, 'Wilmington Priory: historical notes', *Sussex Arch. Collections*, 69 (1928), pp. 44–5.
15 H. E. Salter (ed.), *Newington Longueville Charters*, Oxford Record Series 3, 1921, pp. ix–x.
16 Donald Matthew, op. cit., pp. 116–17.
17 Ibid., pp. 131–2.
18 Ibid., pp. 134–5.
19 T. Taylor, *Saint Michael's Mount*, 1932, pp. 64–5, 70–71.
20 Ibid., pp. 68–70, 82.
21 Marjorie B. Honeybourne, 'The abbey of St Mary Graces, Tower Hill', *Trans London and Middlesex Arch. Soc.*, 11 (1954), pp. 16–26; F. H. Thompson, 'Excavations at the Cistercian abbey of Vale Royal, Cheshire, 1958', *Ant. J.*, 42 (1962), pp. 183–207.
22 A. R. Myers (ed.), op. cit., pp. 782–3.
23 For the unusual sequence of monastic occupation at Denny and for the recent excavations that have helped to sort it out, see Patricia M. Christie and J. G. Coad, 'Excavations at Denny Abbey', *Arch. J.*, 137 (1980), pp. 138–279.
24 A. R. Myers (ed.), op. cit., pp. 783–4; David Knowles and W. F. Grimes, *Charterhouse. The Medieval Foundation in the Light of Recent Discoveries*, 1954, pp. 24–8.
25 Quoted by Aubrey Gwynn, *The English Austin Friars in the Time of Wyclif*, 1940, p. 74.
26 *Religious Orders II*, pp. 132–3.
27 Ibid., pp. 175–84.
28 *Religious Orders III*, pp. 159–60; W. A. Pantin (ed.), *Documents Illustrating the Activities of the General and Provincial Chapters of the English Black Monks 1215–1540. Vol. III*, Camden Third Series 54, 1937, pp. 123–4. For the Observants, see A. G. Little, 'Introduction of the Observant friars into England', *Proc. British Academy*, 10 (1921–3), pp. 455–61.
29 J. A. F. Thomson, 'Piety and charity in late medieval London', *J. Eccl. H.*, 16 (1965), pp. 189–90.
30 For this, see my own *Medieval England*, 1978, p. 210 (quoting Dr N. P. Tanner's unpublished *Popular religion in Norwich with special reference to the evidence of wills, 1370–1532*, Oxford D. Phil. thesis, 1973).
31 M. G. A. Vale, *Piety, Charity and Literacy among the Yorkshire Gentry, 1370–1480*, Borthwick Papers 50, 1976, pp. 20–22; D. M. Palliser, *The Reformation in York 1534–1553*, Borthwick Papers 40, 1971, pp. 2–3.
32 *Religious Orders III*, pp. 224–5.
33 W. Butler-Bowdon, *The Book of Margery Kempe*, 1936, p. 163.
34 W. A. Pantin, 'Two treatises of Uthred of Boldon on the monastic life', in *Studies in Medieval History presented to Frederick Maurice Powicke* (eds. R. W. Hunt, W. A. Pantin and R. W. Southern), 1948, pp. 363–85; *Religious Orders II*, pp. 66–7.

35   Thomas Arnold (ed.), *Select English Works of John Wyclif. Vol. 3 Miscellaneous Works*, 1871, pp. 345–8, from the controversial tract on 'The Church and her Members'.

36   For a useful sorting-out of what Wyclif really intended, see Michael Wilks, 'Predestination, property, and power: Wyclif's theory of dominion and grace', *Studies in Church History*, 2 (1965), pp. 220–36.

37   A. R. Myers (ed.), op. cit., pp. 844–5.

38   Ibid., p. 843.

39   For the text, see Joyce Youings, *The Dissolution of the Monasteries*, 1971, p. 135.

40   M. E. Aston, 'Lollardy and sedition 1381–1431', *Past & Present*, 17 (1960), especially p. 16.

41   H. Peter King, 'Cistercian financial organisation, 1335–1392', *J. Eccl. H.*, 24 (1973), p. 143.

42   R. B. Dobson, *Durham Priory 1400–1450*, 1973, p. 272, and E. M. Halcrow, 'The decline of demesne farming on the estates of Durham cathedral priory', *Ec. H. R.*, 7 (1954–5), pp. 345–56. In R. A. Lomas's 'The priory of Durham and its demesnes in the fourteenth and fifteenth century', ibid., 31 (1978), pp. 339–53, more emphasis is placed on the estates the obedientiaries of Durham still kept in hand.

43   Eleanor Searle, *Lordship and Community. Battle Abbey and its Banlieu 1066–1538*, 1974, pp. 258–66, 324–37; P. F. Brandon, 'Cereal yields on the Sussex estates of Battle Abbey during the later Middle Ages', *Ec. H. R.*, 25 (1972), pp. 403–20, and the same author's 'Demesne arable farming in coastal Sussex during the later Middle Ages', *Agric. H. R.*, 19 (1971), pp. 113–34.

44   Barbara Harvey, *Westminster Abbey and its Estates in the Middle Ages*, 1977, p. 151; also the same author's 'The leasing of the abbot of Westminster's demesnes in the later Middle Ages', *Ec. H. R.*, 22 (1969), pp. 17–27.

45   P. F. Brandon, 'Late-medieval weather in Sussex and its agricultural significance', *Trans Inst. Brit. Geog.*, 54 (1971), pp. 1–17, and the same author's 'Agriculture and the effects of floods and weather at Barnhorne, Sussex, during the Late Middle Ages', *Sussex Arch. Collections*, 109 (1971), pp. 69–93.

46   W. H. St John Hope, 'On the Premonstratensian abbey of St Mary at Alnwick, Northumberland', *Arch. J.*, 44 (1887), pp. 337–46.

47   W. H. St John Hope, 'On the Whitefriars or Carmelites of Hulne, Northumberland', *Arch. J.*, 47 (1890), pp. 105–29.

48   J. S. Richardson and Marguerite Wood, *Melrose Abbey*, 1949, p. 3.

49   J. S. Richardson, *Sweetheart Abbey*, 1951, p. 8.

50   J. Wilson Paterson and David McRoberts, *Inchcolm Abbey*, pp. 7–9.

51   S. F. Hockey, *Quarr Abbey and its Lands 1132–1631*, 1970, pp. 136–9.

52   T. Taylor, op. cit., p. 84.

53   *VCH Sussex*, 1937, ix: 102; *Cal. P. R. 1338–1340*, p. 92.

54   A. B. Whittingham, *Bury St Edmunds Abbey*, 1971, pp. 28–9.

55   Alfred Clapham and P. K. Baillie Reynolds, *Thornton Abbey*, 1956, pp. 11–16.

56   For the calculation, see K. L. Wood-Legh, *Studies in Church Life in England under Edward III*, 1934, p. 73.

57   J. R. Holliday, 'Maxstoke Priory', *Trans Birmingham and Midland Inst., Archaeological Section*, 1878 (for 1874), pp. 55–105; R. M. Haines (ed.), *A Calendar of the Register of Wolstan de Bransford, bishop of Worcester 1339–49*, Worcestershire Historical Society 4, 1966, pp. xlii–xliii.

58   Richard Mortimer (ed.), *Leiston Abbey Cartulary and Butley Priory Charters*, Suffolk Charters 1, 1979, p. 7; J. A. Playle, *Leiston Abbey. A Premonstratensian house in Suffolk, circa 1350–1540*, University of Southampton unpublished dissertation, 1978, pp. 8–9.

59   *Cal. C. R. 1377–1381*, p. 486.

60   A. Hamilton Thompson, *The Premonstratensian Abbey of Welbeck*, 1938, pp. 28–31, 76–7; H. M. Colvin, *The White Canons in England*, 1951, p. 271.

61   Kenneth H. Rogers (ed.), *Lacock Abbey Charters*, Wiltshire Record Society 34, 1978, p. 48.

62   R. H. Hilton, *The Economic Development of some Leicestershire Estates in the 14th and 15th Centuries*, 1947, p. 116.

63   C. T. Flower, 'Obedientiars' accounts of Glastonbury and other religious houses', *Trans St Paul's Ecclesiological Soc.*, 7 (1911–15), pp. 60–61.

64   An eye-witness account of these events is included in John Leland's near-contemporary *Collectanea* (ed. Thomas Hearne, London, 1770), v: 373–81, although Leland himself cannot have been present at the ceremony.

65   Eileen Power, *Medieval English Nunneries c. 1275 to 1535*, 1922, pp. 7, 39–40.

66   *Lincoln Visitations II*, p. 175.

67   *Lincoln Visitations I*, p. 53.

68   Justin McCann, *The Rule of St Benedict*, 1972, pp. 118–21.

69   R. Gilyard-Beer, *Cleeve Abbey*, 1960, p. 16.

70   A. J. Taylor, *Basingwerk Abbey*, 1971, p. 3.

71   J. T. Fowler (ed.), *Rites of Durham*, Surtees Society 107, 1903 (for 1902), pp. 89–90.

72   R. B. Dobson, op. cit., pp. 144–72.

73   Quoted by A. Hamilton Thompson, *The English Clergy and their Organization in the Later Middle Ages*, 1947, pp. 169–70.

74   *VCH Hertfordshire*, 1914, iv: 396. For a word portrait of Thomas de la Mare, see *Religious Orders II*, pp. 39–48.

75   J. T. Fowler (ed.), op. cit., pp. 16–17.

76   This dependency is usefully discussed in *Religious Orders II*, pp. 283–5.

77   Sybil Jack, 'Monastic lands in Leicestershire and their administration on the eve of the Dissolution', *Trans Leicestershire Arch. and Hist. Soc.*, 41 (1965–6), p. 16.

78   Ibid., pp. 16–17; for the very similar experience of the episcopal landowners, see Christopher Dyer's valuable *Lords and Peasants in a Changing Society. The Estates of the Bishopric of Worcester, 680–1540*, 1980, pp. 209–17.

79   G. H. Cook, *Letters to Cromwell and Others on the Suppression of the Monasteries*, 1965, pp. 67–8. Richard Wharton's letter, written at Bungay, was dated 7 November 1535.

Chapter 8   Indian Summer and Collapse

1   Owen Ashmore, 'The Whalley Abbey bursars' account for 1540', *Trans Hist. Soc. Lancashire and Cheshire*, 114 (1962), pp. 51–2.

2   Charlotte Augusta Sneyd (ed.), *A Relation, or rather a True Account of the Island of England . . . about the year 1500*, Camden Society 37, 1847, p. 29.

3   G. H. Cook, *Letters to Cromwell and others on the Suppression of the Monasteries*, 1965, p. 66; for this common Benedictine practice of an abbot living away on his manors, see *Religious Orders II*, pp. 252–3.

4   G. H. Cook, op. cit., pp. 243–4.

5   For Ashbury and its comforts, see Margaret Wood, 'Ashbury Manor, Berkshire', *Trans Newbury District Field Club*, 11:3 (1965), pp. 5–11.

6   For Milton, see *RCHM Dorset*, 1970, iii:191–5; for Muchelney, see Nikolaus Pevsner, *South and West Somerset*, 1958, pp. 249–50.

7   W. A. Pantin, 'Notley Abbey', *Oxoniensia*, 6 (1941), pp. 36–41; Nikolaus Pevsner, *Essex*, 1965, pp. 339–40 (St Osyth).

8   *RCHM Dorset*, 1952, i:240–46.

9   Walter H. Godfrey, 'The abbot's parlour, Thame Park', *Arch. J.*, 86 (1929), pp. 59–68; Jennifer Sherwood and Nikolaus Pevsner, *Oxfordshire*, 1974, pp. 809–11.

10   Owen Ashmore, *Whalley Abbey*, 1962, pp. 10, 18–19.

11   H. M. Colvin and R. Gilyard-Beer, *Shap Abbey*, 1963, pp. 6, 10–12. For Redman as a builder, see *Religious Orders III*, p. 51; and for other towers at houses of the order, see A. W. Clapham, 'The architecture of the Premonstratensians, with special reference to their buildings in England', *Archaeologia*, 73 (1923), p. 126.

12   *Religious Orders III*, p. 37.

13   R. Gilyard-Beer, *Fountains Abbey*, 1970, pp. 34–5, 58–9.

14   J. C. Dickinson, *Furness Abbey*, 1965, pp. 12–14.

15   A. Hamilton Thompson, *History and Architectural Description of the Priory of St Mary, Bolton in Wharfedale*, Thoresby Society 30, 1928 (for 1924), pp. 154–5.

16   Derek Baker, 'Old wine in new bottles: attitudes to reform in fifteenth-century England', *Studies in Church History*, 14 (1977), pp. 193–211.

17   Antonia Gransden, 'Antiquarian studies in fifteenth-century England', *Ant. J.*, 60 (1980), pp. 76, 82.

18   *Religious Orders III*, pp. 91–5.
19   Joan G. Greatrex, 'Humanistic script in a monastic register: an outward and visible sign?', *Studies in Church History*, 14 (1977), pp. 187–91.
20   *Religious Orders III*, pp. 87–90.
21   Ibid., pp. 100–107, 347; Robert W. Dunning, 'Revival at Glastonbury 1530–9', *Studies in Church History*, 14 (1977), pp. 213–22.
22   W. H. Godfrey, op. cit., pp. 64–7.
23   Quoted in *Religious Orders III*, p. 149.
24   Ibid., p. 151.
25   C. H. Williams (ed.), *English Historical Documents 1485–1558*, 1967, p. 657.
26   *Religious Orders III*, pp. 161–2; for a list of Wolsey's suppressions, see p. 470 in the same volume.
27   J. C. Dickinson, 'Early suppressions of English houses of Austin canons', in *Medieval Studies presented to Rose Graham* (eds. Veronica Ruffer and A. J. Taylor), 1950, pp. 63–5.
28   Deirdre Le Faye, 'Selborne Priory, 1233–1486', *Proc. Hampshire Field Club and Arch. Soc.*, 30 (1973), p. 67.
29   C. H. Williams (ed.), op. cit., p. 761. For this and other similar suppressions, see also *Religious Orders III*, p. 157.
30   A. L. Bedingfeld (ed.), *A Cartulary of Creake Abbey*, Norfolk Record Society 35, 1966, pp. xxi–xxiii; A. L. Bedingfeld and R. Gilyard-Beer, *Creake Abbey*, 1970, p. 8; C. H. Williams (ed.), op. cit., p. 762.
31   *Religious Orders III*, pp. 162, 470; S. E. Rigold, *Bayham Abbey*, 1974, p. 10.
32   G. H. Cook, op. cit., pp. 54–5. However, there seem to have been canons still in residence at Shulbred in 1536, when the priory was at last formally suppressed (*Medieval Religious Houses*, p. 153).
33   *Religious Orders III*, pp. 165–6.
34   Ibid., pp. 166–71.
35   C. H. Williams (ed.), op. cit., pp. 771–2.
36   Ibid., p. 773.
37   *Religious Orders III*, p. 329.
38   C. H. Williams (ed.), op. cit., pp. 777–8.
39   *Religious Orders III*, pp. 346–7.
40   Ibid., pp. 352–3, 356; for Hailes and its 'feigned relic', see also G. H. Cook, op. cit., pp. 206–7.
41   For an analysis of these choices, see G. W. O. Woodward, 'The exemption from suppression of certain Yorkshire priories', *E.H.R.*, 76 (1961), pp. 397–8; also Sybil Jack, 'The last days of the smaller monasteries in England', *J. Eccl. H.*, 21 (1970), p. 111, and *Religious Orders III*, pp. 310–11.
42   Quoted in *Religious Orders III*, p. 328.
43   G. H. Cook, op. cit., pp. 107–8, 116.
44   For these, see Elizabeth M. Hallam's 'Henry VIII's monastic refoundations of 1536–7 and the course of the Dissolution', *B.I.H.R.*, 51 (1978), pp. 124–31.
45   *Religious Orders III*, pp. 332–3.
46   C. H. Williams (ed.), op. cit., p. 774.
47   G. H. Cook, op. cit., pp. 62–4.
48   *Religious Orders III*, p. 351.
49   Ibid., pp. 350, 384; G. H. Cook, op. cit., pp. 138–40.
50   Thomas Fuller, *The Church History of England*, 1655, vi: 358.
51   *Religious Orders III*, p. 355.
52   G. H. Cook, op. cit., p. 181.
53   C. H. Williams (ed.), op. cit., pp. 785–6.
54   For this concession, see 'Inventories of goods of the smaller monasteries and friaries in Sussex at the time of their dissolution', *Sussex Arch. Collections*, 44 (1901), passim.
55   C. H. Williams (ed.), op. et loc. cit.
56   *Religious Orders III*, p. 357.
57   Ibid., loc. cit.; G. H. Cook, op. cit., pp. 237–8.
58   A. G. Dickens (ed.), *Tudor Treatises*, Yorkshire Archaeological Society Record Series 125, 1959, pp. 28–32, 123–5.

59   For a discussion of this and further references, see my own *Medieval England*, 1978, pp. 214–15.

60   A. G. Dickens (ed.), op. cit., p. 123n.

61   Mackenzie E. C. Walcott, 'Inventories and valuations of religious houses at the time of the Dissolution, from the Public Record Office', *Archaeologia*, 43 (1871), pp. 221–4.

62   Ibid., pp. 214–17; *Medieval Religious Houses*, pp. 108, 165.

63   A. G. Dickens, 'The Edwardian arrears in Augmentation payments and the problem of the ex-religious', *E.H.R.*, 55 (1940), p. 402; for other discussions of the fate of the ex-religious, see also L. F. Salzman, 'Sussex religious at the Dissolution', *Sussex Arch. Collections*, 92 (1954), pp. 24–36; G. A. J. Hodgett, *The State of the Ex-Religious and Former Chantry Priests in the Diocese of Lincoln 1547–1574*, Lincoln Record Society 53, 1959 (for 1958), passim, and the same author's *Tudor Lincolnshire*, 1975, pp. 39–48; F. C. Morgan and Penelope E. Morgan, 'Some nuns, ex-religious and former chantry priests living in the diocese of Hereford (*c.* 1554)', *Trans Woolhope Naturalists' Field Club*, 37 (1961–3), pp. 135–48; and Michael L. Zell, 'The personnel of the clergy in Kent, in the Reformation period', *E.H.R.*, 89 (1974), pp. 513–33.

64   This was certainly the considered view of Professor Knowles (*Religious Orders III*, pp. 413–14).

65   Ibid., pp. 389–92; Claire Cross, '"Dens of loitering lubbers": Protestant protest against cathedral foundations, 1540–1640', *Studies in Church History*, 9 (1972), pp. 231–7; David Marcombe, 'The Durham dean and chapter: old abbey writ large?', in *Continuity and Change. Personnel and Administration of the Church in England 1500–1642* (eds. Rosemary O'Day and Felicity Heal), 1976, pp. 125–44.

66   H. P. R. Finberg, *Tavistock Abbey. A Study in the Social and Economic History of Devon*, 1969 (2nd edn), p. 268.

67   Mackenzie E. C. Walcott, op. cit., p. 243.

68   John Paul, 'Dame Elizabeth Shelley, last abbess of St Mary's Abbey, Winchester', *Papers and Proceedings of the Hampshire Field Club and Arch. Soc.*, 23 (1965), pp. 69–71.

69   A. G. Dickens (ed.), op. cit. (1959), p. 123n; H. P. R. Finberg, op. cit., p. 267.

70   A. Hamilton Thompson, *Easby Abbey*, 1948, p. 7.

71   *Religious Orders III*, p. 357.

72   *Monastic Sites from the Air*, pp. 32–3 (Muchelney) and 212–13 (Kenilworth).

73   *RCHM Dorset*, 1970, iii: 184.

74   Titchfield was surrendered in late December 1537; Wriothesley's grant of the site was obtained on 30 December; the letter is dated 2 January 1538 (Joyce Youings, *The Dissolution of the Monasteries*, 1971, pp. 246–8 with plan).

75   Sir Henry Spelman, *The History and Fate of Sacrilege*, 1632 (published posthumously in 1698), chapter VI.

76   For this and many other examples of post-suppression conversions, see J. C. Dickinson, 'The buildings of the English Austin canons after the dissolution of the monasteries', *J.B.A.A.*, 31 (1968), pp. 60–75.

77   The quotations are taken from Margaret Aston's useful 'English ruins and English history: the Dissolution and the sense of the past', *J. Warburg and Courtauld Institutes*, 36 (1973), pp. 231–55.

78   D. Knowles, 'Notes on a bible of Evesham Abbey', *E.H.R.*, 79 (1964), pp. 775–7.

Index